Hunters, Herders, and Hamburgers

Hunters, Herders,

and Hamburgers

The Past and Future of
Human-Animal Relationships

Richard W. Bulliet

Columbia University Press   New York

Columbia University Press
Publishers Since 1893
New York   Chichester, West Sussex
Copyright © 2005 Columbia University Press

Library of Congress
Cataloging-in-Publication Data
Bulliet, Richard W.
Hunters, herders and hamburgers : the past and future of human-animal
relationships /
Richard W. Bulliet
p. cm.
Includes bibliographical references and index.
ISBN 0–231–13076–7 (cloth : alk. paper) — ISBN 0–231–50396–2 (e-book)
1. Human-animal relationships.   I. Title.

QL85.B85 2005
179′.3—dc22
2005041381

♾
Columbia University Press books are printed on permanent and
durable acid-free paper.

Printed in the United States of America

c 10 9 8 7 6 5 4 3 2 1

Animals Are Passing from Our Lives

It's wonderful how I jog
on four honed-down ivory toes
my massive buttocks slipping
like oiled parts with each light step.

I'm to market. I can smell
the sour, grooved block, I can smell
the blade that opens the hole
and the pudgy white fingers

that shake out the intestines
like a hankie. In my dreams
the snouts drool on the marble,
suffering children, suffering flies,

suffering the consumers
who won't meet their steady eyes
for fear they would see. The boy
who drives me along believes

that any moment I'll fall
on my side and drum my toes
like a typewriter or squeal
and shit like a new housewife

discovering television,
or that I'll turn like a beast
cleverly to hook his teeth
with my teeth. No. Not this pig.

—Philip Levine

Contents

Hunters, Herders, and Hamburgers

1. Postdomesticity
Our Lives with Animals

Let's start with sex and blood.

In the shock year 1969, half a million young people celebrated drugs, sex, and rock 'n'roll at Woodstock. Tens of thousands more joined campus protests against the secret bombing of Cambodia. In New York, a police raid on the Stonewall Inn in Greenwich Village provoked the first gay protest.

Most Americans responded by shaking their heads in bafflement or disgust and settled for less demonstrative recreations. Sam Peckinpah's *The Wild Bunch* was in theaters, with its shockingly bloody but viscerally electrifying final shootout—body shots only, as squib technology for squirting blood hadn't yet developed a capacity for head shots. Also showing were Vilgot Sjoman's *I Am Curious (Yellow)*, featuring frontal nudity and simulated sexual intercourse, and Paul Mazursky's comic look at the then-titillating practice of wife swapping, *Bob and Carol and Ted and Alice*. On Broadway, the musical *Hair*, which was also known for its full frontal nudity, entered a triumphant second year, and in Philip Roth's *Portnoy's Complaint*, the bestseller list shed comical light on the then taboo subject of masturbation.

President Nixon led the older generation in deploring the national wallow in decadence of all kinds: "Drugs, crime, campus revolution . . . on every hand we find old standards violated, old values discarded, old principles ignored. [This threatens] the fundamental values, the process by which a civilization maintains its continuity."[1]

When the century ended three decades later, campus demonstrations were ancient history and Woodstock the fading, fond memory of the middle-aged. The country's political mood had swung far to the right—almost far enough to remove from office a president more than suspected of hiding the "moral decadence" of 1969 behind his Arkansas folksiness. Crime was down, young people thought more about common stocks than communes, and college bookstores stocked ponderously academic books on queer theory.

Yet even with this backswing of the cultural pendulum, graphic sex and blood were still going strong. Blended together, they guaranteed lucrative sequels for slice-and-dice horror films like *Halloween* (1978), *Nightmare on Elm Street* (1984), *Candyman* (1992), *Scream* (1996), and *I Know What You Did Last Summer* (1997). As the years passed, blood gushed more and more freely. The drenching blood that shocked in *Carrie* (1976) became commonplace and even parodied in the 1998 vampire movie *Blade*. And 2004 witnessed the extraordinary phenomenon of millions of Christian viewers being drawn to a particularly bloody depiction of their Lord's passion.

As for graphic sex, triple-X video rentals, soft-core pornography on hotel TVs, and thousands of Web sites devoted to every sort of sexual taste more than compensated for the eviction of peepshows and porn theaters from Times Square. Estimates of the number of Americans habitually visiting pornographic Web sites ran as high as 25 million, with as much as 57 billion dollars being spent on pornography worldwide.

Why did graphic depictions of sex and blood survive the resurgence of "traditional" values in American culture? Why do conservative Republicans, yuppies, and evangelical Christians seem no less inclined toward pornographies of sex and blood than the hippies and radicals whom they so often blame for initiating a decline in national morality? Psychologists, pundits, politicians, and preachers offer so many different answers that it is evident that no one knows for sure. Most likely, the phenomenon is too complex to be explained by any simple equation.

A hitherto unrecognized part of the answer, I would propose, lies in the dawning of a new era in human-animal relations. At first blush, this may seem implausible, if not absurd. In the context of the many other changes in outlook and behavior associated with the attitudes of "domesticity" giving way to those of "postdomesticity," however, its relevance becomes hard to ignore.

"Domesticity" and "postdomesticity" are key concepts of this book. Both are comparatively straightforward, even though they have never before been identified or defined. "Domesticity" refers to the social, economic, and intellectual characteristics of communities in which most members consider daily contact with domestic animals (other than pets) a normal condition of life: in short, the farming existence of a bygone generation for most Americans, but contemporary reality for most of the developing world. "Postdomesticity" is defined by two characteristics. First, postdomestic people live far away, both physically and psychologically, from the animals that produce the food, fiber, and hides they depend on, and they never witness the births, sexual congress, and slaughter of these animals. Yet they maintain very close relationships with companion animals—pets—often relating to them as if they were human. Second, a postdomestic society emerging from domestic antecedents continues to consume animal products in abundance, but psychologically, its members experience feelings of guilt, shame, and disgust when they think (as seldom as possible) about the industrial processes by which domestic animals are rendered into products and about how those products come to market.

Domestic societies take for granted the killing of animals and experience few moral qualms in consuming animal products. By contrast, postdomestic societies, which include a steadily increasing portion of the U.S. population, an even greater portion of the British population, and significant numbers in Australia and (less so) Europe, are fully immersed in the emotional contradictions inherent in postdomesticity. Meat, leather, and test animals are hard to give up, but details about what goes on behind the scenes to provide these goods and cultural services are revolting. Pets and wildlife evoke deep positive feelings, but domestic animals feeding the consumer market are a morally troubling reality.

Among the unconscious reactions to the changes wrought by the transition to postdomesticity is an increasing fascination with fantasies of sex and blood. To understand this in the American context, we must consider how American relations with animals have changed in the twentieth century. In 1900, some 40 percent of the U.S. population lived on farms. By 1990, the proportion had fallen to 2 percent. The generation that shouldered the burden of World War II, those born between roughly 1900 and 1925, for the most part either grew up on farms or had parents or close relatives who lived on farms. Among immigrant city folk, the parental farming village may have been far away in Europe, but even they grew up seeing live poultry for sale in the neighborhood market and hearing the regular clip-clop of draft horses pulling wagons in the street. Animal-drawn transport flourished in a country that in 1915 still had only 32,000 miles of hard surface roads outside of incorporated towns and cities. Not only had livestock not yet disappeared from urban life, but farm animals were still an integral part of daily existence. Then as now, most children learned the sounds ascribed to domestic animals— "moo-moo," "baa-baa," "cock-a-doodle-doo"—even before they learned real verbs and nouns. But back then they also had opportunities to hear those sounds in real life.

As for animal products, in the first half of the century, most people slaughtered their own chickens and hogs, or watched their butcher carve steaks and chops from a fat-sheathed carcass. When Clarence Saunders opened the first supermarket in Memphis in 1917, his Piggly Wiggly did not carry meat. (The up-to-date version of the chain's smiling Mr. Pig logo is dressed cannibalistically as a butcher.) Not until the second half of the century—after the relaxation of wartime rationing, when large supermarkets sprouted everywhere, getting Americans back in their cars—did meat begin to come prepackaged, with Styrofoam trays and polyethylene film eventually replacing the customary brown butcher paper. Studious cooks may still have known what part of the animal body the words "brisket," "chuck," and "sirloin" referred to, but most younger buyers maintained a studied obliviousness toward the gutted, skinless, headless, and hoofless carcasses hanging from hooks in the cold-room and felt no loss when the meatcutters who carved their steaks and ground their hamburger were shifted from behind the counter to somewhere out back.

Door-to-door milk delivery was another commonplace of American domesticity in the first half of the century and one of the last common roles of the horse-drawn wagon. The milkman kept the buyer in touch with an actual dairy to which the empty bottles had to be returned for refilling. Marketers of animal products assumed a general familiarity with real animals. One mid-century hair cream commercial invited skeptical customers to run their hands through a sheep's wool and feel the natural lanolin that would lend a sheen to the wavy locks of whoever used the product. But by 1969, disposable cardboard cartons on supermarket shelves had long displaced the milkman, and nobody on Madison Avenue was proposing advertising campaigns based on presumed personal contact with a sheep or any other farm animal.

Whatever else might be said of the countercultural youth of 1969, the vast majority of them had grown up entirely removed from the world of domestic animals that their parents had taken for granted in their own childhoods: for them, there was no harnessing of horses, milking of cows, collecting eggs, plucking feathers, or butchering pigs. Some flower children followed their nature-loving consciences by abandoning meat and extolling vegetarianism. A few others bought a goat or two and retreated to communes in New Mexico. But every member of the post–World War II generation, whether hippie or Young Republican, reacted subliminally to the removal of domestic animals from their lives, and in particular to the disappearance of animal slaughter and animal sex from childhood experience.

Postdomestic Fantasies: Sex

Domestic societies around the world have generally had a scornful attitude toward engaging in sexual intercourse with animals,[2] but they have also recognized that it happens—and not all that infrequently. At the turn of the twentieth century, when domestic attitudes toward animals were still largely unquestioned and intellectual interest in sexual behavior was shifting from centuries of religious proscription and legal regulation to pseudoscientific study and classification, the pioneering sexologist Havelock Ellis made the following remarks:

> Bestiality . . . is . . . the sexual perversion of dull, insensitive, and unfastidious persons. It flourishes among primitive peoples and among peasants. It is the vice of the clodhopper, unattractive to women or inapt to court them. Three conditions have favored the extreme prevalence of bestiality: (1) primitive conceptions of life which built up no great barrier between man and the other animals; (2) the extreme familiarity which necessarily exists between the peasant and his beasts, often combined with separation from women; (3) various folk-lore beliefs such as the efficacy of intercourse with animals as a cure for venereal disease, etc.[3]

Though psychologists working decades later surpassed Ellis in many respects, his observation that sex with animals was of "extreme prevalence" probably reflects a degree of acquaintance with rural situations that was rapidly diminishing in Europe. Other reports support Ellis's view. Two surveys of the sexual practices of Soviet university students in the 1920s revealed that eight percent of men from peasant backgrounds admitted to having had intercourse with animals and considered it "a fairly natural part of a peasant childhood."[4] Men from village backgrounds in parts of the world still immersed in the mentality of domesticity readily recall certain companions of their adolescence—never themselves, of course—resorting to intercourse with an animal. On being informed that Americans use congress with a sheep as their bestiality cliché, one Turkish informant, who acknowledged that village acquaintances of his youth engaged in intercourse with donkeys, remarked: "A sheep? That's disgusting!"

Ellis considered the sow the most common sexual companion, but also knew of multiple instances involving mares, cows, donkeys, goats, and sheep. Instances of intercourse with dogs, cats, rabbits, hens, ducks, and geese also showed up occasionally in his research. Though Ellis considered bestiality primarily a male vice, he took note of numerous cases of women seeking gratification with dogs or having sex with dogs or donkeys as an entertainment for men—including in "select circles of Paris," according to one of his informants.

By contrast with the situation in domestic society, in postdomestic society male intercourse with animals appears to be rare. In this one small area, the rural-urban migration of postdomesticity seems to have fulfilled the age-old wish of sex regulators for an improvement in sexual mores, by separating men and boys from their pigs, sheep, and donkeys.

Yet fantasies of exhibitionistic sex involving women—especially intercourse between women and dogs or women and horses—continue to excite the interest of the postdomestic male, at least so far as one can judge from the abundant animal-sex pornographic sites on the Internet. This shift from actually having sex with animals to luridly fantasizing about it is part and parcel of the general shift from real-world carnality to sexual fantasy that is an integral aspect of the societal movement from domesticity to postdomesticity.

From the perspective of the generation of Havelock Ellis, the prime indicator of this shift has been the revaluation of masturbation, which went from being a dangerous habit subject to the sternest disapproval to being considered, by the 1970s, a harmless or even encouraged practice. Contemporary sex advice often observes that masturbation, the handmaiden of sexual fantasy, has never given anyone a sexually transmitted disease or caused an unwanted pregnancy. Rules and warnings about masturbation, from the biblical condemnation of the sin of Onan and the harsh penalties imposed on priests and monks in medieval penitentials to the moralizing paragraphs contained in early Boy Scout handbooks, culminated in the nineteenth century in pseudoscientific determinations that masturbation, primarily male, caused physical weakness and mental deterioration. Popular and scientific opinion alike identified blindness, idiocy, and death as the woeful consequences of habitual "self-abuse."

The first generation of Soviet students, who had openly and shamelessly admitted to having sex with animals, agonized over masturbation. "I may guess that the influence of masturbation has been mainly on the memory, which has begun to get noticeably duller," wrote one. "It sometimes happens when I start to speak that the thought which I had in my mind to say has got lost somewhere." Another wrote: "When I think about masturbation, my hair stands on end. It rises before me like a gigantic monster clutching me in its claws. As result of ten years of masturbation, I myself have turned from a man into a monster."[5]

The transition to postdomesticity contributes to an explanation of both the near disappearance of bestiality in the United States over the first half of the twentieth century and an increasingly benign—even downright positive—attitude toward masturbation in the second half. Moving adolescents off the farm and into the town largely explains the former phenomenon. Boys lost access to farm animals, and the increasing availability of the automobile for dating gained them private access to girlfriends.

The latter phenomenon, with its attendant rise of sexual fantasy, brings us back to Havelock Ellis's description of sex in the late domestic era:

Among children, both boys and girls, it is common to find that the copulation of animals is a mysteriously fascinating spectacle. It is inevitable that this should be so, for the spectacle is more or less clearly felt to be the revelation of a secret which has been concealed from them. It is, moreover, a secret of which they feel intimate reverberations within themselves, and even in perfectly innocent and ignorant children the sight may produce an obscure sexual excitement. It would seem that this occurs more frequently in girls than in boys. . . . The coupling of the larger animals is often an impressive and splendid spectacle which is far, indeed, from being obscene, and has commended itself to persons of intellectual distinction [Ellis footnotes here the Countess of Pembroke, Sir Philip Sydney's sister, whose interest in the mating of her horses his source describes as "very salacious"]; but in young or ill-balanced minds such sights tend to become both prurient and morbid.[6]

The unspoken assumption of this passage, whether one agrees with all its particulars or not, is that in Ellis's day and for many preceding centuries, both children and adults commonly witnessed animal copulation. The conditions of domesticity made this more or less inevitable. Not only did children observe what was going on around them—"the birds and the bees" was a euphemism for "the dogs and the horses" (has anyone outside entomological and beekeeping circles ever paid attention to bee sex?)—but they found it, in Ellis's words, "mysteriously fascinating."

It is hard to see much aesthetic appeal in the sight of dogs or sheep—or even humans—copulating. When the sight is novel, however, the viscera react. Children stare and become mysteriously fascinated. But then it ends. The show is over, even if the memory remains. It is a drama without visible climax and one that after a few repetitions is hardly worth looking at. Nevertheless, experience of sex acquired in this fashion cements the connection between sex and the real world of carnal contact. Animal mating spectacles literally leave nothing to the imagination. Inured to—and conditioned by—animal sexuality through frequent childhood exposure, therefore, adults in domestic societies experienced sex in later life in an overwhelmingly carnal fashion: a matter of smell, exertion, and tactile sensation carried out more often than not in the dark or with most of one's clothes on.

With the carnal reality of sexual intercourse the norm, religious moralists and would-be scientific analysts of sexual behavior understandably came to look upon imagined sex as perverse: the product of an unhealthy and fevered mind. Normal people, they decreed, wanted to engage in real sexual acts with real partners. To that end, they either looked for opportunities or took a cold shower. Normal people, the authorities further opined, shunned masturbation and dissuaded their children from indulging in it either by tongue-lashings or physical restraints, not just because it was nonprocreative (the opinion of thinkers like Immanuel Kant) or because it violated biblical law, but even more because of its attendant fantasizing. Blindness, symbolically a loss of the capacity to fantasize, became the popularly imagined penalty for masturbation, and madness the ultimate destination of the perverse mind absorbed with unhealthy sexual imaginings.

Though the fad for written pornography in Georgian and Victorian times testifies to a developing taste for imagined sex, especially among urban, upper-class sophisticates who were more or less removed from rural life, many well-known works took carnal reality and the portrayal of "real life" as erotic touchstones. John Cleland's notorious *Fanny Hill* (1749) was not the unsatisfied housewife, oversexed cheerleader, dominatrix, or blackmailed ingenue of late twentieth-century pornography, but a prostitute plying her trade while looking for true love, much in the manner of the more sedate confessional novels then enjoying popularity. The hundreds of acts of fornication described by a Londoner named Walter in the thousands of pages of *My Secret Life*, published perhaps in the 1870s, are presented with stupefying tedium as real-life experiences. No Internet-style fantasies about deep-space homosexual couplings between Captain Kirk and Mr. Spock for Walter. And *The Autobiography of a Flea* (1887) was largely devoted to the centuries-old—but always freshly exciting—pastime of uncovering sexual deviation in the Catholic Church, only one of a number of social critiques or problems addressed in nineteenth-century pornography.[7] This is not to say that genuine pornographic fantasies designed solely for sexual stimulation—as opposed to sexual instruction manuals, real or fictional diaries, Tantric devotional tracts, and salacious political satires—were never written in situations of domesticity. But it was notably in the final, postdomestic decades of the twentieth century that pornography came into full flower, and the orgiastic and patently unreal fantasies of the Marquis de Sade finally came to be appreciated by intellectuals as the writings of a man with presciently "modern" sensibilities.

Domestic-era fantasy-centered works like De Sade's do not weigh heavily when stacked up against the staggeringly huge library of fantasy-filled English-language pornography that has appeared in print and electronic form in the past thirty years. The genres into which this library divides—including topics like incest, pedophilia, mind control, science fiction, female domination, and BD/SM (bondage and discipline/sadism and masochism)—seldom evoke the real-life experiences of prostitutes, gigolos, nude dancers, and other actual sex workers.

By hiding the animal sex that in the domestic era was an inescapable component of life, and thereby keeping children "innocent" until their first adolescent encounters with pornographic images, postdomesticity encourages expressions of sexuality that put fantasy in the place of carnal reality. Scarcely do any children in postdomestic society encounter repeated instances of animal copulation. If they do run into a situation at the zoo or happen upon a pair of dogs lustily engaged, their parents are sure to do whatever they can think of to distract them. They certainly do not see animals engaged in sex frequently enough to become inured or bored. Postdomestic families take pains to screen such sights from their children on the assumption that they are revolting, corrupting, or revelatory of something children ought not to know anything about. As a result, the first visual encounters with sexual intercourse for today's postdomestic children come late, typically in early adolescence. Moreover, they most often come from pictorial fantasies in movies, magazines, or more recently, Internet sites. Sexual fantasy takes priority over real-world carnality, and masturbation takes priority over the actual act as a response activity.

In terms of the social benefits that so greatly concern contemporary moralists, whatever may be gained in terms of childhood innocence by postponing exposure to sex until early adolescence and then channeling it—unintentionally, of course, from the parents' point of view—through visual fantasies, must be weighed against the fact that postdomestic children do not have the opportunity to become sexually inured or bored before entering adolescence. When the first viscerally powerful exposure to sex occurs at age twelve instead of age six, a hormonally driven desire for more is inevitable, and the world of visual fantasy, whether hard-core pornography or the nudity and simulated sex scenes in R-rated movies, is there to satisfy it. It makes no difference whether one's upbringing is conservative or liberal. The pattern stems from postdomestic changes in living conditions that have affected virtually all nonrural families. Hence no amount of sermonizing can reverse the trend toward fantasy and away from carnal reality.

Postdomestic Fantasies: Blood

Most humans eat meat when it is available, though most cultures hem in the practice with taboos—no blood, no pork, no beef, no horse, or no dog, for instance. Since meat consumption generally rises with a society's standard of living, it seems apparent that as a species, humans like meat. It follows, therefore, that prior to our postdomestic age, humans looked at domestic meat animals with a clear and unemotional realization that they were destined to be slaughtered. The Oscar-winning movie *Babe* (1995), based on Dick King-Smith's 1983 children's story,[8] hinged on the conceit of an uncommonly bright pig catching on to this simple and horrifying (to the pig) truth. In making this discovery (scarcely present in the novel) the motivating spark of the motion picture, the Australian moviemakers George Miller and Chris Noonan— Australia is a major center of postdomestic thinking—promoted the postdomestic notion that if people could but realize the horror of such animals' lives, they would make short work of the meat industry. The same sentiment pops to mind regarding hunting, a normal male activity in domestic societies, whenever one hears deer hunters being accused of (or bragging about) "killing Bambi," a phrase that emerged as postdomestic code decades after the release of Disney's *Bambi* in 1942.

Whether the animal being killed is domestic or wild, one's first exposure to the real-life (real-death?) spectacle, or even to a realistic fantasy rendition, has a powerful visceral effect—as powerful as first witnessing sexual intercourse. On the sexual side of this comparison, there may well be some variation between the genders (boys perhaps being more affected than girls), but it is common knowledge that the first sight of a lot of blood causes many people, both male and female, to faint or feel sick, even when forewarned. It is also well understood that frequent exposure to the sight of blood tends to harden people to the point where they can tolerate it. The same fall-off of visceral stimulation in response to frequent exposure occurs with sex as well. Whether the spectacle is sex or blood, to keep the feeling strong, the details or vividness of the exposure must steadily intensify. This basic principle has driven the plot lines of hundreds of sex and horror movies. The most exuberant orgies and the bloodiest shootouts show up at the end.

In domestic societies, virtually everyone witnesses animal bloodshed and slaughter more or less frequently from childhood onward. In postdomestic societies, they don't. Even the most unscientific of surveys bears this out. A show of hands in a classroom at the American University of Beirut, in the sophisticated capital of a country still immersed in domesticity, indicated that 90 percent of AUB's students in 2004 had witnessed animal slaughter, as compared to well under 20 percent at Columbia University in New York City.

People living in domestic societies have for centuries considered it only natural to see hogs and sheep butchered, chickens beheaded, and carcasses hacked by meat cleavers. In the days when warfare consisted of soldiers chopping at one another with swords and axes, can it be doubted that the emotional hardening derived from exposure to animal slaughter helped toughen men for battle? Or that a lifetime of watching animals die fed into the popular enthusiasm for gladiatorial combat, public executions, bear-baiting, and other recreations now regarded as barbaric? When World War II–generation Americans talked about someone running around "like a chicken with its head cut off," they knew what they were talking about. A couple of centuries earlier, a parallel simile referred to severed heads with jaws still moving as if the deceased still talked. Today's children understand neither image from firsthand experience.

Postdomestic society hides animal bloodshed just as it hides animal intercourse. Postdomestic urban life is sex- and gore-free—at least as far as animals are concerned. This is part and parcel of the postdomestic contradiction: domestic animals must reproduce and be slaughtered to provide the products the society consumes, but these facts of life must not be witnessed. When cattleman-journalist Michael Pollan sought in 2001 to chronicle the life and death of a calf he had purchased for a story in *The New York Times Magazine*, the manager of the slaughterhouse for which his steer was destined permitted him to observe every stage of the animal's conversion into commercial products except for "the stunning, bleeding, and evisceration process."[9]

The desire to shelter children from violence and bloodshed is not, of course, solely a postdomestic sentiment. It can occasionally be found in other situations. In his *Utopia*, the sixteenth-century writer Thomas More imagined an ideal society in which only slaves kill animals because people "do not want their citizens to become hardened to the butchering of animals. For engaging in such activities, they believe, slowly destroys our capacity for compassion, which more than any other sentiment distinguishes human beings from other animals."[10] An echo of More's concern comes from contemporary India, where despite the vegetarian preference of a large proportion of the population, animal slaughter for meat consumption is common, and everyday close contact between humans and animals marks the society as a whole as a domestic one. In 1998, the Calcutta *Telegraph* reported the plan of the Calcutta Municipal Commission to force butchers to put curtains in front of their shops. According to Commissioner Asim Barman, the "open display of slaughtered animals looks cruel and affects children. . . . The sight of chickens being hacked and cut into pieces is gruesome. . . . As it is done in open marketplaces or on roads, it draws out cruel instincts among children."[11] Despite such scattered humane sentiments, however, only postdomestic societies have populations that are sufficiently removed from regular contact with domestic animals to make possible this understandable desire to shelter children from coarsening experiences.

But would this desire have been so understandable in earlier ages? As predatory animals in a leopard-eat-man environment, the hominid ancestors of *homo sapiens* benefited from visceral arousal at the sight of flowing blood just as they did from constant readiness for sexual intercourse. Success in the hunt hinged on a lust for killing, at least among males, and the reproductive survival of the group, in the absence of a fixed rutting season, depended upon male sexual arousal in response to sensual stimuli. These two forms of lust may not then have been as visually focused as they later became, but these primordial visceral responses to blood and sex certainly continue to exist in our species. Even today, humans are still animals drawn to the consumption of meat, continuously capable of sexual arousal, and vision oriented. Sex and blood are still turn-ons.

However, though human instincts may have changed little, postdomesticity has brought to an end the previously unavoidable witnessing of animal slaughter by small children. The postdomestic movie *The Silence of the Lambs* (1991) correctly assumed that American audiences would empathize with the feelings of a heroine who was traumatized as a child by exposure to the slaughter of lambs, as symbolized by the lambs bleating for their mothers. What the screenplay did not consider is the fact that people who in their younger years *frequently* witness hog butchering or chicken decapitation, and who see these bloody events treated as commonplace by adult role models, eventually come to take them for granted. Repetition, particularly within a cultural pattern in which animal slaughter, like animal sex, is open and normal, dulls the senses. Visceral responses subside. A remnant of what this bygone life was like survives in the annual Miss Navajo Nation competition, where every lovely and well-educated contestant must demonstrate an ability to slaughter and skin a sheep.[12]

When and how does today's postdomestic child encounter killing and bloodletting? From wildlife documentaries on television, or perhaps news reports from crime scenes or battlefields. In terms of visceral impact, however, slice-and-dice horror movies trump these snippets of real life. Just as postdomestic sex focuses on media-aided adolescent fantasy, so the blood and gore that children could not help witnessing in the era of domesticity gives way in postdomesticity to fantasies of blood marketed to adolescents. And since fantasies must be ratcheted up to keep the visceral thrills coming, the imagining of sex and blood in movies, photographs, and fiction steadily increases and pushes the ever-receding boundaries of taste.

This does not mean that domestic or earlier "predomestic" cultures—we'll come to "predomesticity" in the next chapter—knew nothing of the gratuitous violence that marks these movies. Quite the contrary. Some pastoral societies, such as the Central Asian Mongol and Turkic peoples of centuries past, have historically shown a particularly strong propensity to shed blood in the course of conquest. Tamerlane's fourteenth-century pyramids of skulls seem not to have been a myth. Romans and Aztecs reveled in the sight of blood in mortal combat, the sacking of cities, and ritual sacrifice. And public hangings and decapitations drew enormous crowds in early modern England and France. But in these instances, the bloodshed was all too horribly real. Contemporary engravings and descriptions of these ghastly events do not particularly emphasize the gory details that postdomestic filmmakers lavish attention on. Carnal reality made fantasy unnecessary, since everyone already knew what killing looked like.

Paradoxically, postdomestic societies with high levels of sex-and-blood pornography may exhibit a strong and generalized abhorrence for real-life maiming, killing, and sexual predation—alongside a prurient fascination with real excesses that come to public attention through the press. There is a reciprocal relationship, it seems, between doing and fantasizing. Our contemporary engagement in the latter at the expense of the former derives in substantial part from the deferral into adolescence of the visceral responses to blood and sexual intercourse that are innate in our species. Domestic society, by exposing children to sex and bloodshed, hardens them early and causes them to think of sex and blood in terms of real-life carnality rather than fantasy. Grown to adulthood, they prefer—or at least expect—the real thing, the actual bloodshed and intercourse, and thus respond less strongly to fantasized depictions.

Domestic societies kill domestic and wild animals without guilt and according to what they see as their needs. These needs can include sport and entertainment along with the consumption of flesh and skin. Post-domestic society anguishes over both sorts of killing, but cannot escape the demand for animal products that can be satisfied in no other way. It also anguishes over the suspected but unproven effect on children of blood and killing in movies and on television. As with violent sex acts in pornography, optimists sometimes cite the reciprocal relationship between doing and fantasizing to argue that blood fantasies sate violent urges and prevent them from being acted upon. This contention recalls the post–Civil War American argument that the rugged college sporting events then gaining popularity could satisfy young men's yen for violence and thereby lessen the likelihood of war. Appropriately, today's postdomestic attitude toward sports involves less participation and live spectating and more vicarious involvement through the mass media. Professional wrestling, currently a popular staple of cable television, substitutes fantasy violence for the real thing, leaving only meager audiences for the genuine pain and bloodshed of professional boxing. Jesse Ventura and The Rock gain entry into civil society by faking violence; Mike Tyson remains on its margins for actually dishing it out.

Postdomestic Behaviors: Elective Vegetarianism

Whereas the connection of a sea change in human-animal relations to the burgeoning of pornographies of sex and blood is largely subliminal, certain other responses reflect a greater consciousness of changed conditions. Foremost among conscious postdomestic behaviors is elective vegetarianism. Most observant Muslims and Jews do not eat pork because they were brought up not to eat pork in homes that considered this stricture a divine injunction. Many observant Hindus, Jains, and Buddhists do not eat meat (and sometimes eggs and milk products) because they learn as children that these products are forbidden. How they understand this prohibition varies. Some are instructed in the religious doctrine of the transmigration of souls, and conclude that their own soul might be housed in an animal body in its next incarnation. Some subscribe to the doctrine of *ahimsa*, the prohibition of injury to sentient beings. But many are simply told that the cow is their mother and hence not to be harmed, much less eaten.

Other food taboos in domestic societies are less strongly rooted in religious or ethical precept. The Tuareg tribes of the southern Sahara do not eat eggs or chickens. But don't ask them why. The Alevi Shi'ite Muslims of Turkey do not eat rabbits, and the Shi'ites of Iran do not eat eels.

Americans do not eat horses or dogs. The list of actual taboos is extensive, particularly in comparison with the rarity of religious taboos on eating vegetable products.[13]

All of these limitations on the consumption of animal flesh or animal
products have cultural roots that are considered primordial or else stem
from cultural revulsions so general within a particular society that few
households violate the accepted norm. They rarely arise as matters of
debate, though the nineteenth-century passion for rational explanation
did lead to many far-fetched rationales, usually anchoring meat taboos
in precocious notions of health awareness or ecological balance among
ancient ancestors. The fact of the matter is that people who customarily
don't eat pork don't eat pork because their tradition tells them not to,
not because they worry that undercooking will lead to infection by trichi-
nosis parasites. Modern South Americans who invoke a similar fear of
parasitic disease to explain their shunning of llama meat use pseudo-
science for the opposite reason, to separate themselves from the "backward" llama-eating tradition of the country people.

The extreme of not consuming meat we call vegetarianism. Refusal to
consume any animal products at all is sometimes called by the same name
and sometimes labeled "vegan," a term coined in 1944 when Donald Watson and Elsie Shrigley founded The Vegan Society in England. Whatever
the label, there is a world of difference between the cultural meat taboos
of domestic societies and postdomestic elective vegetarianism. No Muslim, Jewish, or Hindu household of, say, the eighteenth century can plausibly be imagined encountering the following American dilemma:

> After seeing the movie "Babe" at age 9 and realizing the source of
> what was on her plate, Lauren Pierpoint of Boulder decided to
> stop eating meat. At age 6, Nathan Kessel of Boston was given a
> choice by his parents between a vegetarian diet and eating meat
> regularly; he has been a vegetarian for three years now.
>
> With a finicky toddler who would spit out any type of meat,
> Heidi Feldman of Norcross, Ga., decided "almost overnight" to put
> her entire family on a vegetarian diet. School lessons about endan-
> gered species combined with a visit to the zoo persuaded 7-year-old
> Laura Grzenda of Boulder to stop eating meat.
>
> "Every time I put a piece of meat in my mouth, I felt like the ani-
> mal was talking to me," Laura, now 12, said. "It was saying 'Moo,
> don't eat me.' "[14]

This, in one permutation or another—compassion for meat animals being raised under inhumane conditions; fear of bacterial, antibiotic, or steroid contamination stemming from those conditions; conviction that eating meat is not conducive to health; unwillingness to consume anything with a face—is elective vegetarianism: a conscious choice, usually contrary to family tradition, to avoid some or all meats. It is spreading in our postdomestic society with such phenomenal speed that most restaurants in major metropolitan areas now offer vegetarian entrees that would not have appeared on their menus a decade ago. Yet it is still only a threat on the beefy horizon in states like South Dakota, where a questionnaire administered to fifty adults chosen at random yielded fourteen who had no familiarity at all with the word "vegan."[15]

Nevertheless, the production of meat worldwide is also spreading fast because of the truism mentioned earlier—economic development results in people eating more and more meat. In 1998, the United Nations Human Development Report noted that Americans, whether postdomestic or still oriented toward yesterday's domestic habits, consume an average of 260 pounds of meat per year, compared with 6.5 pounds in the domestic Muslim society of Bangladesh.[16] American development economists take this human craving for meat as a given in calculating future agricultural patterns worldwide. Yet more and more Americans find the practice of meat eating—indeed, the very concept—revolting.

Paradoxically, the simultaneous expansion of meat consumption and of elective vegetarianism results from the same aspect of postdomesticity: the push to maximize productivity and minimize the cost to the consumer. By raising and processing animals in ways that seem inhumane and revolting to real and potential vegetarians whose lives are entirely disconnected from animal husbandry, meat producers make eating meat more affordable and thus help to expand the market.

Compared with vegetable products, meat has always been costly, one way or another. The hominid ancestors of *homo sapiens* were poorly equipped to run down and kill large animals, at least until they invented stone and wooden tools to substitute for the fangs and claws of true carnivores. Just as modern anthropoid apes, the species most closely related to humans, eat mostly vegetation, so did primeval humanity.[17] To be sure, the big-game hunters of the Ice Age tundra may have relied overwhelmingly on animal products, as the Inuit of the Arctic do today, but judging from the diets of most peoples who still forage for their sustenance and live entirely on wild products, the Inuits were probably the exception rather than the rule. Even after the emergence of domestic species removed the necessity of tracking a wild animal, risking one's life killing it, and hauling its carcass back to the family, meat was not truly abundant. The size of herds and flocks determined wealth, and the pastoral nomads who were most heavily involved in raising animals preferred to husband their wealth by concentrating their consumption on milk products and young male offspring, rather than deplete it by excess meat eating.

Since animals, like humans, convert much of the vegetation they eat into energy or waste, and only a comparatively small portion into edible fat and muscle, more useful calories can be produced per acre by planting grain and turning it into flour than by feeding the grain to an animal and eating the animal. Pastoralists, of course, steered their herds into wasteland not under cultivation, and the animals kept around farms and villages normally gained much of their sustenance from straw, inedible field stubble, or garbage.[18] On the whole, however, there was seldom enough stubble or garbage to provide meat in abundance. If meat was to be more than a seldom-tasted luxury, traditional patterns of animal husbandry had to be supplemented by hunting, or made more productive by the introduction of scientific methods.

Selective breeding, rapid-weight-gain diets, energy-saving confinement of growing animals, motorized transport to prevent weight loss during long drives to market, improved meat preservation, and most recently, treatment with antibiotics and growth hormones are some of the factors that have enabled food producers to increase the amount of affordable meat available per capita. But these are comparatively recent developments. In the early nineteenth century, most consumers, even in a prosperous, industrializing country like France, seldom ate fresh meat. The innovation of licensing horse butchers in France in 1862 was explicitly intended by the scientific commission that advocated it as a means of providing more meat to the working class by harvesting the bodies of superannuated work horses.[19] The largest gains in the efficiency of U.S. meat production, with the corresponding reduction of costs relative to product yield, took place in the second half of the twentieth century, and industrial methods of meat processing continue to be refined every year. Fortunately for postdomestic souls who prefer to keep their feelings of guilt suppressed, these changes have come about more or less invisibly, since rural-urban migration has denuded the agricultural landscape of witnesses.

Nevertheless, exposés of unappealing practices in the meat industry date from *The Jungle* (1906), Upton Sinclair's sensational novel about the Chicago stockyards.[20] More recently, numerous writers have described the poultry, pork, and beef industries in graphic and sometimes stomach-turning detail.[21] For the most part, however, the meat-consuming public turns a selectively deaf ear to these descriptions. Meat comes to the consumer in a paper-wrapped burger or in familiar cuts laid out on Styrofoam trays covered with transparent polyethylene film. And that is the way the consumer wants it: as far removed as possible from the realities of fattening, killing, and dismemberment.

Thus the "improvements" in animal husbandry that encourage predictions of ever-greater meat consumption worldwide are the same processes that provoke revulsion against meat eating among American children. How this paradox will ultimately be resolved is one of the mysteries of postdomesticity.

Postdomestic Behaviors: Hunting and Blood Sports

Watching animals fight one another has riveted the attention of humans since predomestic times. Ancient images of animals in combat amply attest to this fascination. Indeed, it is possible that the wild jungle fowl of southeastern Asia evolved into the domestic chicken more because humans enjoyed cock fighting, which subsequently spread worldwide, than because they needed meat and eggs. Hunting, whether for food, defense of home and family, or just the thrill of the chase, is at least as ancient. On the surface, the fate of these primal fascinations in the postdomestic era is obvious: Down with hunting, fur trapping, and bullfighting! Underneath, the changes in attitude are more subtle.

Take animals fighting: As an artistic motif and as combat in the flesh, animal combat is known in almost every society, with a large variety of animals: cocks, bulls, camels, dogs, quail, insects, and fish combat members of the same species; dogs fought rats, bears, and bulls in Georgian England; carnivores hunted humans and other animals in the Roman arena; and humans have confronted bulls from Minoan times in the thirteenth century B.C.E. down to present-day Spain and Latin America.

The postdomestic mentality takes an extremely dim view of all of these contests, though they have proved hard to stamp out. Yet few aspects of animal behavior attract more viewers to nature documentaries than scenes of animals hunting and killing other animals, or male animals in rut "butting heads" or "locking horns"—notice how vivid these phrases are. Postdomestic society wants to abolish the staged spectacle of animals killing or fighting other animals, just as it wants to hide domestic animal copulation and slaughter—but animal killing continues to fascinate on the screen or the tube.

With hunting, the contradiction is more stark. People who oppose hunting at the same time consume the flesh and wear the hide of slaughtered animals. They often conceive of the animals killed or maimed in hunting and blood sports as innocents, even when those species are themselves carnivores that naturally prey upon other species. Since they live in the wild, and nature's food chain requires that some animals eat other animals, a fox killing a pheasant gets placed in a separate conceptual category from a farmer killing a chicken. Hunters might contend that hominid predation has for a million years been as much a part of nature as have lions gobbling up the old, young, and slow members of grazing herds. However, since people immersed in postdomesticity do not generally believe that anyone in the modern world needs to kill or trap game for livelihood or personal sustenance, the killing of wild beasts (except for vermin and, in some minds, birds and fish) seems worse than unnecessary. It is wanton, excessive, cruel, vicious, and primitive.

The postdomestic conscience thus accords animals in the wild a right to life—a life preferably undisturbed in their natural state. However, the very expression of such an idea betrays feelings of guilt about those species whose usefulness to human beings strips them of an equivalent right. There are many ways of rationalizing this guilt. Some argue that humans created domestic species and therefore have a right of disposal over them. Other defenders of the double standard for wild and domestic beasts maintain that domestic animals are property, with the implication of a similar right of disposal. Comparison with the long-discredited arguments giving a slaveowner the right to take the life of a slave indicates the philosophical problem here.

Still others contend that humans have so transformed domestic species and bred out of them the characteristics needed for survival in the wild that their only remaining claim to life is to provide products for humans. Yet populations of domestic animals living in the wild—the proper term is "feral animals"—abound in many parts of the world and include every domestic species: horses, donkeys, pigs, goats, dogs, cats, camels, cattle, and so forth. Pigeons are domestic animals run wild, and despite their domestic penchant for hanging around humans, they don't seem to have much trouble surviving. None of these rationalizations has proved sufficient to expunge the sense of guilt that comes from society's passive acceptance of the slaughter of domestic animals. Proclaiming the urgent necessity of saving Bambi from the deer hunter is the least a post-domestic person can do to salve a conscience subliminally disturbed by last night's veal scaloppini.

As one would expect, this awkwardness about killing shows up in the world of visual representation as well. From the 1930s to the early 1950s, at the tail end of the domestic era in the United States, big-game hunting and lion-taming movies by the likes of Clyde Beatty (*King of Jungleland*, 1936) and Frank Buck (*Jacare*, 1942) enjoyed great popularity. Postdomestic sensitivities have kept reruns of these films to a minimum in recent years, however. Today's audiences are uncomfortable with portrayals of wild *mammals*—note the stress on mammals—as dangerous to humans. In the *King Kong* of 1933, the heroine, played by Fay Wray, hates the giant ape who abducts her. In the big-budget 1976 remake, Jessica Lange, in her screen debut, tries to save King Kong and weeps over his broken body. Reluctant to present the hunting of mammals as acceptable or to cast wild carnivores as villains, filmmakers have cast less closely related vertebrates—birds, snakes, alligators, dinosaurs, sharks—as frightening animal adversaries, hoping as they do so that audiences will be willing to accept screenplays that locate a malign intelligence in the often peanut-sized brains of these menaces.

An even better postdomestic solution has been to find animal danger in an entirely different zoological class. *Them!* (1954) initiated this trend by infesting New Mexico with ants mutated into giants by nuclear bomb testing. The ants weren't intelligent, but the movie's posters, unlike the film itself, showed them with a decidedly murderous gaze in their humanoid eyeballs. The apotheosis of this genre is arguably 1979's *Alien*. No viewer could possibly object to frightened, endangered humans trying to kill huge, maybe intelligent, insectlike monsters from outer space that planted their larvae in human hosts who subsequently suffered ghastly deaths when the infant monsters burst through their abdomens. After successful sequels in 1986, 1992, and 1997, enthusiasts thrilled to learn of a 2004 showdown, already available in comic books, between the Aliens, the perfect carnivores, and the Predators, the perfect extraterrestrial hunters who debuted in the film of that name in 1987. Paul Verhoeven's *Starship Troopers* (1997) and *Men in Black* (1997), starring Tommie Lee Jones and Will Smith, legitimated insects as targets of human violence by making jokes likening intelligent but murderous insects from other planets to cockroaches. Given the proliferation of postdomestic anxieties, we are likely to see many more films about monstrous insects before another one is made about a man-eating tiger. Silly though they may seem, they feed on one of the deepest of inherited human fears: the fear of being eaten alive.

Postdomestic Science

The famous notion of "paradigm shifts" elaborated by Thomas Kuhn in *The Structure of Scientific Revolutions* (1962) has been applied, borrowed, or critiqued countless times. Simply put, Kuhn maintained that certain sets of scientific ideas, such as Newtonian physics or the Ptolemaic earth-centered universe, constituted "normal science" in their day. They answered most of the questions people had about the world, but the limitations of their own incomplete representations of nature also put limits on the range of questions that could be entertained. Over time, the buildup of questions that could not be answered within the paradigm gave rise to a period of new and multifaceted conjecture and observation, culminating in a shift to a new paradigm: a new model of "normal science." In some respects, the transition from domesticity to postdomesticity resembles the sort of paradigm shift Kuhn had in mind. People think about human-animal relations now in ways that were literally unthinkable two hundred years ago, and the postdomestic mentality finds ridiculous many things accepted as self-evident truths in the bygone domestic era, such as the idea that animals have no feelings. But there is no reason to try to force Kuhn's notions yet again into a historical change that is not fundamentally scientific. Postdomesticity has radically altered the scale of values by which scientific research is popularly appraised, but it has not produced a fundamentally different scientific model.

Beyond creating a greater sensitivity about the humane treatment of animal subjects, postdomestic value changes do not govern the way scientists conduct their research. But they have affected public reception of research results. Systematic if not truly scientific research on domestic animals as species dates to the second half of the eighteenth century, when an English farmer named Robert Bakewell developed the New Leicester breed of comparatively fat sheep by "in-and-in" breeding. The practice involved restricting reproduction that had previously taken place on a free-range basis and selectively mating animals with desired traits, including sires with their own female offspring. Once the trait of excessive fat was established, Bakewell rented his rams to other farmers so they could benefit from the "improved" breed. Bakewell's sheep, and his similarly "improved" breed of longhorn cattle, lost popularity after his death, when gustatory tastes shifted to leaner meat. However, a shorthorn cattle breed developed by his apprentice Charles Colling benefited from this change in tastes, and many other breeders took up selective mating.

"Improvement" of domestic animals—that is to say, intensification of some trait desired by consumers of animal products—has continued to the present day to be a primary goal, along with the treatment of disease, of domestic animal science. But where scientists who could increase egg or milk production or make meat animals grow fatter quicker enjoyed public approval through the first half of the twentieth century, further developments along these lines in postdomestic society have met with vociferous criticism. Feeding techniques that fatten cattle quickly and help lower meat prices evoke complaints that the beef has an inferior flavor. Antibiotics added to the feed to ensure animal health and hormones added to speed fattening excite fears of transmission to consumers. Spatial and organizational schemes designed to limit animal movement and reduce wastage of calories (for example, the infamous "veal-fattening pen") appear to critics to be cruel and inhumane. DNA manipulation ("frankenfoods") inspires diffuse fears and categorical rejection. The underlying rationale of the science hasn't changed, but what was once seen as a public good now seems fraught with liabilities.

Schemes for transferring domestic livestock into new habitats have encountered a similar shift in the evaluation of scientific research. From the days of Columbus onward, explorers and colonists made it a practice of bringing European farm animals with them. These imports commonly decimated local fauna by eating their eggs and young or by competing for grazing room, and they permanently altered the lifestyles of hundreds of non-European peoples.[22] Secure in their domestic mentality and its core principle that the exploitation of domestic animals takes priority over any concern with wild animals, Europeans saw nothing wrong in what they were doing. In the nineteenth century, they embraced the transplantation of species as a progressive scientific enterprise. In the France of Napoleon III, for example, the *Bulletin de la Société Impériale Zoologique d'Acclimatation* reported on scores of schemes for introducing llamas to the Pyrenees, yaks to France, and camels to Brazil. Most of them never came to pass, but people enjoyed reading about such scientific enterprises, and showed little or no concern for the possible effect on native wild fauna.

To today's postdomestic eye, tampering with the faunal diversity of a region looks suspicious. Postdomestic historians vividly recount the worst experiences of centuries past, from the eradication of much of the native wildlife of Hawaii by dogs, pigs, and other European domesticates, to the rabbit infestation of Australia, which began when a single rancher introduced bunnies onto his property in 1859. The domestic animals that were once released into the wild without a second thought, such as the starlings set free in New York's Central Park as part of a campaign to introduce into the United States every bird mentioned by Shakespeare, now raise anguishing questions. Should the feral mustangs and wild burros of the American West be preserved as part of the natural ecology, or should they be eradicated or thinned out to improve living conditions for pronghorn and other indigenous species? Should the feral camels of Australia, the end product of the deliberate introduction of camels for laboring purposes in 1860, be classified as vermin and shot because of their habit of walking through rabbit-proof fences while they graze, or should they be valued as a picturesque feature of the outback?[23] Whatever eventually becomes of such transplants, the current postdomestic mood looks dimly on what was considered a valid avenue of scientific experiment a century and a half ago.

Counterbalancing the declining appreciation of scientific research on improving domestic animals and transplanting them to new habitats has been a meteoric increase in popular enthusiasm for nonlethal scientific observation of wild animal species. European naturalists performed prodigious acts of collection and classification toward the end of the domestic era. John James Audubon, Charles Darwin, and Alfred Russell Wallace thought nothing of killing a woodpecker, fox, or bird of paradise and having it skinned and stuffed for display. A field researcher today can still collect insects in this way, but the preferred technique is patient and detailed observation of species in the wild. The popular appetite for such studies, which in Victorian times would have resulted in a learned paper being read before a scientific society, seems boundless, particularly when the findings touch on possible links with humans.

From 1970 on, field observations of chimpanzees by Jane Goodall, followed by the work of other primatologists, have headed the list of popular accounts;[24] but Edward O. Wilson demonstrated that even the study of ants could lead to conclusions pertaining to humans as a social species when he published *Sociobiology: The New Synthesis* in 1975.[25] In 1973, at the dawning of the postdomestic era, Konrad Lorenz, Karl von Frisch, and Nikolaas Tinbergen put ethology, the zoological study of animal behavior, on the scientific map by winning the Nobel Prize. But their prizewinning studies conducted in earlier decades did not gain them a wide popular following. The contemporary cachet accorded to studies of animals in the wild stems directly from postdomestic changes in the popular appreciation of animal science.

Postdomestic Symbolism

The waning of direct contact with productive domestic animals has been accompanied by a powerful desire to humanize animals of all sorts, including farm animals. From the turn of the twentieth century though the 1950s, the children and grandchildren of people who had exchanged life on the farm for life in town incorporated humanized farm animals into romantic visions of a bucolic past with which they had physically lost touch. The Walt Disney creations most closely connected with farm life, Clarabelle Cow and Horace Horsecollar, date to 1928 and 1929, respectively, which makes them just about as old as Mickey Mouse. However, they virtually disappeared from the silver screen after 1942, while Mickey continued to flourish, becoming more human in dress and manner with every passing year. In fiction, Beatrix Potter created and drew many little animals dressed in human clothes in the several dozen books she authored between *The Tale of Peter Rabbit* in 1900 and *The Tale of Little Pig Robinson* in 1930, but the story that overshadows all the rest is Peter's terrifying encounter with mean Farmer McGregor.

As the post-farm generation aged, humanized wild animals gradually shouldered farm animals off the stage. Disney released *Bambi* in 1942 and gave the chipmunks Chip and Dale to the world one year later. The latter flourished through the mid-1950s, when Clarabelle Cow and Horace Horsecollar were well into retirement. Warner Brothers handled the transition skillfully, if unconsciously. The studio's 1935 release *I Haven't Got a Hat* featured several fresh animal characters, some of them derived domestic-style from paired food items—"Ham and Ex" and "Porky and Beans." The only successful newcomer was Porky Pig, who is clearly based on a farm animal and not on wild swine. He starred in seventeen cartoons in 1936, half the time with Beans the Cat. The next year brought sixteen more, all without Beans. In one of his solo cartoons, *Porky's Duck Hunt*, the humanized pig went hunting for Daffy Duck, an animal with wild coloration, in contrast to the white domestic coloration of Donald Duck, a Disney creation that debuted in 1934. Bugs Bunny, again a wild animal with wild coloration, came to the screen in 1938 in *Porky's Hare Hunt*.

The most successful transition from domestic to wild animals took place in 1949, with the first Wile E. Coyote–Road Runner cartoon by Chuck Jones. Like the "wild" animals Daffy Duck and Bugs Bunny, they did not wear clothes; unlike them they did not talk, though they could read signs (and the coyote could produce them at will). Wile E.'s Sisyphean efforts to catch and eat the innocent but smart-alecky road-runner in thirty-nine cartoons made through 1966 became a metaphor for human hope and frustration that outlived its farm-based predecessors.

By the time American postdomesticity reached full flower in the 1970s, the animated animal cartoon had begun its plunge into decadence and sterility. Not until 1991 and the television debut of Ren and Stimpy, the crazed Chihuahua and moronic cat created by John Kricfalusi, did truly postdomestic cartoon animals reach the screen. Their humanization was so complete that it was difficult to tell what species of animal they were, and their antics strayed as far from the middle-class behavior of Mickey and his friends as taste would allow—and for conservative viewers a bit beyond.

Nevertheless, the heyday of the cartoon animals that had helped bridge the migration from farm life to city life was over. The cinematic future of humanized animals, whether drawn, acted, or filmed in the flesh, lay either in comedies anchored on the conceit that animals can talk and perceive things exactly as humans do—*Antz* (1998), *Dr. Doolittle* (2001), and *Dogs and Cats* (2001)—or in stories that directly engaged postdomestic anxieties. In *Escape from the Planet of the Apes* (1971), intelligent chimpanzees debate the ethics of animal experimentation with their human captors, a subject that was absent from the first film in the series, in 1968. In addition to *Babe* (1995), *Chicken Run* (2000) features claymation hens who plot their escape from a poultry farm designed like a Nazi prison camp, and *Finding Nemo* (2003) focuses on aquarium fish who live in terror of a little girl whose finny pets inevitably go belly-up.

Specific release dates make tracing the history of animals in cartoons and movies easy. Other manifestations of postdomestic animal symbolism are harder to pinpoint chronologically. Take atavistic longing for farm life: when did nonfarming people with homes on rural roads adopt the practice of putting life-size, naturalistically painted, plastic farm animals in their front yards? Or take substituting an animal for Jesus at Christmas: when did the simple outline of a reindeer in lights become a Christmas lawn decoration symbolizing the whole team drawing Santa's sleigh?

In some instances, such as Beat Seeberger-Quin's project to display 800 large fiberglass cows, bizarrely painted by local artists, on the streets of Zürich in 1998, which was imitated with great success in "cow parades" in Chicago (1999) and New York (2000), the meaning of the animal symbolism is almost impenetrable. As *New York Times* reporter John Kifner wrote: "In Chicago, more than 10 million people saw the exhibition, called CowParade, generating more than $500 million in tourist revenue. Of course, Chicago, of stockyards fame, has a long connection with cattle. New York's relationship with cows is more tenuous, particularly since the recent shrinkage of the bull market."[26]

I believe that any person brought up in domesticity with no previous exposure to postdomestic peculiarities, if miraculously translated across time and space to New York for a viewing of its "cow parade," would be completely baffled. The statues were fun to look at, but they were utterly devoid of meaning. Nothing remained to connect the gaudy beasts with the culture of cattle utilization that may just barely have retained some resonance in Zürich and Chicago. The conjectural time traveler would have been as amazed as was the erudite, British-educated Pakistani scholar who once expressed to me his complete bewilderment, tinged with disgust, at the gratitude toward a pet dog expressed by an American scholar in the introduction to a scholarly monograph. For people who live within the postdomestic worldview, it is hard to grasp how odd many contemporary attitudes toward animals seem from a domestic perspective.

Postdomestic Philosophy and Religion

Intellectually inclined readers might object to my beginning this chapter with sex and violence and leaving the animal rights movement to the end. However, my purpose has been to show that postdomestic attitudes affect everyone in this country, and in a few other countries as well. Though most Americans (myself included) are not vegetarians, everyone is aware of the growth of vegetarianism. Though many Americans hunt, everyone is aware of the outcry against hunting. And everyone goes to the movies, where pornographies of sex and blood fascinate the youth audience, and stories directed specifically at children contain the most eloquent expositions of postdomestic concern.

By comparison, espousal of animal rights has not yet permeated the United States as deeply as it has Britain, and its philosophical and religious complexities do not attract most nonacademic readers. Australian-born Peter Singer, an Oxford (and now Princeton) philosophy professor, revealed the world of postdomestic moral anxieties for the American intellectual public with his 1973 review of *Animals, Men, and Morals: An Enquiry into the Maltreatment of Non-humans* (1972) in *The New York Review of Books.*[27] The book itself had much less effect. Nevertheless, the books that followed over the next few years showed a movement already in full swing in Britain. Singer's own book *Animal Liberation: A New Ethics for Our Treatment of Animals* appeared in 1975.[28] By 1985, when he again addressed human-animal relations in *The New York Review*, he commented on ten recent books dealing with everything from animals as victims in experimentation to antibiotics and hormones in the meat industry to animal rights and environmentalism. Singer pursued his scrutiny of the ethics of experimenting on animals in a review of two further books in 1989, brought out a revised and updated version of his own book a year later, and reviewed five more books on animal rights, the cattle industry, and animal husbandry and the environment in 1992.

Though the positions advocated in these works were passionately held, both for and against animal rights, the debate that Singer's writings summarized was intellectually elevated and for the most part deeply informed. It also tapped philosophical roots that had previously been largely ignored. In evaluating animal exploitation, Singer himself followed utilitarian principles that harked back to Jeremy Bentham. In 1781, Bentham wrote:

> Other animals, which, on account of their interests having been neglected by the insensibility of the ancient jurists, stand degraded into the class of *things*. . . . The day has been, I grieve it to say in many places it is not yet past, in which the greater part of the species, under the denomination of slaves, have been treated . . . upon the same footing as . . . animals are still. The day may come, when the rest of the animal creation may acquire those rights which never could have been withholden from them but by the

hand of tyranny. The French have already discovered that the blackness of skin is no reason why a human being should be abandoned without redress to the caprice of a tormentor. It may come one day to be recognized, that the number of legs, the villosity of the skin, or the termination of the *os sacrum*, are reasons equally insufficient for abandoning a sensitive being to the same fate. What else is it that should trace the insuperable line? Is it the faculty of reason, or perhaps, the faculty for discourse? . . . the question is not, Can they *reason*? nor, Can they *talk*? but, Can they *suffer*? [29]

Arguing that animals above a certain level of neurological complexity share with humans a capacity for suffering, Singer followed Bentham and maintained that their suffering should be considered in any moral calculus of the benefits and drawbacks of experiments on animals and other painful impositions. On his right, philosophers including Michael Leahy of England's University of Kent defended the traditional deep divide between humanity and animality.[30] On his left, Tom Regan of the University of North Carolina, Keith Tester of the University of Portsmouth in England, and others took more absolutist positions in favor of animal rights. In *Animals and Society: The Humanity of Animal Rights* (1991),[31] Tester outlined six moral desiderata:

1. Animals should have complete freedom from human interference, with total separation from pets, wild animals, [and] farm animals.

2. It is unequivocal—no . . . slippage is possible on any site of human-animal relations.

3. Vegetarianism is essential.

4. It is asserted as a natural right. Animals are individuals with feelings; freedom is a natural need; they can suffer and their ability to suffer stems from their nature.

5. The expression of rights for animals is concerned with what it is to be properly human and implies the moral turpitude of disbelievers.

6. Believers are morally obliged to further the cause of animal rights; it is their responsibility as humans.[32]

Theologians entered into the debate with a special concern for finding bases for animal rights in Christian and Jewish writings.[33] This proved to be a daunting task, given the degree to which the worldview of domesticity was rooted in scripture. Jesus and his disciples were not vegetarians, and the temple rituals described in great detail in the Torah put animal sacrifice front and center.

As compelling and passionate as the philosophical and theological debate became for intellectuals, the animal rights movement also attracted activists, though in rather limited numbers. Animal liberation seemed to some like a worthy, if fuzzily conceived, successor to black liberation, women's liberation, and gay liberation. To many others it resonated more with the abortion debate but seemed more black and white. An animal destined for slaughter, after all, was as defenseless as a fetus, and no one could claim that preventing its slaughter would infringe or usurp a woman's or anyone else's right of choice—except at the dinner table.

In the background of the animal rights debate stood the meat industry: the great killer, the ultimate agent of human exploitation of animals. Outcries against the meat industry may not formally call upon the philosophical premises of animal liberation, but they are part of the movement nevertheless. Upton Sinclair's *The Jungle* is now remembered more for its description of filth and disgusting ingredients in the Chicago meatpacking industry than for its primary purpose: the exposure of unfair labor practices. Today, hundreds of journalists want to be Upton Sinclair. Newspaper and magazine broadsides regularly strafe the meat industry with exposés: stinking lagoons of pig manure, unsafe hormones and antibiotics in cattle feed, mutilation of chicken beaks to facilitate growth in overcrowded conditions, encroachment on the Amazon rainforest for the sake of grazing cattle, unnecessary killing of whales and porpoises, and so forth. Researchers in the cosmetic and pharmaceutical industries and in university biology laboratories endure their own salvos.

The outcry resonates so profoundly with deep moral feelings that it has even seeped into comic books. Dark Horse Comics published the third installment of the graphic novel *Give Me Liberty: An American Dream* by Frank Miller and Dave Gibbons in 1990. The story, set in the year 2011, opens with a brief news report: "Congress approves a health enforcement crackdown on illegal 'beefeasys' [picture of a wary eye peeping through a keyhole as a fist knocks on a featureless door] . . . while the outlaw Fat Boy Burgers Corporation warns that protest suicides by beef addicts will continue [picture of a man in a Fat Boy sweatshirt frying on the electrified fence surrounding the White House, a "Protein Power" placard by his side]." The American armed forces go to war to protect the Amazon rainforest against Fat Boy Burgers and face the fiendish enemy tactic of suicide cattle girdled with belts of dynamite.

Consciousness of animal rights may not yet pervade the mainstream of American life, but it is flourishing in the less frequented byways. Consider the Web site of the book *Eternal Treblinka: Our Treatment of Animals and the Holocaust* (2002) by Charles Patterson. The author's apologia is an eloquent statement of conversion to postdomestic sensibility:

> My awareness of the scope of our society's exploitation and slaughter of animals has been a more recent development. I grew up and spent most of my adult life oblivious to the extent to which our society is built on institutionalized violence against animals. For a long time it never occurred to me to challenge or even question the practice or the attitude behind it. The late AIDS and animal activist Steven Simmons described the attitude: "Animals are innocent casualties of the world view that asserts that some lives are more valuable than others, that the powerful are entitled to exploit the powerless, and that the weak must be sacrificed for the greater good." Once I realized this was the same attitude behind the Holocaust, I began to see the connections that are the subject of this book.[34]

Much of the book recounts, from an animal rights point of view, the main features of animal exploitation under conditions of domesticity. Following Bentham, it represents the domestic presumption of an unbridgeable gulf between humans and animals as nothing less than a license to enslave, torture, and kill. But Patterson's argument goes further. The Web site's summary of chapter 5, "Killing Centers in America and Germany," illustrates its far-reaching ambitions:

> The chapter describes features which American and German killing centers have in common, whether they be a slaughterhouse or death camp. Similar features include: making the operation as speedy and efficient as possible; streamlining the final part of the operation (chute/funnel/tube) which takes the victims to their deaths; processing the old, sick, and injured; and coping with the problem of killing young victims. The chapter also discusses the role of animals in the German camps (Auschwitz had its own slaughterhouse and butcher shop; Treblinka had a "zoo") and Hitler's relationship to animals.

The final part of the chapter looks at Nazi letters and diary entries which reveal that eating meat and hunting animals were the chief rewards granted to German death camp personnel. The letters of SS-Obersturmführer Karl Kretschmer, leader of a Sonderkommando killing squad, to his wife show that eating well was the most satisfactory part of his job. Entries from the diary of Dr. Johannes Paul Kremer, an SS doctor at Auschwitz, praise the meals at the SS officers' mess and the wealth of human body parts available for his medical experiments. The chapter closes with a discussion of "humane slaughter"—the need of the killers to find ever more efficient and less stressful ways to conduct their operations.

Patterson portrays animal eating and genocide as part and parcel of the same horror. Vegetarianism is not just a postdomestic preference here; it is an obligation on every person who wants to escape the guilt of the Holocaust, which our society accepts as the most terrible manifestation of inhumanity ever imagined.

Provided by the site is a list of 180 organizations that "have expressed support for the idea of the book." Whether this "support" includes the equation between killing animals and killing Jews is unclear. The list includes branches of well-known groups like the Animal Defense League, the American Society for the Prevention of Cruelty to Animals, and People for the Ethical Treatment of Animals, along with many less familiar bodies, such as Animal Commandos (Mesa, Ariz.), Bunny Huggers Gazette (Temple, Tex.), Feminists for Animal Rights (Amherst, Mass.), Heartland Vegetarians (Hoffman Estates, Ill.), and Vegan Resistance for Liberation (Concordville, Penn.).

Animal liberation advocates in Britain lead the world in taking direct action to achieve their goals. One news report from August 30, 2000, reported the following:

"Animal liberation is a fierce struggle that demands total commitment. There will be injuries and possibly deaths on both sides. That is sad but certain." So wrote Ronnie Lee, founder of the Animal Liberation Front (ALF). In the two decades since its birth, the organisation has proved itself more than willing to stand by these words. St Andrew's University terrorism expert Professor Paul Wilkinson says animal rights now tops the list of causes which prompt violence in the UK. A dubious honour won following the easing of tensions over Northern Ireland. With 1,200 fire bombings, acts of vandalism and physical attacks last year perpetrated in the name of animal "liberation," the government is planning a clampdown on the extremist groups responsible.

In both its loose structure and tactics the group has been likened to a wartime resistance movement. Any detailed examination of the group is notoriously difficult, as the authorities have found out. While these extremists have indulged in potentially deadly attacks for many years, the police fear that their campaign is moving towards full-blown "urban terrorism." Although poorly financed and lacking resources, Mr Wilkinson says these extremists have gained bomb-making expertise from manuals and via the Internet.[35]

The rage over animal exploitation felt by British activists and their willingness to take action to stop it probably forecasts the future of human-animal relations in the United States. The Press Office of the North American Animal Liberation Front issued a forty-seven-page report on five types of direct action undertaken in 2001: animal liberation (targeting industries that abuse animals), animal release (largely the freeing of minks—3000 in total), animal rescue (removing animals from laboratories or factory farms to homes or sanctuaries), earth actions (obstructing logging and habitat destruction), and genetix [sic] actions (going after genetic engineering companies). Illegal direct actions numbered 137, a small fraction of those carried out in Britain. As for the future, the report states:

The fallout from the Sept. 11 terrorist attacks will be felt for many years to come in the animal rights and environmental activist communities. The American public, and to a slightly lesser extent, Canadians, are seemingly willing to lose a large chunk of their basic freedoms and liberties in exchange for extremely broadened police powers, at least if the corporate media and politicians are to be believed. . . . The impact from all these new [anti-terrorist] laws will, contrary to their stated intended purpose, not stem the flow of economic sabotage actions or animals being liberated. . . . By acting anonymously and in extremely close-knit groups of trusted associates, the ALF [Animal Liberation Front] and ELF [Earth Liberation Front] remain impervious to infiltration, and will continue to remain beneath the radar of police agencies. . . . In 2002, the ALF, ELF, and other underground groups and activists will continue to take action across this continent. It won't be old or new laws that shut them down. . . . The only way to stop the ALF and ELF is for our society at last to seriously deal with the issues which have brought these people to take such dramatic actions, and that does not seem to be happening very quickly.[36]

The following groups claimed responsibility for actions in 2001:

Animal Liberation Front
Animal Liberation—Tactical Internet Response Network
Bakers for Animal Liberation
Coalition to Save the Preserves [*sic*]
Concerned OSU Students and Alumni
Earth First!
Earth Liberation Front
The Frogs
Guerrilla Advertising Contingent
Kangaroo Wilderness Defense
Lawn Liberation Front
Pirates for Animal Liberation
Santa and His Elves[37]

Postdomesticity and the Stages of Human-Animal Relations

We are today living through a new watershed in human-animal relations, one that appears likely to affect our material, social, and imaginative lives as profoundly as did the original emergence of domestic species. I have attempted in this chapter to sketch some of the main characteristics of postdomesticity. Space has permitted but the briefest of discussions, and the number of topics touched upon has been limited. A few others will arise in other contexts in later chapters. Hopefully, however, what has been said has been sufficient to show that a new episode in the history of human-animal relations opened fairly recently but has not yet been recognized. What will happen with postdomesticity over the course of the twenty-first and subsequent centuries can only be a matter of speculation. On the basis of past experience, however, I predict that vestiges of domesticity will hang on for a very long time and that the ultimate trajectory of postdomesticity will only appear when future generations arise that have as little appreciation of the values and practices of the domestic era as Victorians had of the predomestic "savage" era that preceded it.

Though hindsight on the happenings of the far distant past often make them seem rapid in their development, slow evolution has characterized the three previous great transitions: The first transition took place when our hominid predecessors, at a time unknown, consciously began to distinguish themselves from what they came to think of as animals. I shall refer to this transition as the era of "separation." The next transition saw a gradual evolution from initial separation to the era I shall term "predomestic." The mark of this transition was the appearance of new forms of social life, aesthetic sensibility, and spiritual contemplation based on human-animal relations. The third and most obvious transition was from the era of predomesticity to the era of domesticity. This featured the epoch-making and still mysterious transition of certain animal species from wild to domestic forms.

We can appreciate best where we stand today by looking at these past transitions, partly because a historical view will help us understand how great transitions come about, and partly because one of the emerging avenues of *postdomestic* development is a recrudescence, under modern conditions, of *predomestic* feelings about animals—feelings that domestic societies have largely suppressed for thousands of years. Before domesticity, we lived with wild animals and knew no other kind. After domesticity, we still depend upon, though we no longer live with, domestic animals. Those who become guilt-ridden about the productive beasts we cannot humanize feel a corresponding yearning to reconnect with the wild animals that our human ways are rapidly driving to extinction.

2. The Stages of Human-Animal Relations

I can well imagine the horror in the minds of readers who resent being asked to digest yet another new "post-" word, with an equally new "pre-" word on the horizon. However, this "post" is not like other "posts." "Postdomesticity" is meant to be descriptive. It does not stake out a position in our contemporary culture wars the way "postmodernism" does, nor does it signal a politically charged, intercultural state of mind the way "postcolonial" does. It simply brings together everyday aspects of contemporary life—aspects that affect not just intellectuals, but everyone in our society. This network of relationships has never before been singled out for examination.

The purpose of this chapter is to enlarge upon the ideas of separation, predomesticity, domesticity, and postdomesticity—and the transitions between them—outlined at the end of the last chapter. I will confess, however, that in the 1970s, when I first began to think about the history of human-animal relations, I did not see it as having such a clear-cut structure. "The magnitude of the change that has taken place in the relationship between human beings and other animals over the last half century or so . . . cannot be overstated," I wrote in 1975, "but because it is only a part of the vast complex of changes associated with the term modernization, it is seldom singled out for specific recognition."[1]

Contrary to what I thought then, I am now convinced that the changes that are taking place in human-animal relations are *not* an intrinsic part of modernization. As we shall see in the concluding chapter, attitudes toward animals do not seem to be evolving in the same postdomestic direction in Japan. Moreover, European countries like France and Germany that have been at the forefront of modernization for the past two hundred years do not exhibit nearly so many postdomestic traits as Australia. In point of fact, the most striking manifestations of postdomesticity are so far largely confined to the English-speaking world, most notably Britain, Australia, and the United States.

Modernization refers to a comparatively recent, one-time transformation of human societies from a variety of preceding conditions to a condition marked by a substantial measure of sameness in all parts of the globe. People interested in modernity feel little need to concern themselves with deep antiquity. Their time horizon typically extends back to the Enlightenment and no farther.

By contrast, the attitudes of humans toward animals in deep antiquity may count heavily in the shaping of postdomesticity in different parts of the world. Prehistoric humans and before them prehuman hominids not only related to animals in ways that are affecting the changes we are encountering today, but the pathways by which different parts of the world went through the earlier stages of human-animal relations—from the era of separation, to the era of predomesticity, and on to the era of domesticity—seem as likely to determine the future of these relations as the spread of industry, the advent of mass communications, or any other particular aspect of modernization.

Decreasing farm populations and the extension of efficiency standards derived from industrial mass production to the raising of animals and the harvesting of their bodies, which are both part of the American experience of modernization, have unquestionably contributed to the emergence of postdomesticity. But some of the philosophical (for example, animal rights) and psychological (for example, elective vegetarianism) aspects of postdomesticity do not depend on modern conditions. Indian religious thinkers have concerned themselves with the moral problem of killing animals for thousands of years, and pro-vegetarian arguments based on a variety of principles are equally venerable.

The new postdomestic paradigm of human-animal relations is the latest in a four-step sequence of profound transformations in human attitudes toward animals. In saying this, however, I acknowledge that this book is itself a manifestation of what it seeks to describe. A cardinal characteristic of postdomesticity is the opening of a wide-ranging debate over what separates humans from animals, and over the moral consequences of that separation. Domestic societies past and present harbor few doubts on such issues. In domesticity, the gulf between humans and animals is typically wide, deep, unbridgeable, and not discussed.

Predomesticity, however, by which I mean the condition of human societies *before* the appearance of domestic animals, allowed for greater ambiguity. In some respects, the questions we are now beginning to ask restate, in modern terms, some vital questions that have not been asked for thousands of years. Do both humans and animals have souls or spirits? If so, are these souls of the same kind, or are they fundamentally different? Are human traits and abilities unique or simply at one end of a continuous spectrum of animal characteristics? What is the relationship of animals to the sacred? The future of human-animal relations directly depends on how we answer these questions.

Since my last foray into animal history, concerns with human-animal relations have grown exponentially. Vegetarianism was merely a glimmer on the horizon when I published *The Camel and the Wheel* in 1975. Now it defines the menu for as many as 15 million Americans. In that same year, Peter Singer's book launched the animal rights movement in the United States. The Animal Liberation Front (ALF), which started out in Britain, began its activist work in the United States in 1979. People for the Ethical Treatment of Animals (PETA) was founded in 1980, In Defense of Animals (IDA) in 1982, and the Animal Legal Defense Fund (ALDF) in 1984. In 1978, the Supreme Court put teeth in the Endangered Species Act passed five years earlier by halting construction of the Tennessee Valley Authority's Tellico Dam in order to save a three-inch fish known as the snail darter.

Postdomestic science grew at the same time. In the late 1970s and 1980s, reports came of chimpanzees named Washoe and Nim Chimsky and a gorilla named Koko learning to communicate in American Sign Language.[2] Though many scientists did not deem the reports credible, popular interest in the experiments—and indeed in everything involving great apes—was intense. And by the end of the century, the thought that humans and chimpanzees share most of their DNA—claims range from 96 to 99 percent—had deeply affected popular notions of where humans stand with respect to animals.[3]

Though all of these developments strike me as manifestations of postdomesticity, it is clear that postdomesticity is far from reaching a point of equilibrium. More changes surely lie in store as debates over animals play out through the twenty-first century. Global trajectories of development that at the present moment seem unavoidable will inevitably intensify and politicize the debates, already underway, over human-animal relations. Here is a short list of currently crucial issues:

- Population growth, urbanization, industrialization, and overuse of forest resources, accompanied by myriad forms of environmental pollution, will progressively shrink the habitats that sustain wild animal populations.
- Extinctions will become increasingly common and will include many large and familiar species. By 2100, elephants, rhinoceroses, orangutans, and gorillas may be as scarce in the wild as giant pandas are today.
- Conversely, herds and flocks of domestic animals will grow. The long-term worldwide correlation between increasing prosperity and per capita consumption of meat will lead to the expansion of pasture at the expense of wild habitats and to an even greater expansion of the acreage devoted to corn and other grain crops used for fattening meat animals. The countervailing tendency toward vegetarianism currently observable in the United States and other postdomestic societies is unlikely to offset increased meat eating elsewhere, though it will certainly contribute to a growing moral debate at an international level.
- Animal rights movements and environmental movements advocating the preservation of wild species will flourish and become increasingly enmeshed with other sorts of national and international political advocacy. This will contribute to courses on animal rights and environmentalism claiming an ever greater presence in university curricula.
- Cloning, genome analysis, and the bioengineering of modified animal breeds will generate cascading moral and legal debates about the definition of "species," the ownership of species modifications, and the rights of genes.

To this short list of obvious pressures, I might add three less apparent potentialities:

- Human extermination of predator species and restrictions on hunting are generating an unanticipated increase in tameness among species that are learning to cohabit with humans: in America, raccoons, opossums, coyotes, Canada geese, and white-tailed deer, among others. In time, the difference between certain of these species and the species we now label "domestic" may lie solely in our disinclination, at least for the moment, to exploit them for commercial products.

• Habitat fragmentation through deforestation and economic development may eventually foster the appearance of new species. Evolutionary theorists maintain that small isolated populations cut off from the general gene pool of their species may sometimes adapt rapidly to catastrophically changing environments. New species may also evolve from small populations introduced into new ecological niches. This has happened thousands of times over the last several centuries and continues today, either through intentional species transplantation—import of an insect species to combat another insect pest, for example—or accidental transfer through such things as insect infestations in imported fruit or the flushing of water-dwelling species from the ballast tanks of ships.

• By the end of the twenty-first century, our children or grandchildren are likely to see the departure of faunal DNA from planet Earth through space exploration projects intended to establish permanent colonies elsewhere in the solar system. Whether that faunal DNA will be exclusively human—including the microbial DNA in the human gut and in human parasites—or whether it will include suites of animals chosen to complement a selection of plant species (bees, caterpillars, root bacteria, and so forth), to provide companionship (dogs and cats), meals (pigs and cattle), or to evoke memories of home (wild birds, reptiles, mammals, and the like) is likely to become a matter for serious debate.

As we think about these and other issues that lie ahead, and of the intellectual and moral dilemmas that they will pose, the need for a historical understanding of human-animal relations will become manifest. As an animal species, we have always lived with other animal species and have even defined ourselves by our separateness from them. We are humane. They are bestial, animalistic. But the categories and boundaries we have invented to reinforce, symbolize, or rationalize our separation have fluctuated over time.

We can only speculate about when and why our ancestors, whether already humans or prehuman hominids, became self-aware as a species, a process that I shall refer to as *separation*. Did they think of themselves as members of a category distinct from all other animals—the point of view later enshrined in Genesis? Did they group related hominid species (or human subspecies) living in the same environment as beings like themselves, or did they class them as animals? Did they categorize animals in practical terms—those they had sex with (mostly themselves, but possibly related hominid species), those they ate (prey), those they ran from (predators), and those they were indifferent toward? Or did they categorize them in ways unrelated to such mundane practicalities—for example, into those they thought of as ancestors, those they thought of as somebody else's ancestors, or those their customs prohibited them from killing or eating? Did they think of individual animals in the same way they thought of individuals of their own group, or were animals not strongly individualized, and thought of simply as members of a species?

The transition from the era of separation to that of *predomesticity*, the next great watershed in human-animal relations, is difficult to conceptualize. Tens or even hundreds of thousands of years may have elapsed before human groups went beyond their initial species consciousness and began to think of animals as objects for artwork, storytelling, and religious reverence. To oversimplify matters, separation-era perceptions like "I am a human; I am not an animal" do not readily convert into predomestic thoughts like "God appears as a human with the head of a jackal; I must revere the sacred jackal." Separation implies a feeling of superiority: in seeing themselves as distinct from animals, our remote ancestors presumably considered themselves more capable and important than animals as well. By contrast, predomestic thought surely contained an element of humility in the face of an animal world charged with symbolic and spiritual power. Predomestic thought also works at a much more sophisticated level of abstraction and symbolic communication than the possibly pre-linguistic, primal conceptions of hominids dealing with separation.

Predomestic peoples categorized animals in complex ways, as we know from studying groups of foragers still living today. Some drew uncertain boundaries between humans and animals and revered shamans that could pass from one realm to the other. Others rooted their social relations in beliefs that one or another group descended from a specific animal ancestor. Still others thought that people could be reborn as animals. In each case, the people in question drew pictures, made masks, devised dances, and narrated stories and legends to reinforce their beliefs. Predomestic human-animal relations were particularly rich in symbolic expression.

Eventually, however, some human societies came to see the "animal kingdom"—the phrase itself betrays its emergence in a socially complex human society—as divided more simply into wild species and tame species. This transition to *domesticity* is the next great watershed in human-animal relations. It may be that humans had always shared living space and food with a few animals, particularly young ones that they could more easily tame. But after perhaps tens of thousands of years of this sort of predomestic coexistence, some peoples began to protect the animals they lived with, breed them with one another instead of with wild stock, and eventually exploit them for specific products or uses. Domestic animals were the result.

Domesticity became set as a pattern of human-animal relations at different times in different places. Those groups that developed a reliance on domestic animals gradually lost much of the expertise about wild animals that their ancestors had. Wild species that might earlier have been considered ancestors or embodiments of sacredness were increasingly classified as predators (on humans and their domestic livestock), quarry for human hunts, competitors for space and resources, vermin, or spectacles for observation as captives or in staged fights. The more sophisticated categories and conceptions and the expert knowledge of nature that went with them lived on in the groups that refused, sometimes down to the present day, to make use of the domestic species they had access to. But people living in domesticity generally looked down upon people living in predomesticity.

When the era of domesticity dawned, it was not obvious that the spiritual and imaginative aspects of human-animal relations would not survive. Predomestic residues dominated attitudes toward animals in early domestic times. As domestic animals became more useful, however, their spiritual qualities evaporated. If a yoke of oxen could pull a plow, wasn't it inappropriate to think of a god as a bull? Thinking about wild species became simpler as well. As contact with wild animals diminished, a lion might still be a symbol of might, but the idea that anteaters or lizards might represent important spiritual forces fell by the wayside.

Using animals gradually triumphed over revering them and playing with them in the imagination. It took many centuries, but this fateful trend is what set the stage for the final transition to postdomesticity. Pets aside, humans and animals no longer live together. Industrialization and rural-urban migration has taken care of that, at least in the United States. A gulf has opened up between city-dwelling humans and the domestic species whose products they consume. These changing relationships have nurtured the growth of all the postdomestic peculiarities and anxieties described in the last chapter.

Though many of the ideas I will bring together in discussing the four eras and the transitions between them are my own, I make no claim to being a scientific researcher in the field of animal studies. My goal is synthesis. Moreover, I am a historian by training and inclination. I have the utmost respect for the many accomplishments of the anthropologists, archaeologists, zoologists, ethologists, environmentalists, economists, and philosophers who have concerned themselves with animal issues and whose works have stimulated my own thinking. But I also believe the historian has a role to play in piecing together the many parts of the puzzle that they so skillfully delineate.

I have already taken one of the liberties historians resort to in works of synthesis. I have artificially divided the unbroken sequence of historical time into four eras and coined names for those eras. Moreover, I have simultaneously engaged in another historian's subterfuge. The names I have given to three of my four eras rest on a concept that is less than two hundred years old: domestication. It is hard to imagine someone living in pre-Darwinian times conceiving of a similar developmental sequence.

As an English word designating an animal species that the Oxford English Dictionary calls "tame and useful" in contradistinction to "wild," *domestic* first appears in 1620. The new meaning then put into circulation represented but a slight extension of the previous meanings of "domestic": living in or pertaining to a house (Latin *domus*), or belonging to a household as a family member, retainer, or servant. While not all English domestic animals lived in the houses of their owners in the seventeenth century, a surprising number did, and it was similarly apt to conceive of them as servants or as retainers—the animal analogue of the human retainer is "pet"—particularly in distinguishing them from wild animals.

"Domestic" gave specificity, both literally and figuratively, to the much earlier word "tame." Tameness was the defining trait of domestic animals. Animals captured in the wild could also become "tame" or be "tamed," to use the verbal form, but everyone knew that the offspring of a tame bear, unlike the offspring of a domestic sheep, would grow up to be as wild as its parent was before being captured. Though "tame" remained the opposite of "wild" in many locutions, the word "domestic," by being rooted in the idea of animals and humans living together, implied that tameness could be a species characteristic—what we today call a genetic characteristic—and not just the particular trait of an individual beast. The boundary between "domestic" and "tame" was blurred. "Domestic" animals could act "wild" and "wild" animals could be "tamed," but whenever the opposition "wild or domestic" was used in the place of "wild or tame," it fundamentally altered the way English-speakers thought about animals in general. Other European languages went through a similar development, but Chinese, Arabic, and many other languages around the world did not.

Humans had known for thousands of years, of course, that the animals that plowed their fields, pulled their carts, and provided their milk were born tame. But they did not know why. They could see that dogs and wolves were similar, and they could raise a wolf puppy to be more or less tame. But the descendants of that puppy still did not manifest the domestic tameness of dogs. The semantic nuance introduced by the word "domestic" did not signal, therefore, a new discovery. The idea that a wild animal could *become* genetically tame—the key idea of "domestication"—did not appear before the nineteenth century.

Nevertheless, another idea that gestated in the seventeenth century, in a totally unconnected setting, had a similarly fateful effect on human-animal relations. René Descartes did not interest himself in the particulars of animal species either wild or domestic. From his point of view, all animals were the same. As he argued in several of his writings, animals should be understood as Nature's machines—"automata" was the word he used—rather than as thinking beings like humans. In a letter to Henry More in 1649 he wrote:

But the greatest of all the prejudices we have retained from infancy is that of believing that brutes think. The source of our error comes from having observed that many of the bodily members of brutes are not very different from our own in shape and movements, and from the belief that our mind is the principle of the motions which occur in us; that it imparts motion to the body and is the cause of our thoughts. Assuming this, we find no difficulty in believing that there is in brutes a mind similar to our own; but having made the discovery, after thinking well upon it, that two different principles of our movements are to be distinguished—the one entirely mechanical and corporeal, which

depends solely on the force of the animal spirits and the configuration of the bodily parts, and which may be called corporeal soul,
and the other incorporeal, that is to say, mind or soul, which you
may define as a substance which thinks—I have inquired with
great care whether the motions of animals proceed from these two
principles or from one alone. Now, having clearly perceived that
they can proceed from one only, I have held it demonstrated that
we are not able in any manner to prove that there is in the animals
a soul which thinks. . . .

That men should be able to construct divers *automata* in which
there is movement without any thought, nature, on her part, might
produce these *automata*, and far more excellent ones, as the brutes
are, than those which come from the hand of man, seeing no reason anywhere why thought is to be found wherever we perceive a
conformation of bodily members like that of the animals, and that
it is more surprising that there should be a soul in every human
body than that there should be none at all in the brutes.[4]

Just as the use of the word "domestic" did not immediately change
thinking about animals, Descartes' view of animals did not differ signif-
icantly from accepted Christian doctrine. Verse 10 of the Letter of Jude
in the New Testament, for example, says of those who reject Jesus
Christ: "These men revile whatever they do not understand, and by
those things that they know by instinct as irrational animals do, they are
destroyed." Basing their arguments on this and other Biblical passages,
St. Augustine, St. Thomas Aquinas, and many other theologians con-
curred on the principle that reason fundamentally distinguishes humans
from animals.

By restating this distinction in explicitly rationalistic terms, however,
and by turning nature into a master craftsman, Descartes made the
human-animal divide a building block of Enlightenment thought.
Descartes also went beyond a biblical understanding of the superiority
of reason over instinct by implicitly extending humanity's right, in its
quest for mastery over nature, to manipulate, exploit, and ultimately
consume or discard nature's machines. An animal that is like a cuckoo
clock can be discarded without the slightest guilt—even though some
Christians, such as St. Francis of Assisi, had taught a reverence for God's
animate creations that transcended the distinction between instinct and
reason.

If Descartes had lived to witness the improvement of domestic animals through the selective breeding techniques developed by Robert Bakewell and other English breeders a century later, he might have argued that certain animal automata are crafted by nature and humanity working together. Charles Darwin relied heavily on the experience of domestic animal breeders in his exploration of how species come into being. But the word "domestication," which is first attested in a nonanimal context in 1774 and came to be used for animals only a century later, depended on the Darwinian notion that one species could evolve into another.[5]

Once the idea gained currency that species are malleable and not limited by a God-given uniformity, thinkers who chose to speculate on the origin of domestic species easily—too easily—concluded that prehistoric humans must surely have created domestic cows, pigs, horses, sheep, and chickens through selective breeding. These conclusions ignored, of course, the fact that careful selective breeding and the record keeping it requires were then of recent vintage. Moreover, it attributed to prehistoric humans something that no modern breeder had ever accomplished: the creation of a separate species. In other words, "domestication," a word that in its earliest usage signified the humdrum process of becoming acclimated to a home, came to denote a watershed in human-animal relations: the creation of domestic species from wild species by a process that prehistoric human societies carried out with conscious deliberation. But was this a sound definition of the word?

Though Darwin himself believed that the origins of domestic species would always remain obscure, subsequent generations of scientists and scholars have struggled to date and describe the process of domestication for various species. Many of them assume that domestication was a conscious process, one that was tried out on many species but only worked with some. In opposition to this idea, I will argue that in most cases, domestication came about as an unintended, unremembered, and unduplicatable consequence of human activities intended to serve other purposes. In other words, though domestication looms as the crucial turning point in the history of human-animal relations, we can make no safe assumptions about how and why it occurred.

3. Separation
The Human-Animal Divide

Asked today what separates humans from animals, most people raised in western cultures include in their reply some or all of the following: speech, reason, large brains, upright posture (bipedalism), the opposable thumb, the use of tools, cooked food, cooperative social life, or the prolonged nurturing of young. The first two answers, speech and reason, have long histories in philosophical speculation. The others reflect the revolution wrought by Darwin in thinking about human-animal relations. The anthropologists and archaeologists who uncover and analyze the pertinent data assume that they are investigating human evolution. Most people living in postdomestic society share this assumption. To the degree that they think about human origins at all, they believe that their distant ancestors were once "just animals." Then something happened, and the human-animal divide began to open. The question is: What was it that happened?

A definitive answer to this question will probably never be found. But the way different societies have approached answering it reveals a good deal about how the people proposing the answer think about themselves and about animals. Three hundred years ago, for example, most Christians, Jews, and Muslims would probably have mentioned that humans uniquely possess a soul, that God created animals separately from humans, and that God gave Adam the power to name the animals and thus assert dominion over them. The human-animal chasm implied by these teachings is obviously profound.

Five thousand years earlier in Mesopotamia, so far as we can tell from the Sumerian epic of Gilgamesh, other answers would have been advanced. The myth dates to a time when, after centuries of development, agriculture had become sufficiently productive to support a literate culture in several small city-states. Yet farming and herding had not yet entirely supplanted foraging. Gilgamesh was a superman, the harsh and demanding king of the city of Uruk. Chafing under his rule, his people called on Aruru, the goddess of creation, to create his opposite, his reflection, with whom he should contest for power.

She dipped her hands in water and pinched off clay, she let it fall in the wilderness, and noble Enkidu was created. There was virtue in him of the god of war, of Ninurta himself. His body was rough, he had long hair like a woman's; it waved like the hair of Nisaba, the goddess of corn. His body was covered with matted hair like Samuqan's, the god of cattle. He was innocent of mankind; he knew nothing of the cultivated land.

Enkidu ate grass in the hills with the gazelle and jostled with the wild beasts at the water-holes; he had joy of the water with the herds of wild game. But there was a trapper who met him one day face to face at the drinking-hole . . . and the trapper was frozen with fear . . .

[Later] with awe in his heart [the trapper] spoke to his father: "Father, there is a man, unlike any other, who comes down from the hills. He is the strongest in the world, he is like an immortal from heaven. He ranges over the hills with wild beasts and eats grass; he ranges through your land and comes down to the wells. I am afraid and dare not go near him . . .

His father . . . said to the trapper, "My son, in Uruk lives Gilgamesh; no one has ever prevailed against him, he is strong as a star from heaven. Go to Uruk, find Gilgamesh, extol the strength of this wild man. Ask him to give you a harlot from the temple of love, a child of pleasure; return with her, and let her woman's power overpower this man. When next he comes down to drink at the wells he will embrace her, and then the wild beasts will reject him . . .

Now the trapper returned, taking the harlot with him. After a three days' journey they came to the drinking-hole, and there they sat down; the harlot and the trapper sat facing one another waiting for the game to come . . . On the third day the herds came; they came down to drink . . . and Enkidu with them, who ate grass with the gazelle and was born in the hills; and she saw him, the savage man, come from far-off in the hills. The trapper spoke to her: "There he is. Now, woman, make your breasts bare, have no shame, do not delay but welcome his love. Let him see you naked, let him possess your body. When he comes near uncover yourself and lie with him; teach him, the savage man, your woman's art, for when his love is drawn to you the wild beasts that shared his life in the hills will reject him . . ."

When [Enkidu] was satisfied [with the woman] he went back to the wild beasts. Then, when the gazelle saw him, they bolted away; when the wild creatures saw him they fled. Enkidu would have followed, but his body was bound as though with a cord, his knees gave way when he started to run, his swiftness was gone. And now the wild creatures had all fled away; Enkidu was grown weak, for wisdom was in him, and the thoughts of a man were in his heart . . .

And now the harlot said to Enkidu, "When I look at you, you have become like a god. Why do you yearn to run wild again with the beasts in the hills? Get up from the ground, the bed of a shepherd." He listened to her words with care. It was good advice she gave. She divided her clothing in two and with the one half she clothed him and with the other herself; and holding his hand she led him like a mother to the sheepfolds, and to the feeding place of the shepherds. There all the shepherds crowded round to see him, they put down bread in front of him, but Enkidu could only suck the milk of wild animals. He fumbled and gaped, at a loss what to do or how he should eat the bread and drink the strong wine. Then the woman said, "Enkidu, eat bread, it is the staff of life; drink the wine, it is the custom of the land." So he ate till he was full and drank strong wine, seven goblets. He became merry, his heart exulted and his face shone. He rubbed down the matted hair of his body and anointed himself with oil. Enkidu had become a man; but when he had put on man's clothing he appeared like a bridegroom. He took arms to hunt the lion so that the shepherds could rest at night. He caught wolves and lions and the herdsmen lay down in peace; for Enkidu was their watchman, that strong man who had no rival.[1]

Civilized life based on agriculture and herding forms the context of this myth. Gilgamesh is a civilized man, the opposite of the wild man who does not distinguish himself from the animals. The gods of Uruk include divinities defined by domesticity, namely, the god of cattle and the goddess of corn (that is, grain). Though the myth portrays Enkidu as being created after the rise of civilization, the way he is described probably reflects a Sumerian awareness in the fourth millennium B.C.E. of predomestic foraging peoples then still living in the Zagros mountains bordering Mesopotamia on the east and inhabiting the deserts to the west. Seeing these foragers as the middle term between the wild animals and the civilized subjects of Gilgamesh and taking civilization to be intrinsic to humanity, the myth asks how humans came to separate from animals.

The answer it gives has several components: First, civilized humans wear clothes, grow crops, and consume bread and wine. Second, humans possess a self-consciousness about sexuality and wisdom that animals lack. Third, and in specific relation to the job Enkidu was expected to do as a civilized man, humans hunt to protect domestic livestock from wild beasts. I will discuss hunting later in this chapter, but as for the other components, it is hard to resist comparison with the myth of Adam and Eve in the Garden of Eden, which biblical tradition locates in Mesopotamia. Adam and Eve had no self-knowledge as humans and lived off the bounty of the garden until the Serpent seduced Eve into eating the forbidden fruit, telling her that it will make her "like God, knowing good and evil."[2] She and Adam consumed the fruit. "Then the eyes of both were opened, and they knew that they were naked."[3] They proceeded to don clothes and produce children. Their sons Cain and Abel became respectively the first farmer and the first herder.

Like Enkidu, until their fall, Adam and Eve led innocent lives that were substantially indistinguishable from those of wild animals. The termination of this innocence is associated in both myths with sexuality linked to knowledge. After engaging in sex, "Enkidu would have followed [the wild beasts], but his body was bound as though with a cord, his knees gave way when he started to run, his swiftness was gone. . . . Enkidu was grown weak, for wisdom was in him, and the thoughts of a man." Similarly, Adam and Eve first experience their newly acquired knowledge of good and evil through an awareness of nakedness and shame, qualities not known among animals. Farming and animal husbandry follow in due course.

Enkidu is killed when he and Gilgamesh go hunting for a great wild bull in the mountains, an animal that would once have been Enkidu's peaceful companion at the water-hole. A more dire fate befalls Adam and Eve, at least in the biblical (though not the Quranic) account. They

carry with them into civilized life the burden of sin from their disobedi-
ence to God. Both outcomes hint at the thought that separation from
wild animals and the acquisition of a civilized way of life may not have
been unalloyed blessings.

Sexual awareness as the agency of separation in these two myths can
be contrasted with other ancient myths and legends that embody notions
of humans mating with animals. Though it seems self-evident that every
species accurately and consistently identifies members of the same
species for mating purposes, myth and folklore abound in stories and
images of miscegenation between humans and animals. In the Mediterranean area alone, Minoan artists of the second millennium B.C.E.
depicted a type of demon that was half human and half donkey, and
Greek bards, following Minoan sources, recounted the tale of the half-
human, half-bull Minotaur haunting the labyrinth beneath the royal
palace of Minos. This was only one of the many Greek legends involving
half-human centaurs, fauns, satyrs, silenoi, and werewolves. At the divine level, Zeus, the chief god of Olympus, repeatedly took animal forms
when seeking intercourse with humans: a bull with Europa, a swan with
Leda. And across the sea, Egyptian art teemed with humanoid gods
bearing the heads of animals.

Nor were these ideas confined to the mythic imagination. During the
Vedic age in India, the sacrifice of a horse that confirmed a king in his
possession of his domain climaxed with an act of sexual intercourse
(concealed beneath a blanket) between the slaughtered horse and the
king's wife, as if the same animal force that fulfilled the king's claim to
the land could be transferred to his royal progeny.

Of course, the actual era of hominid separation from animals is far
too remote in time—possibly going back to the Australopithecines of 2.5
to 4 million years ago—for any human society to have preserved the
slightest recollection of it. What these and other myths around the world
indicate is the recurring interest people have taken in distinguishing
themselves from or linking themselves to animals. Some traditions
understood humanity to be a distinctive order of creation; others conceived of humans mating with other species. Some thought of human
lineages descending from animal ancestors and inheriting their characteristics; others conceived of the souls of humans being reborn in animal
bodies, or vice versa.

By arguing persuasively that humans evolved from animals, Charles
Darwin decisively reformulated the problem of separation for the mod-

ern scientific world and thereby displaced most earlier types of speculation. The Darwinian idea of an evolutionary metamorphosis of one
species into another occurring so slowly that no one could ever see it
happening opened the door to new types of speculation about the crite-
ria of separation and the point in the evolutionary process when separation occurred. Qualities like sexual shame and the divine creation of animals as servants to humankind disappear from scientific discussions of
separation, while capacities like speech, reason, and skill at hunting
retain their importance only insofar as they can be conceived of in evolutionary terms.

The archaeologists and anthropologists who reconstruct the course of
hominid evolution can at best identify the material, social, and physiological factors that may have accompanied separation. However, the
conceptual component of human-animal relations in the era of separation is beyond recovery. Take the modern conjecture that hominids decisively separated from animals when they first availed themselves of
sticks and stones for hunting. Bones and stones from archaeological sites
may well support this, but they cannot tell us whether those hominids
were *thinking* of themselves as different from (other) animals when they
stabbed an antelope with a stick or used a stone to crush its femur to get
at the marrow.

This does not mean, however, that conjectures about bygone psychological states are unimportant. As myth and folklore make clear, human
societies have repeatedly conceived and reconceived of their differences
from animals in ways intended to explain or reinforce their current social
and spiritual circumstances. The myth of Enkidu honored the life of wild
humanity but set civilized life above it. The myth of Adam and Eve provided a basis for later Jewish and Christian notions of sexuality. The
story of Theseus slaying the Minotaur served as a foundation myth for
the city of Athens, which counts the hero among its first kings.

Darwin's reframing of human origins within an evolutionary paradigm is no different. It both informs our present-day understanding of
human-animal relations and circumscribes the range of topics we are
willing to consider in thinking about separation. No one thinking within
a Darwinian paradigm, for example, can entertain notions of particular
human groups descending from kangaroos, bears, or any other nonpri-
mate ancestors, or of humans mating with other species and producing
hybrid offspring. We consider these limitations logical and scientific, and
find their presence in earlier cultural traditions puzzling and contrary to

common sense. But we must also recognize that even within the Darwinian paradigm, certain hypotheses about prehistoric living conditions and psychological states have given rise to ideological arguments that are used primarily to further the ideological interests of their proponents. The most notable case concerns ideological interpretations of the phrase "survival of the fittest," which was coined by the philosopher Herbert Spencer but is usually taken as a pithy summary of Darwinian theory. Theories of racial superiority and inferiority at the end of the nineteenth century were firmly rooted in the supposed struggle for survival.[4] "Social Darwinism" soon lost its scientific credibility, but it was a powerfully influential doctrine when it was in vogue, and it drew a good part of its influence and legitimacy from the appearance of being scientific in Darwinian terms.

As each new hypothesis undergoes testing through scientific research and intellectual debate, it simultaneously contributes to and influences our contemporary reflections on the nature of humanity. This is particularly important when the advent of postdomesticity has called into question many centuries of thinking on human-animal relations generated under conditions of domesticity. It may or may not be coincidental that the dawning of postdomestic attitudes in England coincides with the first flush of Darwinian thought, but a close linkage later develops between, on the one hand, thinking about evolution, and on the other, experiencing postdomestic anxiety about the morality of human exploitation of animals.

Scientific researchers and lay thinkers alike are given to proposing what are essentially educated guesses about the emergence of self-conscious human society. This propensity is rooted in the Enlightenment. Recall how Thomas Hobbes (who died in 1679) and Jean Jacques Rousseau (who died in 1778) thought about human beings in the state of nature, the former viewing it negatively and the latter positively. After two centuries of post-Columbian explorers and colonizers regaling people at home with stories of savages in exotic lands, reflection on what these reports of savagery might imply for the emergence of civilization could hardly be avoided. People who read Hobbes and Rousseau knew of such reports and saw them as supplying empirical evidence for the authors' theories. Yet subsequent ethnographic research has made it clear that the information then available abounded in inaccuracies, distortions, and fantasy. Thus no one today would consider Hobbes's vision of a war of all against all or Rousseau's depiction of idyllic life in a world that did not yet know property to be anything more than philosophical postulates designed to support arguments of contemporary relevance about property, government, and the social contract. The same can be said of the Enlightenment conceit that primordial humans were autonomous individuals without siblings, in-laws, or cousins. This wedding of a philosophical reverence for individualism with the biblical account of humans originating from a single couple was logically absurd, but it was nevertheless useful for devising myths about the origin of organized society.

In the same way, the little that is known today about early hominid life is sufficient to stimulate dozens of theories, but is not abundant or reliable enough to lend much certitude to any of them. The search for human origins and the consensus that at some point in the past the fore-runners of *homo sapiens* were "just animals" makes consideration of the causes and consequences of separation unavoidable. But the particulars of such consideration often relate more to our contemporary postdomestic anxieties and puzzlements than to prehistory. A consideration of two of the most common topics, meat eating and speech, will illustrate both the current freedom to speculate and the tendentious purposes that are so often served by such speculation.

Meat Eating

Putting myself into a venerable Enlightenment frame of mind, let me simply apply my reason, eighteenth-century style, to speculating on the origins and significance of eating meat. Why should I do this? Because judicious speculation is as good a method as any for trying to understand aspects of early hominid life for which concrete information may always be lacking.

To start with, was it easier for our pre-toolmaking hominid ancestors to kill an animal or to eat it? When I ask students in my course on the history of domestic animals about killing and eating a rabbit without using tools or fire, they have much less difficulty thinking of ways to dispatch the creature than of ways to consume it. But asking the same question about a large and dangerous animal, such as an elk, elicits greater uncertainty—except among the football players, who imagine themselves grabbing it by the horns and breaking its neck by a sudden powerful twist (one presumes to the admiring applause of a bevy of fetching cheerleaders).

Like ourselves, our hominid ancestors lacked the claws, teeth, and fleetness of attack of true carnivores. Like anthropoid apes today, they could surely kill other animals, particularly when they acted in concert; but before their adoption of sticks and stones as weapons, the size of the prey they could realistically attack must have been limited. Male chimpanzees, for example, team up to prey on smaller red colobus monkeys, but they do not hunt leopards or crocodiles.

We may safely assume that like the apes, early hominids had some taste for animal protein and fat, or at least were not averse to consuming flesh on occasion. Among the easier tidbits to acquire would have been shellfish, eggs, and small beasts that could be caught by quickness of hand, such as insects, reptiles, amphibians, fish, or small birds and mammals. Such small game could not only be killed without great danger or difficulty, but fingers and teeth could probably rend the body and expose the edible portions. Most of the fifty-three contemporary predomestic foraging societies described in the *Cambridge Encyclopedia of Hunters and Gatherers*[5] derive all or a substantial part of their animal sustenance from such small game.

Now consider a goat, antelope, or wild pig. Surrounding the animal, driving it to a killing spot, bringing it down, and dispatching it by brute force are readily conceivable—though far from simple. Prior to the deployment of tools, however, how did our animal forebears gain access to the meat? Without claws, teeth, hooves, beaks, or horns to penetrate the dead animal's hide, butchering a larger animal would have been a formidable task, though one instantly made easier by recourse to a sharpened stick or rock blade or by scavenging a kill made by another animal.

After butchering, mastication must similarly have posed a problem. While the liver, brain, testicles, eyeballs, bone marrow, and other soft portions could be chewed up raw, tearing off and chewing up a strip of uncooked muscle without a cutting instrument or even putting the mouth directly to the carcass and chewing the flesh on the bone would have been a challenge to teeth and jaw muscles. It is ironic that today many meat lovers shun the soft portions that our hominid ancestors probably preferred.

Cooking was not the only way to make muscle easier to consume. Delaying consumption to permit enzyme activity to begin the breakdown of muscle fiber, analogous to today's "aging" of the best steaks, would have helped, at least in cool weather. This might have enhanced the desirability of eating the leftovers from another animal's kill. But the use of cooking fires, which scholarly reports variously date to sometime in the enormous gap between half a million and two million years ago, indicates a growing preference worldwide for cooked meat as well as cooked vegetable matter.

The notion of meat eating as an important form of subsistence, therefore, involves three conceptually separable operations: killing, butchering, and cooking. Among these three, does it make any difference which came first? It might. Stone weapons and butchering sites marked by bone assemblages may present straightforward evidence of hunting, but hearths might indicate a desire for warmth rather than for cooked food. One might imagine, of course, that the desire to kindle a fire started with a desire to cook. A lightning bolt might have set a forest ablaze, and our hypothetical hominid ancestors might have chanced to eat some charred animal remains. In 1822, Charles Lamb cast this logical supposition in its classic form in "A Dissertation Upon Roast Pig."

Mankind, says a Chinese manuscript, which my friend M. was obliging enough to read and explain to me, for the first seventy thousand ages ate their meat raw, clawing or biting it from the living animal, just as they do in Abyssinia to this day. . . . The manuscript goes on to say, that the art of roasting, or rather broiling (which I take to be the elder brother) was accidentally discovered in the manner following. The swine-herd, Ho-ti, having gone out into the woods one morning, as his manner was, to collect mast for his hogs, left his cottage in the care of his eldest son Bo-bo, a great lubberly boy, who being fond of playing with fire, as younkers [i.e., youths] of his age commonly are, let some sparks escape into a bundle of straw, which kindling quickly, spread the conflagration over every part of their poor mansion, till it was reduced to ashes. Together with the cottage (a sorry antediluvian make-shift of a building, you may think it), what was of much more importance, a fine litter of new-farrowed pigs, no less than nine in number, perished. . . .

While he was thinking what he should say to his father, and wringing his hands over the smoking remnants of one of those untimely sufferers, an odour assailed [Bo-bo's] nostrils, unlike any scent which he had before experienced. What could it proceed from?—not from the burnt cottage—he had smelt that smell before—indeed this was by no means the first accident of the kind which had occurred through the negligence of this unlucky young fire-brand. Much less did it resemble that of any known herb, weed, or flower. A premonitory moistening at the same time overflowed his nether lip. He knew not what to think. He next stooped down to feel the pig, if there were any signs of life in it. He burnt his fingers, and to cool them he applied them in his booby fashion to his mouth. Some of the crums of the scorched skin had come away with his fingers, and for the first time in his life (in the world's life indeed, for before him no man had known it) he tasted—crackling! Again he felt and fumbled at the pig. It did not burn him so much now, still he licked his fingers from a sort of habit. The truth at length broke into his slow understanding, that it was the pig that smelt so, and the pig that tasted so delicious.[6]

This conceit works well in a humorous essay, but is not otherwise plausible. The odor of cooked meat, today so delectable to humans, is not nearly so enticing for most carnivores as is the odor of raw meat, so it is unlikely that appetizing smells made fire victims seem especially toothsome. Then there is the question of where one gets the animals to cook. Lamb takes the easy route by making his Chinese farmer a pig-keeper, without telling the reader what he was keeping the pigs for. As for hypothetical hominid ancestors scavenging after a forest fire, the notion that they would have started deliberately preserving and then kindling fires just to cook meat without first becoming expert at acquiring game defies logic.

So logic seems to put cooking in a secondary position in relation to killing and butchering. Of the latter two, killing was more dangerous if large animals were involved. Butchering could have been practiced on carrion left by other carnivores. This line of reasoning has given rise to the speculation that a period of scavenging probably preceded the development of full-scale hominid predation. It visualizes the Australopithecines of, say, three million years ago swiping the leftovers from a lion's dinner plate and escaping with the scraps to the safety of a tree limb, out of reach of the hyenas bent on scavenging the same remains. But postulating a period of scavenging still does not explain how the taste for carrion developed in an evolutionary line whose teeth and digestive tract are better adapted to eating fruits and vegetables. Surviving species of anthropoid apes, after all, do not scavenge lion kills and break bones to extract marrow.

A carrion-eating background further fails to explain why our hominid ancestors eventually took to killing big—and often dangerous—animals. Some of the answers to this question that logically suggest themselves do not depend on a developmental period of scavenging carrion, nor, indeed, on eating meat of any kind:

1. Killing big animals could have begun as self-defense against predators.

2. Killing big animals could have begun with hominids of the same or closely related species killing one another for control of territory, females, or resources.

3. Killing big animals could have begun for the purpose of securing hides for ornament and protection from the elements, or for appropriating living space in caves.

4. Killing big animals could have resulted from a desire to assert domination.

5. Killing big animals could have been a source of pleasure, emotional release, or bonding within a hominid band.

Several or all of these factors could, of course, have been in play simultaneously, with or without an accompanying desire to kill big animals in order to obtain larger amounts of meat. Over hundreds of thousands of years, however, hominid/human killing came to differ markedly from most forms of animal predation. In its targeting of members of the same species, its extension to large carnivores not usually consumed (such as lions), and its apparent involvement of mass slaughter, as evidenced by kill sites in Eurasia and North America where scores of animals appear to have been stampeded over cliffs, our ancestors' killing went well beyond the plausible parameters of mere food acquisition. Did a prehuman hominid killing tradition prefigure these later developments? Or did they develop as distinctively human traits, intrinsic aspects, perhaps, of whatever separated *homo sapiens* from its forebears?

The time frame in which meat grew to be a major component of the hominid diet may possibly be associated with the extension of the habitation range of *homo erectus*, the most successful descendant of the Australopithecines. *Homo erectus* seems to have wandered away from its African homeland around 1.7 million years ago. Monkeys, apes, and human foragers may eat the leaves, stems, roots, shoots, or fruits of scores of different plants. However, they choose with care what they put in their mouths. Many plants, and some parts of most plants, are vile tasting, indigestible, or poisonous. Unlike cattle, sheep, and other ruminant herbivores, for example, animals in our ancestral line could not digest grass, but they could eat ripe grass-seed—so long as they knew when the seed was ready and had a way to separate it from its stem. Deriving sustenance from the vegetation in one's environment, in other words, required a good deal of knowledge and experience. Twenty miles away, where the familiar forest gave way to prairie, desert, or swamp, and the array of plants changed, purely vegetarian foragers may have lacked the knowledge of the local flora they needed to survive.

Flesh, on the other hand, is pretty consistently edible, even if it doesn't all taste like chicken. Hominids foraging into new environmental zones might be justifiably wary of newly encountered plants, but fish, birds, shellfish, reptiles, and mammals could almost all be eaten, no matter how unfamiliar they might look. Thus a capacity to live from hunting or fishing could hypothetically (I'm still in eighteenth-century Enlightenment mode) have been key to the wide-ranging travels of *homo erectus*, enabling migrating bands to survive in new regions long enough to discover which plants were nutritious and which were inedible.

As a hypothesis for explaining why *homo erectus* was able to spread from Africa throughout Europe and Asia, this is not implausible. There is no way of testing it, of course, but it fits reasonably well with the use of simple stone tools and of fire, evidence for both of which can be traced at *homo erectus* archaeological sites. On this basis, therefore, one might speculate that the domination over animals represented by the ability to cook the meat of animals killed with fabricated weapons was well established by 1.7 million years ago.

Does this signify that *homo erectus* had by then achieved separation from animals at a cognitive level in the context of hunting and eating them? Had *homo erectus* developed a way of designating, verbally or otherwise, various animal species? Did these early hunters think of themselves not just as meat foragers but as powerful beings dominating their prey through the use of weapons? Or had the slow course of evolution simply instilled in *homo erectus*, or in certain bands of *homo erectus*, a taste for meat and an instinct for hunting analogous to that of a cheetah's or a tiger's? Was meat eating a choice? Or had it become a compulsion? Was killing an occasional activity, as it is among chimpanzees? Or had it become a calling?

The purpose of these meandering speculations about hunting and meat has not been to present defensible scientific conclusions. Rather, it has been to demonstrate a manner of approaching the question of separation in the Enlightenment tradition. Though I had no ideological axe to grind, the limits of logical inference and the presumption of evolution kept my argument from wandering into spiritual byways. In this way, my arguments differed dramatically not only from those arising from scripture, but also from those reported ethnographically from predomestic traditions around the world. Anthropologist Mary Douglas, for example, has written extensively about human-animal relations among the Lele of central Africa.[7] At no point do the Lele views of the animal world or their manner of expressing those views overlap mine. Thus the very choice of thinking about separation in "rational" terms of meat and hunting constitutes a commitment to ways of thought that were born in the domestic era, while in fact, there is no certainty that the framing questions I concluded with would be more meaningful to a *homo erectus*—assuming communication were possible—than a parallel set of questions patterned on the Lele view of animals.

Debates about Stone Age (and earlier) life that have recently arisen in postdomestic circles, therefore, should not be casually dismissed when they depart from conventionally logical exposition. Speculating about animals at the dawn of humankind should be understood as a way of talking about human-animal relations today.

I will take as an example the views of the respected ecological philosopher Paul Shepard, whose *Nature and Madness* (1982) argued that the domestication of plants and animals in a Neolithic revolution brought an end to the primal human harmony with nature and generated in its place a myriad of psychological ills. In his final book, *Coming Home to the Pleistocene* (1998), Shepard pleaded for a recovery of a predomestic lifestyle on the grounds that evolution had made humanity fit only for hunting and migratory foraging. Far from being an improvement, settled life based on farming and herding constituted a fall from what is natural and proper for the human species. His theory brings to mind the myth of wild but noble Enkidu and civilized but depressed Gilgamesh. Shepard lists seventy-one characteristics of the healthy existence to which he thinks humanity should return. Those directly pertaining to animals include:

6. All-age access to butchering scenes
7. All-age access to birth, copulation, [and] death scenes
9. Early access via speech to rich species taxonomy

18. Little storage, accumulation, or provision
21. No monoculture [i.e., dependence on a single crop]
22. Independent family subsistence plus customary sharing
28. No domestic plants or animals
47. Periodic mobility, no sedentism
50. Dietary omnivory
55. Celebration of [the] social and cosmological function of meat eating
66. Immediate access to the wild, wilderness, [and] solitude
70. Participation in hunting and gathering[8]

Current debates about human-animal relations percolate throughout Shepard's construction of his Pleistocene (or Stone Age) utopia:

Domestication is a kind of alchemy whose animals reshape the character of people who have tamed them. Remembering that the opposite of wild is not civilized but domesticated, the best in our-selves is our wildness, nourished by the wild world. To be in a community with crops is to feel like a crop, to have the edges all dulled. As Konrad Lorenz observed of sheep and domestic rab-bits, they are not only dull but mean.[9]

A foraging society is not one in which a particular group or gender is more kind, moral, ethical, or informed than another. Among hunters/gatherers there is no religious minority in the form of a Great Mother or goddess cult. The modern attempt to associate feminism, vegetarianism, and animal liberation in any historical or anthropological framework is unfounded. Primal society is not grounds for a new "me first" between men and women or between vegetarians and meat eaters. The human digestive system and physiology cannot be fooled by squeezing a diet from a moral. We are omnivores: our intestines and teeth attest to this fact.[10]

Shepard attacks not only certain new theories—for example, solidar-ity between exploited women and exploited animals[11]—unleashed by the transition to postdomesticity, but some of postdomesticity's hall-mark characteristics, including what he sees as a perverted love of ani-mals manifested in pets, zoos, entertainment, and popular images. The connection between his denunciations of feminist and vegetarian theo-reticians and modern life in general seems at first blush to have no direct connection with the separation of hominids from animals and the eating of meat, but separation and meat eating are actually at the very core of Shepard's thought.

Some crucial social and intellectual mileposts had to be passed in order for our ancestors to hunt cooperatively and share large animals. Our hunting began two million years ago with the 500-cubic-centimeter brain that reached 1,500 cubic centimeters about fifty thousand years ago—and with this increase in brain size came a concomitant ability to conceptualize. Very early in the story, for example, the recognition of other species at a distance would have simply extended a preexisting ability of all large vertebrates in the circumstances of savanna life. Soon after would come a quickness for attaching sounds or smells to those same species, even when they were not visible. And, like wolves, the human predators would have expanded these recognitions to subgroups within the species in order to know which antelopes or zebras were old, sick, pregnant, and very young and which would defend themselves dangerously or flee with ease . . .

As our hominid ancestors increasingly moved into open country, often in sight of prey for hours at a time, it was possible to recognize a kind of daily round of other species, if one had the memory for it, to know when the prey slept, grazed, watered, or changed locations for special feeding, courtship, or bearing young . . .

Having learned from the animals and the nonliving surround, our primal forebears emerged from the Pleistocene wary, able to discern advantage in chance encounters as well as skilled in planning ahead, keenly sensitive to the environment and its signs, communicative, cooperative, and sharing.[12]

This scenario of separation resembles in argumentative form the speculations I indulged in earlier in this chapter, except that it is centered entirely on hunting large game. Shepard has nothing to say about the daily activities that make up the lives of many foraging societies still active in the twentieth century, activities that variously include fishing, collecting honey, digging for edible roots with digging sticks, and capturing small game like lizards, birds, and bats. Ideologically, hunting is all that matters. Hunting gave rise to the distinctive characteristics of humankind. Hunting is an inborn and indelible human trait.

Though he bases his ideas on extensive erudition, Shepard harnesses his scholarship to his message. But he does so with a rhetorical passion that often departs from the syllogistic reasoning of a Hobbes or Rousseau. Feminist assertions that women did most of the work in primal human societies and vegetarian claims that eighty percent or more of early hominid calorie consumption was vegetarian show a similar mixture of traditional scientific style and contemporary ideological passion.

Though the science writers stick to reports of a newly found skull here and a freshly dated campsite there, in postdomestic circles there is a war being fought over who defines the nature of primal humanity. The question of separation is embedded in that war, and meat eating is its prime battlefield.

Speech

The front in the culinary war recedes into the far distance when one turns to speech as a criterion of separation. All modern human societies, whether they eat at McDonald's or forage in the Amazon jungle, use speech. Furthermore, it is generally assumed that regardless of where and when speech first appeared, it rapidly became a hallmark of hominid/human life. One might disagree on the innateness of the human desire or capacity to hunt, but no one denies that all human children, regardless of parental lifestyle, learn to speak without special effort.

Explorations of the role of speech in separation have proceeded in three directions. Physical anthropologists have investigated the anatomy of the speech-producing organs to determine when speech may have first made its appearance. Linguists, notably Noam Chomsky, have explored the common linguistic bases of speech to determine whether syntactic linkages between symbolic utterances—sentence-making, in short—are sufficiently universal and immutable to justify thinking of speech as deriving from genetic changes in the brain that took place at a specific point in human evolution. And students of animal behavior have sought to determine whether human speech and animal communication—for example, dolphin whistles, whale moans, birdsong, or bee dancing—simply lie at different points on a continuous spectrum of communication, or whether they are fundamentally different. As an extension of these studies, some researchers have tried to teach chimpanzees and other primates to communicate by linking symbols syntactically.

The 1960s saw an increase in activity in these areas, and the burgeoning postdomestic market of the decades that followed revealed considerable popular interest in the subject. Indeed, fascination with the question of whether communication is a real or false indicator of human-animal difference has become a major feature of postdomestic science. Nevertheless, the lines of research that led Noam Chomsky to publish *Syntactic Structures* in 1957 and John C. Lilly to publish *Man and Dolphin* in 1961 were not at all rooted in postdomesticity. But while Chomsky has pursued very different interests in his later career, Lilly caught the moment. "Eventually," he wrote, "it may be possible for humans to speak with another species. I have come to this conclusion after careful consideration of evidence gained through my research experiments with dolphins."[13] Statements like this enthralled an emerging postdomestic audience who no longer believed in an unbridgeable chasm between humans and animals, and it whetted their appetite for the experiments of Roger and Deborah Fouts and others in teaching American Sign Language to apes in the 1970s.

Scientific research on the capacity for speech, human or otherwise, provided grist for postdomestic ideological debates, but the issues did not involve feminism or vegetarianism. On the one side, advocates of a human-animal continuum that would erase the sharp ontological divide characteristic of domesticity found encouragement in research reports about dolphin and chimpanzee communication. On the opposing side, people who adhered to the view that humans differed from animals in profound and morally significant ways took Chomsky's theory of an inborn and unique human capacity for syntax—a language gene—as proof of their position.

The two sides brought their scientific guns to bear on issues like animal rights, a cause that shot into prominence with the publication in 1975 of Peter Singer's *Animal Liberation: A New Ethics for Our Treatment of Animals*. The pro-rights camp could see no moral basis for human exploitation of animals since humans were themselves only the most recent evolutionary link in a chain of animate creatures—and a minor link at that, considering the massive and oft-cited overlap between human and chimpanzee DNA. Opposing voices, such as Michael Leahy in *Against Liberation* (1991), saw the human capacity for syntax and thus for symbolic reasoning as constituting an unbridgeable and genetically based gulf between humans and animals. Accordingly, he accused the liberationists of erroneously, unscientifically, and sentimentally attributing to animals mental processes of which their brains were incapable.

The question of whether speech played a central role in the separation of humans from animals has become a pawn in postdomestic ideological debates, but its place in those debates has almost no overlap with the arguments over meat eating. Physical anthropologists are in agreement that our Australopithecine ancestors of 4 to 2.5 million years ago lacked the anatomical equipment needed for speech. Indeed, they debate how clearly even the Neanderthals who lived in Europe as recently as 40,000 years ago might have spoken. This means that hunting, the earliest phases of stone tool making, and the taming of fire all seem to have long preceded speech. Consequently, those who want to make speech the hallmark of humanity are forced to argue that those earlier attainments did not kick the animals that achieved them over the threshold into self-conscious humanity. On the other hand, those who argue with Paul Shepard for humans evolving as a species innately adapted for hunting and meat eating have to explain how the social aspects of human life they associate with early hominid hunting groups, such as mastery of the patterns of plant and animal life in their environment, were developed and perpetuated without the benefit of speech.

Lost in this confrontation is the distinction between what theorists today think defines the difference between humans and animals and what the first humans thought constituted that distinction. It may well be true that humans have a genetically transmitted capacity for speech that is categorically different from the vocalization capacities of any other species; but whether true or not, presyntactic hominids may already have set themselves apart from the animals because of their ability to hunt the most fearsome predators, make tools, control fire, or something else that is lost on us today.

The question of possible way stations between acquiring a physical capacity to speak and emitting the syntactically complex utterances we now define as human language complicates matters. Reassuming the guise of a naïve Enlightenment man with an inquiring eighteenth-century mind, I would suggest a consideration of two such way stations: (1) song and (2) imitation of animal vocalization.

The archaeologists who disagree about whether the Neanderthals of 40,000 years ago were physically capable of making the full range of sounds that later humans employed in speech also disagree about whether a perforated cave bear femur from a Neanderthal site is a flute. Some musicologists support the flute interpretation of Ivan Turk, the archaeologist who published the find in 1997.[14] But skeptics say the round holes aligned on one side of the bone were made by carnivore teeth and only coincidentally occur at intervals needed to produce a diatonic scale.

Let us suppose, as seems likely, that the bear femur really was used as a flute. From this we might infer that the Neanderthal who made it found musical tones appealing. Why not also assume that he or she knew how to produce musical tones vocally to make a wordless song? Lack of speech could still have been a key factor in why the Neanderthals were eventually superseded by *homo sapiens sapiens*, for the language gene may have developed in a separate evolutionary line that led to modern humans. So there may be no reason to continue caricaturing the Neanderthals as grunters and growlers when they might, in fact, have been singers.

As whimsical as this string of suppositions may seem, it is not implausible to suppose that modulated tone-making—song—probably did precede syntactic speech, and that the Neanderthals are good candidates for being the original *Meistersingers*. What would have inspired their song? Sexual desire and spiritual emotion, most likely. These are the things that move us to song today—even when we don't understand the words. To Neanderthals in full voice, the speech sounds of their upstart rivals— our direct ancestors—may have seemed pathetically lacking: weak, hesitant, tuneless, articulated at the lips and the tongue instead of flowing freely from the throat. Much is sacrificed vocally for the sake of speech. Even today a fine singing voice is prized above a good speaking voice.

The role of speech in separating humans from animals fits awkwardly into this fanciful hypothesis of Neanderthal vocalization. After all, such a late appearance of the language gene would put the period of separation at only 30,000 to 40,000 years ago. By then, humans had long known how to make tools, hunt big game, control fire, and adapt to any environment. Surely they had also come to distinguish themselves from animals.

An alternative conception might see the language gene putting in the late appearance that the evolution of the tone-making capacities of the skull suggests, but would make it only a secondary feature in the psychological separation of humans from animals. Song, such an alternative might imagine, could have distinguished humans from animals long before speech did. We like to think, in our prideful verbosity, that speech is an unalloyed blessing. But it is songs, not speeches, that run constantly through our heads, cause our hearts to pound, and bring tears to our eyes.

The second hypothetical way station between nonspeech and speech: imitation of animal vocalization. How do modern human societies represent the vocalizations of animals? At a primary level not commonly encountered outside the orbit of hunters and animal trainers, humans closely imitate the sounds made by animals.

This is occasionally done as an entertainment. One late nineteenth-century variety performer played "The Cat Piano." "It comprised a number of live cats confined in narrow boxes with wire netting on the front ends. Artificial tails extended from the rear. This performer was a marvelous cat imitator and miaowed the 'Miserere' by pulling the cats' tails. Spits, snarls, and plaintive mews added to the effect of the back-fence serenade."[15]

In postdomestic society, this "art" has degenerated into the cinema cliché where the good guys hidden in the forest call to each other in hoots and whistles that are invariably mistaken by the bad guys for natural animal noises. More realistically, people who work closely with animals often address them using various clicks, grunts, and other noises that are not only not words, but do not utilize the standard phonemes of their own language. In schooling horses, for example, the voice of the trainer plays an important role. Some trainers always use words, but others prefer clucks or other nonwords. In both cases, the rhythm and tone of the vocalizations are the key to their effectiveness.[16]

Moving to the secondary level of representation, humans again "imitate" the sounds the animals make, but they only use the phonemes in their own language in making these imitations. As a result, secondary-level representations of animal vocalizations differ quite substantially from actual animal sounds. Indeed, the same animal vocalization sounds different according to the language of the speaker. To an English-speaker, a dog "says" *arf-arf* or *bow-wow*, but Koreans represent the sound as *wong-wong*, Bengalis as *vak-vak*, Moroccans as *hab-hab*, and Japanese as *wan-wan*. Roosters "say" *cock-a-doodle-do* in English, but *ko-ko dag ko-ko-ko* in Korean, *caw-caw-CAW-CAW-CAW* in Bengali, *ger-GER-ger* in Mandarin Chinese, *ko-KE-ko-ko* in Japanese, *ü-ürü-ü* in Turkish, *ququli ququ* in Persian, and *koo-koo-ree-koo* in Hebrew.

In addition to fitting the accepted phonemic structure of the particular language, these secondary-level representations, drawn from ten informants reporting on as many languages, generally involve duplicated or rhyming syllables, irrespective of language. The representations also, for the most part, fall short of being true words. That is, they cannot easily be declined, conjugated, or otherwise incorporated into syntactic utterances except as nonverbal sounds. For example, in English, you can say "the dog went *arf-arf*," but you cannot say "the dog arfed." You can say "the rooster went *cock-a-doodle-do*," but you cannot say "the rooster cock-a-doodle-doed" (or maybe cock-a-doodle-did?). This is not absolutely invariable, but exceptions are sometimes strained. You can say "the cow went *moo-moo*" and also "the cow mooed," but you cannot say "the cow moo-mooed."

There are indications that this modern situation is of great antiquity. The ancient Greeks, for example, represented non-Greek speakers as making the sound *bar-bar*, using duplicated syllables as they would for animal sounds. From this they derived the word "barbarian." Classical Arabic represents the unintelligible whispering of magicians by the verb *zamzama*, which can also mean "the horse neighed." Duplication of syllables not only imitates animal sounds but also suggests that the people making the sounds—barbarians and magicians, for example—should not be considered fully human.

At the tertiary level, fully conjugatable and declinable words like "bark," "cackle," "bray," and "low" take the place of *arf-arf*, *cluck-cluck*, *hee-haw*, and *moo-moo*. These words are normally thought of as onomatopoetic in origin—that is, imitative of the actual animal sounds. This they share with utterances on the primary and secondary levels. But they are far less likely to contain duplicated syllables. Their level of imitation is a giant step away from the semi-words they take the place of, which are in turn a giant step away from animal reality.

One might not query these different levels of representing animal vocalizations further were it not for the fact that infants often acquire the secondary-level semi-words before they acquire the fully formed words at the tertiary level. Parents in American society assume this and feel quite pleased when their little ones call the family dog a "bow-wow" or identify a cow in a picture book as a "moo-moo."

This peculiar situation calls to mind the research of Brent Berlin and his colleagues first published in 1969 as *Basic Color Terms: Their Universality and Evolution*. The authors' examination of color terms in scores of languages worldwide revealed a seemingly fixed order of acquisition. This is, languages that had only two terms saw things, literally, in black and white. Languages that had three terms divided the spectrum into black, white, and red. Languages that had four terms added green or yellow to the previous three. This sequence of basic color terms in vocabularies that expanded from the simplest to the most complex societies turned out to correspond to the sequence of acquisition of colors in the visual perception of human infants.

Without attempting to deal with the research in this field that has been undertaken since 1969—I am, after all, merely spinning out a conjecture as one might have done in an eighteenth-century salon—I would hazard the guess that the representations of animal utterances we have today at the secondary level might be fragmentary remains of a presyntactic phase of human speech. Babies learn these semi-words before they learn real words and before they learn to link words in syntactic strings. Moreover, the semi-words themselves all refer to animals and take the place in infant speech of nouns naming those animals. For Mom and Dad, the dog "goes bow-wow"; for baby, the dog *is* "bow-wow."

Just as my speculations on Neanderthal song rested on the strong likelihood that an anatomical capability of vocalization preceded the evolution of the hypothetical language gene—let us assume that syntactically complex sign language came after rather than before vocal speech—it stands to reason that not just song but some sort of speech preceded the development of syntax attributed to that gene. What did our presyntactic ancestors use their new-found vocal capability for prior to the development of syntax? Primary level imitation of animal sounds for hunting purposes could have been a first application. Then, as human groups settled on a limited set of phonemes to convey simple meanings among themselves, a representation of animal identities by semi-words—proto-nouns—that constrained imitation of the actual animal utterances within the bounds of these sets of phonemes would have been quite useful. An early forager might have been able to represent actions efficiently by hand signs, but having a way of signaling to someone else that the animal over the crest of the hill was a dangerous lion rather than an edible antelope may have been as good a reason as any to start making up word-like sounds—even before they evolved the ability to say, "Let's get out of here!"

These concatenations of conjecture have surely proceeded far enough. Their purpose has not been to present sophisticated research findings. My goal, rather, has been to introduce the notion that some capacity for vocalization—song in the one case and a vocal "naming" of animals in the other—might have come into being prior to the appearance or development of the syntax gene. If so, it could have been sound-making rather than speech *per se* that contributed to the separation of humans from other animals.

In the final analysis, we do not know and probably never will know how and when our ancestors developed a consciousness of being human, and our lack of certainty will continue to leave room for tendentious (or frivolous) theorizing, whether of a postdomestic kind or of an Adam-and-Eve-in-the-Garden kind. Two million years ago seems too early; forty thousand years ago seems too late. But there's a long time in between. Whenever it happened, the humans that crossed the threshold from the era of separation to the era of predomesticity found themselves in the new and unfamiliar situation of thinking about animals generically and categorically, whether altogether (Us-versus-Them) or species by species, and of thinking of themselves as being different. This situation inevitably gave birth to thoughts of how humans and animals might be related, and this eventually became a serious preoccupation and a hall-mark of predomestic societies around the world.

4. Predomesticity

Anthropologists and archaeologists like the phrase "hunters and gatherers." They use it as a blanket term to characterize human lifestyles over the tens of thousands—if not hundreds of thousands—of years that elapsed between separation and the emergence of domestic species. And it serves equally well for the lifestyles of small groups of people around the world who still live by foraging. However, the phrase does not appeal to me. It strikes me as conveying the improbable message that human groups that did not or still do not make use of domestic species focus their involvement with animals primarily on their place on the dinner menu.

Perhaps no anthropologist or archaeologist would accept this crude simplification of their phrase's meaning, but my distortion of it reflects the way the transition from "hunting and gathering" (what I call "predomesticity") to the "Neolithic revolution" (a code word for the onset of domesticity) is commonly narrated. Though it is recognized that societies in different parts of the world developed techniques of domestic plant and animal management at different times and in different ways, the original notion of a Neolithic revolution focuses on the Fertile Crescent and on a few domestic varieties of plants and animals that appear in the archaeological record at about the same time, some ten thousand years ago.

The human groups involved in that archetypal transition seem first to have hunted wild animals and harvested fields of wild wheat and barley. Then they began cultivating domesticated strains of wheat and barley and keeping flocks of sheep and goats, while still relying extensively on foraging and hunting, until the new food production techniques became sufficiently developed. These changes in food consumption patterns in the Fertile Crescent came to be broadly associated with the idea of the Neolithic as a cultural period, wherever and whenever it appeared. Other changes in Neolithic material life, such as pottery making and the crafting of tiny stone microliths, took second place to the transformation in food consumption. At least this is the general depiction of the Neolithic food revolution enshrined in world history textbooks.

As every anthropologist and archaeologist knows, however, there is no general association between the appearance of domestic plant species and the appearance of domestic animal species. Dogs became domestic tens of thousands of years before the first crop was planted, while the human groups that first utilized domestic horses, donkeys, camels, water buffalo, and yaks had been consuming farm crops for thousands of years. Moreover, most plant domestication, including chili peppers, manioc, cacao, and corn in Mesoamerica; peas, flax, and olives in the Mediterranean area; and yams, bananas, and breadfruit in southeastern Asia, seems to have had little or nothing to do with the appearance of domestic animals. Indeed, some ancient social systems that depended heavily on one or another form of agriculture, from Bantu farmers in the tsetse fly–ridden forest zones of sub-Saharan Africa to Maya orchard keepers in the Yucatan, thrived without domestic animals, while others that depended almost entirely on herding domestic animals, notably the desert and steppe pastoralists of the Afro-Eurasian arid zone, grew no crops.

The classic Neolithic transition in the Fertile Crescent, therefore, is not typical, and neither is the association between plant and animal domestication so often deduced from it. Domestic wheat and barley first appear in regions adjoining the mountains of southern Turkey, where the grains grow wild. Evidence of domestic sheep and goats first shows up not too far away in northern Iraq and Iran. Specialists debate whether cattle and pigs fit into the same complex. Cattle may have first become domestic in the areas where wheat and barley were first cultivated, but other evidence points to northeastern Africa or western Pakistan. Or they may have become domestic by separate processes in all three places.[1] What is certain, however, is that wheat and barley farmers did not start using cattle to plow their fields until thousands of years later, which renders the intuitively obvious relationship between the origin of grain farming and the domestication of cattle wildly anachronistic. As for the pig, its wild ancestor, *sus scrofa*, was so widespread, and the evidence for pig raising diffusing from a single locale so scarce, as to strongly suggest multiple domestication events from Europe to southeastern Asia.

The special attention accorded to the wheat-barley-sheep-goat complex grows from three facts: first, it is the earliest complex currently known and the most thoroughly studied; second, the Nile and Tigris-Euphrates valleys that neighbored the hillier parts of the Fertile Crescent where the complex originated became the sites, four to five thousand years later, of early civilizations; and third, western culture has constructed for itself an ancestral lineage that goes back to those early civilizations in Mesopotamia and Egypt.

The importance of the first of these facts is undermined by the general agreement that strict chronology tells us little about domestication. Early human societies located at great distances from one another developed according to their own local circumstances. If jungle fowl turned into domestic chickens in southeastern Asia, or guanacos into domestic llamas in the Andes, in both cases hundreds or thousands of years after sheep and goats became domestic in the Iranian highlands, no one supposes that the earlier event triggered the later ones. Except in cases where there is clear evidence of interregional influence, such as the appearance of a plant or animal far from its wild habitat, domestication complexes—that is, groupings of domestic plants and animals in particular regions—should be treated as independent phenomena regardless of their chronology.

As for the other two facts, the venerable tradition of starting accounts of world history with descriptions of Egyptian and Mesopotamian civilizations does not justify glossing over the thousands of years that elapsed between the domestication of wheat, barley, sheep, and goats and the emergence of those civilizations. One could well argue, for example, that intermediate developments, rather than the original domestication events, were the determining factors that enabled those civilizations to take shape.

The yoking of cattle to plows could have been one such development. Plowing, however, developed long after—probably several thousand years after—cattle, wheat, and barley first became domestic. No one contests that the ox-drawn plow greatly increased production of these crops, thus making possible the agricultural surpluses commandeered by the priests and kings of the first city-states. But plowing was not an inevitable consequence of cattle domestication nor even of bringing domestic cattle into conjunction with domestic grain plants. In the Sahara, the cattle-herders of the eighth and seventh millennia B.C.E., a period when a rainier climate supported grasslands from the Red Sea to the Atlantic Ocean, never subjected their animals to the yoke. Unlike wheat and barley, sorghum and other locally domesticated grains did not particularly benefit from plowing. Hence the cattle culture of the Sahara, from which today's cattle-herding cultures in the Sahel zone just south of the Sahara probably derive, centered primarily on valuing the animals as a form of wealth, and used the cattle as a source of meat, milk, and other animal products. In this case, the cattle did not contribute to a civilization-supporting agricultural surplus.

There is no cogent reason, therefore, to think of the wheat-barley-sheep-goat complex as a model form of domestication, or one that led ineluctably to urban civilization. Once we strip away this special attention paid to the Fertile Crescent and scrutinize, as scientific specialists normally do, each domestication event, the idea that eating the harvest of deliberately planted crops correlates closely with eating domestic animals largely evaporates. It is incontestable, of course, that the domestication of grains along with other plants changed human society once and for all, by increasing food supplies and making population growth inevitable. It is similarly incontestable that in some instances, societies that largely sustained themselves on domestic plants witnessed the appearance of domestic animal species. This does not mean, however, that humans living on the fruit of their harvests deliberately domesticated animals as an extension of their agricultural activities.

I will examine the transition to domesticity more closely in the next three chapters, but in looking at predomesticity in different parts of the world, I believe it is more important to ask how specific predomestic societies conceived of animals in general than how they fitted them into their diet. What and how much animal flesh a society was consuming when it began to deliberately plant crops, and when the first evidence of animal domestication appears in relationship to agricultural production, are important data. But so is the status accorded animals in the social, aesthetic, and spiritual life of those societies.

Once the food nexus is challenged as the predominant cause of domestication, evidence of nondietary attitudes toward animals takes on new significance. The possibility arises that while plant domestication probably did emerge, as is commonly argued, from population growth exerting environmental pressure, animal domestication may have arisen from long-developing attitudes toward animals that involved meat consumption only partially or not at all.

Students of domestication agree that when there is a relationship between agriculture and animal domestication, the former facilitates the latter by causing previously migratory foraging groups to settle in villages. Settled life makes it easier to pen and protect animals and to keep them from breeding with wild stock. (Nonagricultural settlements such as fishing communities around lakes and on seashores might also have provided good environments for domestication.) But the emergence of farming may not have *caused* people to domesticate animals. Since the transition from hunting to herding took place slowly, the predomestic ideas that people had about animals probably did not change much until domesticity was well established.

Art, myth, and folklore provide windows onto predomestic attitudes toward animals. What they tell us offers insights not just into the transition to domesticity, but also into some of the thoughts about animals that are now recurring in postdomesticity.

Predomestic Art

The artistic accomplishments of predomestic peoples everywhere in the world, from Paleolithic times to the present day, testify to the urge humans have to draw, paint, and sculpt. Though the circles, cup-like indentations, and outlines of hands found at prehistoric sites in Australia may prove to be the earliest evidence of this urge, the best known prehistoric art consists of cave paintings in northern Spain and southern France. Perhaps as early as 60,000 years ago, European Neanderthals scratched simple patterns of geometric lines. Fully developed images begin some 30,000 years later, when our direct ancestors, *homo sapiens sapiens*, were beginning to supplant the Neanderthals.

Almost all of Europe's Paleolithic cave paintings depict animals, and the first scholarly attempts to explain their subject matter focused on hunting. It was proposed that early humans painted pictures of the animals they ate, possibly to magically enhance their success in the chase. Yet very few images explicitly suggest hunting, and by and large, human artwork has seldom focused strongly on food.[2] Thus more recent scholarship has revised earlier views. To take just one example, André Leroi-

Gourhan concludes a survey of images from seventy caves as follows: "There are good reasons to suppose that the drawings of Palaeolithic animals constitute a bestiary rather than a collection of edible species."[3]

The bestiary is strongly skewed, for reasons one can only guess at, toward certain species. Horses account for 30 percent of the images and are found in all assemblages. Bovids—four-fifths bison and most of the rest aurochs (*bos primigenius*), the ancestor of domestic cattle—make up another 30 percent. Then come harts and hinds, the male and female of the red deer (11.3 percent); mammoth (9.3 percent); ibex, the progenitor of the domestic goat (8.4 percent); reindeer (3.8 percent); bear (1.6 percent); felines, presumably lions (1.3 percent); and sundry others, including rhinoceros (.07 percent), birds (.02 percent), and fish (.03 percent). Wolves and hyenas are absent, and there is but one dubious representation of a pig.

Horses and bison provided meat, to be sure, but this alone can hardly account for their disproportionate representation, not to mention the enormous skill lavished on their portrayal. Examination of postures, association with other animals, placement in the caves, and other variables have inspired a variety of conjectures as to the purpose of the images. Many of these center around notions of ritual and suggest linkages between hunting, consumption, and sacredness. But if providing meat for the group was the sole objective, then the absence of fish, birds, and pigs is puzzling, given the preferred place on the menu these animals had in later European societies. Whatever the correct explanation of the artists' selection of subjects, it seems clear that the people who frequented the caves had strong and distinctive feelings about certain animal species and not about others. And peoples living in other regions had their own special feelings. Nothing in the French and Spanish caves, for example, brings to mind the foot-tall mammoth-ivory statue of a standing man with a lion's head found in southern Germany and dated to 30,000 years ago.[4]

Prehistoric artwork from different parts of the world displays no more unity of conception than the art of more recent times, beyond the fact that animal images play an important role everywhere. Different societies exhibited different tastes and concerned themselves with different subject matter. Sometimes, as in the European cave paintings, the animals most frequently represented are among those that were hunted for meat in the artist's society. Sometimes they are not, as is the case with the jaguars and jungle birds so commonly represented in pre-Columbian art. Sometimes they are shown in isolation, sometimes they appear in half-human, half-animal form, and sometimes they are purely imaginary. All predomestic human groups evolved sophisticated ideas about animals, and many created visual representations to convey those ideas. But the nature of the ideas varied widely. Only occasionally is there a correlation between an animal species portrayed and the subsequent emergence of a domestic form of that species in the same environment. Take the dog, for example. Though it is the earliest and most ubiquitous of domesticates, it rarely appears in prehistoric art—even in areas where dogs formed a part of the human diet.

The conclusion that food needs did not necessarily dictate artistic preferences leads to a second conclusion: human imaginings of animals in late predomestic times involved many factors unrelated to food. What those factors were varied greatly and are often impossible to determine from the images themselves. But they collectively attest to an era in human-animal relations that was much less centered on food production than one would surmise from conventional descriptions of the "Neolithic revolution" or characterizations of predomestic groups as "hunters and gatherers."

Predomestic Myth and Folklore

There is no way of telling whether the myths and tales of the Australian Aborigines and other contemporary foraging peoples reflect views of the world that formed before the advent of domesticity. The traditions of these peoples could have been influenced, after all, by those of peoples with domestic outlooks, such as missionaries, with whom they came into contact. But without specific evidence, there is no reason to presume that they do not reflect a predomestic worldview, particularly inasmuch as foragers in widely separated regions share many traits. These shared traits sometimes lead anthropologists to treat all foraging societies categorically:

Common features in hunter-gatherer religions find considerable explanation in the lifeways of the people and their proximity to nature. Living within and off nature, foragers have both their practical and conceptual consciousness focused on animals, plants, the landscape and seasons, and meteorological and astronomical phenomena. At the metaphysical level, hunter-gatherers regard nature as pervasively animated with moral, mystical, and mythical significance. . . . Shamanism is a technique and a thought system for entering and conceptualizing such a universe and for relating to, channeling and transforming its beings and forces for the benefit of humans.[5]

Some archaeologists and art historians call on notions of shamanism to explain the occasional animal-headed human images [from Paleolithic times] . . . that resemble later rock art from several parts of the world showing humans with animal heads or animal masks. Yet there is no definitive way of determining whether these represent shamans. Some foraging peoples in Africa and North America have creation stories that conceive of the "first people" as being half human and half animal either externally or internally, with separation occurring either case by case or in one creative act.[6]

As for ancient foragers, some myths and stories preserved in texts or transmitted orally almost certainly contain residues from predomestic times, though identifying these residues can be difficult and controversial. In *Muelos: A Stone Age Superstition About Sexuality* (1984), anthropologist Weston La Barre argued that historical accounts of headhunting, drinking from the skulls of enemies, and conceiving of brain matter, spinal fluid, and semen as constituting the precious vital stuff of masculinity reflect cultural concepts that first appear in carefully arranged groups of human skulls found at Paleolithic sites. Humans wearing animal horns and horns being shown on images of gods played a part in the myth complex he describes, and were carried over into the era of domesticity.

Le Barre's case for a Paleolithic origin for these practices may not be entirely convincing. But it shows how combining archaeological finds with reports about ancient customs and modern ethnographic data can lead to plausible and unexpected hypotheses. Though the transition from predomesticity to domesticity does not arise as such in his argument, his views may help explain why skulls and horns are so evident in some early domestic situations. I will return to this matter in a later chapter.

While myths tend to become frozen, folklore shows greater flexibility as it passes by word of mouth from generation to generation. The Br'er Rabbit stories collected by Joel Chandler Harris surely reflect the animal trickster at the center of much of the folklore of African foraging peoples, and the dangerous wolves that haunt European fairy tales are probably part of a storytelling tradition that predates the arrival of domestic animals in Europe. But the adaptation of these tales to changing conditions continues down to the present day, when most societies have long forgotten their ancient myths of gods and heroes. For these reasons, the vast amount of animal imagery contained in myths and stories is hard to date. In the aggregate, however, it amply confirms the importance of animals in the spiritual and imaginative life of predomestic peoples everywhere.

However, myth and folklore rarely touch on the process of domestication, if such a process was ever consciously recognized. Moreover, the animals that eventually became domestic show up less often than one might suspect, given their eventual economic utility. This is not to say that myths and stories about cattle, sheep, goats, pigs, and horses don't exist, but they are surprisingly uncommon when compared to the number of stories about lions, bears, wolves, jackals, foxes, deer, and other nondomesticates. Wild bulls occasionally show up as emblems of power, but when horses appear, they are usually already domestic (and pulling chariots) or being tamed by a hero, as in the case of Pegasus and Bellerophon. The "wild" stallion of modern romance is a feral animal, not a member of a wild species.

Meat eating similarly plays a limited role in myth and folklore. The people who invented the stories, like those that painted on the walls of caves, did unquestionably acquire meat by hunting and wild vegetable products by gathering, but their thinking about animals went far beyond their stomachs. Hence the assumption implied by the phrase "hunting and gathering" that preoccupation with food was the sole or primary stimulus behind animal domestication cannot be taken for granted. Animals loomed larger than any other aspect of nature in the mental landscape of predomestic humans. So when some of those humans decided to capture wild animals and keep them in their communities long enough for them to breed, there is no certain way of knowing what motivated them.

5. Where the Tame Things Are

No one knows for sure how at the end of predomestic times, in one place or another, certain animal species came to be domestic. Common to many theories and scenarios, however, are assumptions (1) that domestication was a process, (2) that it was a process that involved purposeful human activity, and (3) that it was roughly the same process for all species. This is why the verb "to domesticate" is taken to be transitive—that is, *domestication* is something done *to* animals *by* humans. With respect to the purposefulness of the human actions involved, it is further commonly assumed that the humans who carried out domestication understood what they were doing, and that after the fact, they understood what they had done. Or at least they understood it well enough to try it out on other species.

Questions follow from these assumptions: If humans purposely initiated the process of domestication, why did they decide to do so only after tens of thousands of years of not doing so? What exactly was the process they implemented to accomplish the domestication? And why did they domesticate so few species?

I don't believe these questions can be answered on the basis of the usual assumptions. Rather, an altogether different set of questions should form the starting point for understanding domestication: How did the domestication process differ from species to species? To the extent that human actions contributed to domestication, did the humans realize what they were doing? When domestication had been accomplished, were the humans involved sufficiently aware of what had happened to attempt repeating the process with other animals? Does the small number of domestic species indicate that most (or all) other species cannot become domestic?

The domestic animals that are today most associated with products for human consumption—sheep, goats, cattle, pigs, chickens—underwent domestication a very long time ago. However, as we have seen, the common notion of a discretely bounded Neolithic revolution in which the domestication of plants and animals are closely linked, as is so often described as occurring in the Fertile Crescent some 10,000 years ago, accords poorly with the archaeological evidence of domestication. Animals more closely associated with providing labor than with products for consumption—horses, donkeys, camels, water buffalos, yaks, llamas—became domestic thousands of years after the advent of farming. Dogs, on the other hand, became domestic thousands of years before farming, and reindeer seem to have become domestic in fairly recent times in nonagricultural northern Asia.[1]

Despite these inconsistencies, the idea of a connection between farming and animal domestication has a strong intellectual pedigree. Nineteenth-century materialist reconstructions of human social evolution maintained that humans were first hunters, then herders, and finally farmers. Animal domestication came about as a consequence of human groups turning the wild animals they preyed upon into domestic animals to be managed in the interest of a more systematic harvesting of meat, milk, and other products. Only subsequently did some of the herders settle down and take up farming. This three-step developmental hypothesis, largely born of a centuries-old European prejudice that pastoral nomads were more primitive and "savage" than farmers, could not withstand the growth of knowledge about genetic processes. It could not explain nor did it seek to explain how wild instincts like excitability, wariness, combativeness, and flight from predators gave way to traits of domestic tameness: docility, acceptance of human presence, tolerance of saddling and harnessing, and acquiescence in being herded, milked, sheared, and slaughtered.

Darwin's theories created the topic of domestication by laying out a vision in which one species could transform into another, implicitly including the notion of a wild species transforming into a tame one. But the inheritance of tameness traits from generation to generation, a defining characteristic of domestic species, did not fit very well with Darwin's idea of natural selection, since tame beasts were more vulnerable to predators than wild ones. Explaining why domestic animals transmitted tameness and manageability to their offspring while seemingly related wild species did not called for some sort of reproductive selection. Either certain wild populations became tame or domestic through the action of natural selection—as improbable as tameness might seem as a success-ful survival strategy in the wild—or purposeful human intervention gradually changed the behavior (and appearance) of selected groups of wild animals. Since scientific breeding to produce desired physical traits in domestic animals was well known in nineteenth-century England—Darwin himself studied breeding practices intensively—scientific human selection as the mechanism of domestication did not seem illogical. Yet no one had ever observed the generation of a domestic species from a wild one through scientific breeding. Wild animals were commonly tamed, but they did not pass the quality of tameness to their offspring. Nor did dogs cease to be dogs even when breeds differed as dramatically as a St. Bernard and a Chihuahua.

Since early versions of Darwinian theory considered every species to be highly uniform in genetic inheritance, domestication as a process of species change was originally thought of in terms of one or a small hand-ful of mutations. But as Mendel's demonstration of the action of domi-nant and recessive genetic traits became better understood in the twen-tieth century, it was realized that wild populations harbor many genetic variations. Evolutionary theory's cofounder, Alfred Russel Wallace, had always stressed this in contrast to Darwin's views. Accordingly, it seemed that many generations would have to pass before any mutation of the wild prototype could become so well established as to be a uni-versal characteristic of a new domestic species. In a large, freely inter-breeding population, the tendency would be for mutations to disappear as the animals carrying them bred with the dominant type of the species. During the generations of gradual change needed for domestic traits to appear, therefore, the breeding population originally drawn from the wild would have to be kept reproductively isolated from its wild kin, or nearly so, to prevent the desirable mutant or recessive characteristics from becoming diluted by dominant wild traits.

These considerations gave rise to the notion that sedentary life and deliberate human breeding selection were prerequisites for domestica-tion. After all, how could peoples who followed and preyed upon wild herds simultaneously maintain a separate group of the same wild species in reproductive isolation long enough for it to evolve into a domestic breed, much less a domestic species? Always on the move and without speedy transportation (the horse being a comparatively late domesticate), how could they have guarded their semi-wild captive herds of sheep, goats, cattle, and pigs to keep them from straying, being snatched up by lions and wolves, or mating with wild cousins—and still have devoted themselves to hunting as a basic mode of animal exploitation?

Imagining the necessity of corrals, strictly controlled access to pasture, and constant protection from predators and would-be wild mates, domestication theorists rejected the early three-step sequence—first hunting, then herding, then farming—and speculated instead on the implications of agriculture. Agriculture, they maintained, provided a new basis for human sustenance that permitted or entailed sedentary life and thus provided the presumed prerequisite for animal domestication. Corrals and pens and close management of herds and flocks seemed much more compatible with farming life than with migratory foraging.

Visualizing domestication as a process carried out by sedentary agriculturists posed new problems, however, even leaving aside the fact that dogs became domestic long before the emergence of farming and sedentary life. If a people had no experience of domestic animals, why would they have wanted to keep a group of wild animals in reproductive isolation? Or, if they already had one or more domestic species, how would they have known that reproductive isolation was the source of their tameness? Or that reproductive isolation of a different wild species might result in similarly tractable beasts? Short of assuming an amazingly precocious (and subsequently forgotten) grasp of Darwinism, how could domestication be anything other than the unanticipated outcome of practices engaged in for other purposes?

Rats and Foxes

Historian Jared Diamond in his book *Guns, Germs, and Steel* quotes this observation by Francis Galton, a nineteenth-century scientist and cousin of Charles Darwin:

> It would appear that every wild animal has had its chance of being domesticated, that [a] few . . . were domesticated long ago, but that the large remainder, who failed sometimes in only one particular, are destined to perpetual wildness.[2]

To this Diamond adds:

> Dates of domestication provide . . . evidence confirming Galton's
> view that early herding people quickly domesticated all big mam-
> mal species suitable for being domesticated. All species for whose
> dates of domestication we have archaeological evidence were do-
> mesticated between about 8000 and 2500 B.C.—that is, within the
> first few thousand years of the sedentary farming-herding societies
> that arose after the end of the last Ice Age. . . .
> In the 19th and 20th centuries at least six large mammals—the
> eland, elk, moose, musk ox, zebra, and American bison—have
> been subjects of especially well-organized projects aimed at do-
> mestication, carried out by modern scientific animal breeders and
> geneticists . . . Yet these modern efforts have achieved only very
> limited successes. While bison meat occasionally appears in some
> U.S. supermarkets, and while moose have been ridden, milked,
> and used to pull sleds in Sweden and Russia, none of these efforts
> has yielded a result of sufficient economic value to attract many
> ranchers.[3]

Note that Diamond's dismissal of modern efforts to domesticate
large mammals hinges not on success in instilling in them inherited qualities of tameness, but on ranchers' perception of their commercial value.
In fact, people who raise domestic bison do not shy away from calling
them "domestic bison," as an Internet search will quickly reveal, even if
their flesh is not commonly sold. Diamond further loads his case in favor
of Galton's declaration by omitting the reindeer from his list of large
mammals domesticated before 2500 B.C.E., along with the fact that reindeer and elk belong to the same species, *Rangifer tarandus*, interbreeding freely when they are brought into contact, as they were during a
failed effort to establish reindeer herding in Alaska.[4] The failure of that
experiment, which had little to do with the animals and much to do with
the disinclination of indigenous Alaskans to adopt a pastoral nomadic
life, should prompt us to question whether it is correct to assume that
prehistoric humans necessarily wanted to domesticate the wild animals
they came in contact with. Just as today, aversion to migration may
always have prevented the fishing peoples in the Pacific Northwest from
even thinking about living from elk or reindeer herding.

Galton's assumption that all large mammals were tested for domestication potential thousands of years ago and that only a few passed the

test is a key element in Diamond's thesis that "the fates of human societies" lie not in human difference but in the historical and geographical accident of living in proximity to a major domesticatable species. But the Galton assumption strains credulity, not least because it suggests that groups that already had a few domestic species would certainly have tried to acquire more by experimenting with the local wildlife.

Thomas Bewick's *A General History of Quadrupeds*, published in 1790, enjoyed great popularity and was the standard English-language work on mammals of its time. Bewick has this to say about "The Peccary, or Mexican Hog," known in the American Southwest as the javelina:

> Like the Hog, the Peccary is very prolific. The young ones, if taken at first, are easily tamed, and soon lose all their natural ferocity; but can never be brought to discover any signs of attachment to those that feed them. They do no mischief, and may be allowed to run about at pleasure. They seldom stray far from home, and return of their own accord. . . . The flesh of the Peccary, though drier and leaner than that of our Hog, is by no means disagreeable, and may be greatly improved by castration. . . . Although the European Hog is common in America, and in many parts has become wild, the Peccary has never been known to breed with it. They frequently go together, and feed in the same woods; but hitherto no intermediate breed has been known to arise from their intercourse.[5]

Rather than arguing species by species, Diamond adduces six general reasons to explain why most large wild mammals "failed," to used Galton's term, to become domestic: "Diet," meaning inefficient conversion of plant matter to meat; "Growth Rate," meaning too long a wait for the appearance of useful mature animals; "Problems of Captive Breeding"; "Nasty Disposition"; "Tendency to Panic"; and "Social Structure," meaning that the animal is too migratory, too territorial, or too competitive. None of these would seem to apply to the peccary, which Diamond mentions in passing but does not specifically discuss.

A more reasonable explanation for the nondomestication of the peccary would start with the idea that the Native Americans who lived around and hunted peccaries never "experimented" with domestication at all, and that the European colonists already had domestic pigs and had no need of another domestic swine that could not be used for interbreeding. Does this explanation imply that the Native Americans were incapable of figuring out how to domesticate an animal, and were thus inferior to people living in the Fertile Crescent or China? Only if it is assumed that domestication was an obvious scientific process just waiting for a bright person to come along and discover it. It is this assumption that I propose to take issue with.

Diamond's core argument concentrates on large mammals. He recognizes that many small mammals—he might have added birds—were domesticated long after 2500 B.C.E.; but these he dismisses. "The continuing development of domesticated small mammals isn't surprising, because there are literally thousands of wild species as candidates, and because they were of too little value to traditional societies to warrant the effort of raising them."[6] His argument is not persuasive. Chickens and pigeons probably do go back to his chosen time period, and humans have valued them enough to have spread them around the globe. More importantly, however, the underlying assumption remains that very few species are susceptible of domestication and most are not.

We shall consider, then, the cases of two animal species, rats and foxes, that have been successfully domesticated in the twentieth century—and under laboratory conditions. The careful experiments that produced domestic rats and foxes point not to a somewhat mysterious natural susceptibility, but to a more straightforward genetic basis for domestication.

One popular theory has it that the strain of docile laboratory rat used for experiments since the nineteenth century descends from rats caught around 1800 by ratcatchers servicing the English ratting craze. Most of the captured rats were thrown into pits to be killed by dogs for the entertainment of spectators. But the story goes that the few rats that exhibited the not uncommon mutation of albinism were set aside for breeding and exhibition. These became the original stock from which tame white laboratory rats derive. One might question whether human selection for a mutation affecting hair color, if that's what was involved, should eventuate in an inheritable trait of tameness, but in any case the entire story has never been verified, and alternative theories exist.

An effort to replicate the domestication of laboratory rats and to study the process scientifically began in 1919 when Dr. H. D. King captured thirty-six wild rats, sixteen males and twenty females.[7] In the first generation, few of the captive rats—only six of the twenty females—proved capable of reproduction, and such young as were born had to be fostered on domestic mothers. By the eighth generation, nonreproduction among the descendants of those few who reproduced in the first generation had fallen dramatically, and from the thirteenth generation onward all females were fertile. In other words, for the first twelve generations, fertile females continued to produce some offspring that were too "wild"—making use here of Diamond's category of "Problems of Captive Breeding"—to reproduce under conditions of captivity. Throughout this period, the "captive-grays," as the experimenters called them, still looked like wild rats and retained their wild hair coloration.

Not only did fertility increase with each generation, but the rats became more and more tame, though even after forty-three generations the captive-grays were measurably less tame than long established albino breeds of laboratory rat. Experiments with introducing genetic variations in the color pattern of the rats' hair through interbreeding with albino domestic strains resulted, in some mixes, in levels of docility equivalent to the domestic breed. These experimentally introduced hair-pattern genes seem to have had a pleiotropic effect—that is, the introduced gene probably altered some internal biochemical process that triggered several quite different changes, some visible, like albino coloration, and some behavioral, like tameness.

Compared with the original wild stock, the captive-grays came to show a significant reduction in the weight and output of certain endocrine glands. The adrenal glands of laboratory rats are only half to three-quarters the weight of those of wild rats, and unlike their wild cousins, fighting exhausts their supply of adrenalin very quickly. Their tameness, therefore, seems attributable to a drastic reduction in the "fight-or-flight" behavior triggered in wild stock by adrenalin and other hormones.

One conclusion drawn from the captive-gray experiment was that even though the skeletal measurements archaeologists often use to distinguish wild from domestic stock—such as the configuration of horn cores and the length and maturation of long bones—may reliably signify domestication, skeletal changes may have nothing directly to do with the increase in tameness that is central to the process of domestication. Skeletal changes may equally have little to do with the onset of domestication. In other words, the earliest archaeological evidence of a species becoming domestic, to the degree that the evidence depends on the measurement of hard tissues like bones or on external characteristics like hair or feather color, may yield substantially incorrect dates. As the captive-gray experiment indicates, genetically transmitted tameness may arise without major changes in the bony material or visible characteristics of the species.

But what are we to make of the progressive diminution of adrenal output in the captive-gray population? Though human selection for tameness was not part of the experiment, tameness came about anyway. Two possible explanations spring to mind: Either the rats with high adrenal output failed to reproduce in captivity as efficiently as they normally would in the wild, or the rats with low adrenal output reproduced more efficiently in captivity than they would have in the wild. The need for foster mothers in the first generation would lend support to the first explanation. Few of the captive-grays reproduced at all, and those that did failed to mother their young. The most likely cause of this reproductive inefficiency is the constant state of agitation produced by living in captivity. Those few who were placid enough to reproduce were still too flighty or distracted to act as mothers.

The second explanation finds support from common sense. In the wild, it seems likely that the rats with the lowest fight-or-flight response are the ones most often eaten by predators. With respect to adrenal output, natural selection in a high-predation environment would tend to winnow out in every generation the rats most capable of passing the trait of docility to their young. The very fact of laboratory captivity, therefore, would favor the transmission of low adrenal output because captivity guarantees protection from predators (other than the experimenters).

These observations have suggestive implications for the origins of domestication. Given the well-known fact that some species reproduce readily in the predator-free captivity of zoos while others reproduce poorly, it seems reasonable to hypothesize that many animal species would react to confinement the way the wild rats did. On the one hand, the most aggressive or flighty animals would reproduce poorly because of the agitation induced by the captive environment, while the calmer ones would have a greater chance of reproducing because of the absence of predators. In this scenario, a substantial degree of tameness might emerge after several dozen generations, regardless of why the humans decided to keep the animals confined and regardless of any human interference in the form of selective breeding specifically to produce tameness. Simply keeping a small number of animals confined and preventing them from mating with wild stock, in combination with a constant and disturbing human presence, would in and of itself be the mechanism leading toward domestic tameness.

Another scenario that has been imagined does not even require confinement. The animals in question are considered self-domesticating. Take the example of the domestic cat, an animal that is genetically little different from its wild forebears. According to the scenario, with the beginning of farming, humans began to store grain to eat during the fallow season and to provide seed for the next planting. The stored grain attracted large numbers of rodents, the favorite prey of small wild felines. Some of the wild cats, probably those least given to running away at every rustle of leaves or ominous shadow, began to skulk around human settlements because of the abundance of delicious rodents. The humans tolerated the furtive cats because they were eating rats and mice but were leaving the stored grain alone.

The humans, naturally, would have killed or driven away from the settlement all larger predators, the ones that posed threats to human children and incidentally to the cats as well. They would similarly have killed any cats that acted too aggressively. Over a period of generations, protection from animal predators and human culling of the most aggressive cats would have enhanced the reproductive efficiency of the cats with the lowest adrenal output. After fifty generations or so, the result could well have been a species of domestic cat. Thereafter, further intrusions of wild cats would have been seen as a nuisance, if not a danger, since the rats and the mice were being satisfactorily controlled by the domestic cats. Thus human discouragement of further visits by wild cats would have sharply reduced the probability of the domestic cats interbreeding with their wild cousins and reacquiring wild genetic traits.

In this scenario, cat domestication—dog domestication might be substituted with scraps from the Paleolithic hearth taking the place of stored grain—occurs without human deliberation. Since there is no human deliberation, that is to say, no decision to engage in a conscious process of domestication, the same scenario could occur in more than one settlement, perhaps with a mutation such as yellow fur color becoming established in one place and another mutation for black fur in another. Exchange of such tame cats would then foster the development of distinctive breeds.

The implication of this hypothetical scenario is that domestication may not in all cases have resulted from purposeful human activity. If this should prove to be the general or even the predominant case, and not just one applicable to hypothetical cats, then obviously it cannot be maintained that humans discovered the "process of domestication." This possibility requires exploration, because instances of inadvertent or unanticipated domestication would undermine the arguments of those archaeologists and historians of technology who are strongly inclined to believe in single instances of invention or discovery followed by geographical diffusion of the new knowledge or technique. If a major change in human-animal relations can come about inadvertently, then it is much more probable that that change will take place in several unconnected places.

With regard to cats, Egypt has generally been accepted as the locale of first domestication.[8] Pigs, however, pose a more challenging problem. The wild porcine species *sus scrofa,* from which all domestic pigs are believed to descend, is widely spread geographically in Eurasia and North Africa. Over this vast territory, several patterns of pig domestication came into being. Some societies grazed pigs in forests where they could eat acorns and hazelnuts and root for tubers. Other societies kept them close to human settlements and fed them on kitchen waste or shared with them the roots and tubers eaten by the people themselves. Some societies involved pigs in their religious rituals and observed rigid restrictions on eating them. Others regarded pig meat as a staple food. Some treated piglets as pets, even to the extent of women letting them suckle at their breasts. Others considered them embodiments of filth, even though they might be willing to consume their flesh.

It is difficult to imagine such a wide variety of pig cultures resulting from a single instance of domestication and a subsequent diffusion over vast geographical distances. Getting domestic pigs to trek long distances to establish breeding herds in new territories would in itself have been a major problem. How much easier it would be if one were to postulate multiple locales for pig domestication! This is most easily done if pig domestication is treated as a naturally arising symbiotic relationship, rather than an extraordinary discovery made by one group of humans who figured out how to achieve domestication.

Carl O. Sauer, in his *Seeds, Spades, Hearths, and Herds*, visualized a scenario for pig domestication in southeastern Asia that he felt yielded utilization patterns entirely different from those in, for example, southeastern Europe.[9] He argued that sedentary fishing communities gained their basic sustenance from the harvest of the sea and from yams and other root crops. Not needing pigs for food, they let them clean up the garbage in their settlements and even adopted piglets as pets, feeding them with the same roots and tubers they themselves lived on. Over dozens of generations, the pigs that voluntarily visited human settlements to scavenge food became domestic. Eventually, these domestic pigs were incorporated into religious rituals as sacrificial animals.

Sauer did not discuss genetic issues in this scenario. However, if life in the fishing village provided protection from wild predators as well as abundant food, the pigs with the lowest fight-or-flight responses may have reproduced with much more efficiency than they would have in the jungle. By contrast, if the most aggressive pigs had difficulty reproducing in proximity to humans or were systematically culled through killing or castration, there would have been fewer and fewer in each generation capable of passing on the genes for high adrenalin production. These circumstances are quite logical corollaries of Sauer's basic scenario and provide another hypothetical example of domestication taking place without deliberate human agency.

But human agency cannot be discounted in all instances. In cases where human interference with natural selection was deliberate, we must ask: What did the humans do, and what objectives were they trying to achieve? The most efficient case would involve humans deliberately selecting for mating the tamest captive animals in each generation to produce the next generation. At the present time, long-term experiments are continuing in Russia to determine whether captivity, combined with selecting for reproduction the animals that exhibit the least aggression toward humans, is sufficient to produce domestication. But insofar as this program consciously conceives of a domesticated species as an end product and aims at no other utility, it is firmly rooted in Darwinian science and is therefore hard to project as a model of prehistoric domestication.

In 1959, Dimitry K. Belyaev, a domestication theorist who directed the Institute of Cytology and Genetics of the Siberian Department of the Soviet (now Russian) Academy of Sciences, inaugurated an experiment that has lasted for over forty years.[10] Unlike the captive-gray experiment, Belyaev drew his initial breeding stock of thirty male foxes and one hundred vixens from a commercial fur farm in Estonia. Though not subject to selective breeding, these animals were already tamer than wild foxes. They had, after all, already survived the pressures of a certain degree of confinement. Belyaev's experiment included comparisons with other species designed to see how much of an animal's fight-or-flight reaction was genetically determined. Of fifty otters caught in the wild, only eight (16 percent), all showing weak fight-or-flight reactions, were able to produce offspring under captive conditions. Among a group of wild rats tested the same way, only 14 percent produced young that lived to adulthood. Through crossbreeding fox strains, cross-fostering newborns, and transplanting embryos between donor and host mothers, Belyaev estimated the contribution of genetic inheritance to fight-or-flight reactions to be 35 percent.

Belyaev's working hypothesis was that human selection based solely on the apparent tameness of a young animal would not only produce a line of domestic foxes, but also yield foxes that would come to exhibit some of the visible physiological traits commonly associated with domestication—traits such as floppy ears, curled tails, and altered fur patterns. In each generation, therefore, as the foxes reached sexual maturity at seven to eight months, they were separated into categories according to their defensive attitude toward humans. Only the most docile were allowed to reproduce. In the sixth generation, a category of super-tame foxes had to be devised to account for foxes that were eager for human contact from their first month of life on, whimpering to attract attention and sniffing and licking their handlers. Before that, tail-wagging and whining, as opposed to biting and flight, had been the strongest indicators of tameness. By the tenth generation, 18 percent of the pups were put in the super-tame category. This proportion increased to 35 percent in the twentieth generation, and 70 to 80 percent in the thirtieth.

As for visible physical changes, Belyaev's prediction proved true. Piebald coloration in the form of a white blaze on the forehead, a trait also found in domestic dogs, horses, pigs, and cattle, showed up in the eighth, ninth, and tenth generations. Then came floppy ears and curled tails. Shorter tails, shorter legs, and overbites and underbites showed up after fifteen to twenty generations. These mutant traits remained uncommon, but their incidence was an order of magnitude greater than among the commercially farmed foxes that provided the original breeding stock. It is not hard to imagine a less scientific breeder beginning to select for such visible traits once they began to appear. As for nonvisible physical changes, the rise in the output of hormones relating to stress and fear that typically accompanies maturity among wild foxes became increasingly delayed as the generations progressed.

What the captive-gray rat and Russian fox experiments clearly demonstrate is that all species capable of domestication were not domesticated in the natural course of human prehistory. Quite to the contrary, they strongly imply that the prehistoric societies that first came to know domestic animals had no idea how domestication came about, and therefore could not possibly have undertaken deliberately to add a new species to their repertoire of domestic livestock. Among both rats and foxes, the time span for the emergence and general spread of genetically determined tameness was more than thirty generations. For a species that matures in a few months, thirty generations can pass within the life-span of a single individual, although Belyaev himself died in 1985, when his experiment had been underway for approximately twenty-five gen-erations. But with animals that mature more slowly and have longer ges-tation periods, like cows and horses, thirty generations constitutes a cen-tury or two of elapsed time, or four to six human generations.

Given this time span, the total absence of recordkeeping before the development of writing, and the ignorance of rational, scientific, and ex-perimental methodology that may fairly be assumed for prehistoric human societies, it is unimaginable that the humans who ultimately reaped the benefits of domestication had any clear recollection of how their domestic stock originated. To ascribe to them an understanding of the process of domestication solid enough for them to attempt it suc-cessfully with another species is beyond the realm of credibility. To the extent that they may have realized that their domestic stock originated as wild captives, any attempt they may have made to replicate the process with other large mammals would probably have been aban-doned as futile after a limited period of time, unless there were interim advantages to be realized from half-wild stock.

Tame in the Wild

The marvel of domestication is not that early humans discovered a process that is only today yielding to experimental understanding. They didn't. But some groups did engage in long-term practices that resulted in the totally unexpected development of genetically transmitted tame-ness. What those practices were and why they were sustained long enough to give rise to domestication lies at the root of our enquiry. But just as we have raised the possibility that species like cats, dogs, and pigs may have become domestic because of the genetic consequences of vol-untarily frequenting human camps and settlements, so we must ask which other species may have entered the roster of domestic animals without significant human agency. Once these have been accounted for, we will be left with a crucial inventory of species whose domestication seems to have depended on centuries-long commitments to captive reproduction with no expectation of behavioral change. An inquiry into why people made these commitments will illuminate the epochal transition from predomesticity to domesticity.

Scenarios that envision wolves developing a symbiotic relationship with human hunters or cats becoming tolerated as rodent-catchers by early farmers are hard to develop for herd animals like cattle, sheep, goats, horses, llamas, camels, and donkeys. Where these animals are present in large numbers, they require such extensive grazing lands that they must shift territory frequently enough to allow the plants to recover from their depredations. Yet grasses and shrubs are no more abundant around humans than elsewhere, nor is there any reason to think that natural vegetation in the near vicinity of human settlements would have been enough to maintain more than a few animals. Moreover, as humans began to plant and harvest grain, they are more likely to have driven off wild grazers than to have adopted them. Thus not only is there no reason to suppose that grazing animals would have been particularly attracted to an abundance of food around a human encampment or village, but there is good reason to think that the animals that fell into human hands suffered nutritionally. Archaeologists commonly take a reduction in average body size as an indicator of early domestication and surmise that it most probably resulted from captive stock receiving inadequate nourishment in comparison with their wild cousins.

In thinking about the domestication of herd animals, one must start with the fact that sheep, goats, and cattle became domestic four to five thousand years before horses, camels, donkeys, onagers, and water buffalo. Under the conventional formulation of domestication history, it would be legitimate to ask: If people had deliberately domesticated sheep, goats, and cattle and understood what they had done, why should they have waited thousands of years before applying the same process to these other species? As we have seen, however, the presumption of human understanding of a domestication process involving a large mammal is almost unimaginable. Instead, we should consider whether the time gap between the earlier and later groups of domesticates signifies either a difference in process or a difference in human purpose.

The Indian elephant affords an instructive comparison. Elephants have been used on the Indian subcontinent for labor and warfare for at least 2,500 years, but they are not a domestic species. Indian elephants are born and bred in the wild, captured as adults, and then trained to their tasks. There are practical reasons for this, most notably the enormous cost of feeding an elephant during its immature years. The system works, however, because of the natural tractability of adult Indian elephants (a trait probably shared by the now extinct elephants of North Africa that were apparently used in Hannibal's invasion of Italy in the second century B.C.E.).

The domestication experiments performed with rats and foxes provide a possible insight into elephantine tractability. As we have seen, in the absence of predators, rats and foxes with low levels of excitability reproduced more efficiently than flighty and aggressive rats with high adrenal output. One might ask whether the absence of predation has the same effect on other species. In other words, is the edginess and volatility of a given population of a species in some measure a function of predation insofar as the individuals least inclined to bolt and run at the first hint of danger are also the ones most likely to be eaten prior to producing offspring, and thus least likely to pass their comparatively calm proclivities and lower adrenal output on to their offspring?

Several sorts of observations seem to support this hypothesis. First, species that evolve on islands that have few indigenous predatory animals often appear entirely tame. The Galápagos islands offer many examples. Birds and reptiles descended from related species on the South American mainland are totally oblivious to human presence. The reason for this is not that they don't know enough about humans to be afraid of them. Humans have been visiting the islands for almost five hundred years. The reason is that there are virtually no predatory species (one hawk, no mammals) in the entire island group, save on those few islands where pigs were introduced by European sailors.

The famous dodo on the island of Mauritius, where the native fauna included no predatory mammals or snakes, was similarly devoid of a fight-or-flight response and thus easily killed off by sailors stocking up on meat. One might object that birds and reptiles afford poor examples—though they too, like mammals, must stay alive long enough to reproduce—but one could also cite a distinctive fox species on the island of Chiloe off the coast of southern Chile. Charles Darwin was able to dispatch one with a blow of his geologist's hammer because it failed to react to his approach. Along with a feline the size of a house cat, the fox was the largest native predator on the island and hence had never had to run from danger.

If docility becomes a characteristic of island species that experience very low levels of predatory threat, does the same thing happen among continental populations? The Indian elephant has already been cited.

The adults protect the young, but the adults themselves have little fear of being attacked. The same can be said of lions, tigers, and bears. Carnivores at the top of the local food chain can afford to spend most of their day drowsing in the open or gazing at the strange doings of human beings, since no other animal is going to attack them. Like elephants, these large carnivores can be quite tractable, since they have not inherited extreme fight-or-flight reactions. The fact that they may choose to attack a meddling human makes them wild and dangerous, but the lack of an inbred inclination to flee other animals explains why we see them in circuses. Like elephants, they can be trained for certain tasks. Small prey species like prairie dogs and gazelles can't, which is why we don't see gazelle and prairie dog acts under the big-top.

In these three situations, then—human confinement, isolation on predator-free islands, and local food-chain supremacy—species that have virtually nothing to fear from predation sometimes develop diminished fight-or-flight characteristics. The reason for this, however, cannot be that they know from inheritance to be unafraid of other animals (including humans) in their surroundings. It is a cardinal tenet of Darwinism that acquired characteristics cannot be passed on genetically. Therefore, since animals are born with no knowledge of other species and acquire such knowledge only through upbringing and experience, their comparative docility under the conditions listed is most likely the consequence of reproduction in a predator-free environment. From a human perspective, they appear tame in the wild, though for dangerous carnivores, "unexcitable" may be a better word than "tame." Individuals with comparatively low excitability live to reach maturity and over time these individuals seem, for some reason, to have a higher rate of reproductive success than their flightier relatives.

Camels and Llamas

The tame-in-the-wild phenomenon may contribute to understanding how camels, llamas, asses, and onagers came to be domestic. The camelid family (camels, llamas, guanacos, alpacas, and vicunas), like the equid family (horses, asses, onagers, and zebras), originated in North America, though ancestral forms reached Eurasia in the late Miocene period some 13 million years ago. Several species from both families were still roaming North America when the first humans hiked in from Asia or pulled their canoes onto a Pacific beach. Soon thereafter, it appears, they became extinct, along with many other large Western Hemisphere animals. However, two camelids, the guanaco and the alpaca, continued to flourish in South America.

Since the 1960s, a scientific debate has raged over Paul S. Martin's hypothesis, based on quantitative models, that the extinction of the large animals of the Americas (as well as extinctions in Australia, Madagascar, and various Pacific islands) came about as a result of massively superfluous killing inflicted by the incoming humans upon the defenseless local fauna—defenseless because they were not yet familiar with human predation.[11] Though little archaeological evidence of such overkill has materialized and the proposed method of stampeding herds over cliffs is hard to visualize in the cliff-free prairies of the Great Plains and the swamps of Florida and Georgia, computer simulations demonstrate that a slowly advancing killing front of human hunters *could* have done the job if they were determined enough.

I do not have the scientific qualifications to enter into this debate, but my sympathies lie with those who argue that the extinctions in the Americas resulted from climatic change or from epidemic diseases being imported from Asia.[12] A conception of predomestic hunters being so devoted to killing that they would exterminate countless millions of animals just because it was within their power runs counter to so many other indications of predomestic reverence for animals, including those of the Native American descendants of the first humans in the Western Hemisphere,[13] that more is needed to prove the case than a computer simulation and a rough synchronization of human migration and animal extinction. As Donald Grayson, one of the active participants in the debate, puts it:

> While the initial presentation of the overkill hypothesis was good and productive science, it has now become something more akin to a faith-based policy statement than to a scientific statement about the past. . . . Martin's theory is glitzy, easy to understand and fits with our image of ourselves as all-powerful. It also fits well with the modern Green movement and the Judeo-Christian view of our place in the world. But there is no reason to believe that the early peoples of North America did what Martin's argument says they did.[14]

The megafaunal extinction theory also has difficulty accounting for the survival of guanacos and alpacas of the South American plains and mountains. It is hard to credit this to a precocious fear of humans when even after twelve thousand years of being felled by spears and arrows, guanaco herds in some areas still evinced no particular fear of humans. From early Spanish reports to the present day, observers maintain that wild guanacos not only do not run from humans, but manifest an apparent curiosity about their activities. Whenever the male leader of a herd is killed, it seems the remainder of the herd simply stands around waiting to see what will happen next.

Like their cousins who migrated to the Old World and successfully spread as far as the Atlantic Ocean, the South American camelids lack the horns, fangs, claws, and sharp hooves used for protection by so many animals. Camels and llamas can neither run like horses nor leap like impalas. The key to camelid survival in both hemispheres seems to have been the exploitation of ecological niches that were unattractive to potential predators, such as deserts and high mountains. Darwin found enormous guanaco herds on almost barren lava fields and discovered that they could slake their thirst with salty water. They also flourished in the high Andes mountains.

The physiological secrets of camelid survival in punishing environments have been carefully studied in the case of domestic one-humped camels. Because they recycle essential nitrogen compounds that other animals take in through eating and then excrete, they can live well on nitrogen-poor vegetation. Because they lose very little moisture through excretion or through sweating, the latter trick being managed by toleration of an eleven-degrees Fahrenheit increase in blood temperature before sweating begins, they can stay away from watering holes much longer than other animals, and they can lose as much as one-quarter of their body weight in water loss before suffering ill effects. And because two-humped camels and the South American camelids can grow long, dense wool—think camel's hair and vicuna coats—they can endure the intense cold of a Central Asian winter or the chilly heights of the Andes.

These adaptations for living in barren environments do not mean that camelids take no interest at all in the safety of the herd. They are generally watchful animals, and in recent decades llamas have been effectively substituting for dogs in guarding North American sheep flocks. But they would rank fairly low on any scale of flightiness.

The possibility thus arises that the ancestral camels from which the domestic one-humped and two-humped varieties derive, as well as the ancestral guanacos and vicunas from which domestic llamas and alpacas derive, may have been comparatively tame in their wild state. That is, someone who wished for whatever reason to capture one might have approached close enough to put a rope around its neck without frightening an entire herd into panic flight. We have no direct evidence with respect to camels, but in the early twentieth century it was reported that "guanaco are readily domesticated, and in this state become very bold and will attack man, striking him from behind with both knees."[15] The word "domesticated" here should undoubtedly be understood to mean "captured in the wild and subjected to human control."

This possibility of camels being tame in the wild because of their adaptation to barren environments is particularly intriguing with respect to domestic one-humped camels, since no wild one-humped camels are ever mentioned in the historical record of their native Arabia. How could it be that the aurochs, the wild form of domestic cattle, survived in heavily populated Europe down to 1627, and the wild species that are ancestral to our domestic horses, pigs, sheep, and goats still survive today, while the Arabian desert, one of the most sparsely populated regions of the earth, is devoid of wild camels? Could it be that there is no genetic difference between wild and domestic camels? Did domestic camelids (one-humped in the Arabian desert, two-humped in the Gobi desert of Mongolia, and llamas in the Andes) originate from a human decision to assume control over a more-or-less tame wild species, rather than from a period of long-term captivity and reproductive isolation from wild stock, as presumed in standard theories of domestication? And could this exploitation of the quality of being (more or less) tame in the wild similarly help explain the domestication of two other desert animals, the Nubian wild ass of the Sahara (the ancestor of our donkey) and the onager (also called a *hemionus*, meaning "half-ass") of the Syrian, Arabian, and Iranian deserts, which seems to have been used domestically only from about 3500 to 500 B.C.E.?

This scenario, in which a wild species comes easily and quickly under human control because from a human point of view the animals are virtually tame in the wild represents a second pathway (along with the cat, dog, and pig scenario of unplanned domestication through voluntary cohabitation) by which a domestic species might have come into existence without a lengthy and premeditated process of domestication. Such scenarios suggest that each domestic species has a separate history and that no systematic domestication process devised by humans and experimented with for a wide array of species has ever existed. This conclusion is not inconsistent with much of the detailed scientific study of domestication. What I am challenging is the widely believed overview that equates domestication with farming and maintains that early humans mastered a technique of domestication that their descendants subsequently forgot.

6. Domestication and Usefulness

By concentrating on genetically transmitted tameness as a defining characteristic of domestic animals, I have until now ignored the fact that most people think "domestic animal" means "useful animal." That is the equation that I shall explore in this chapter.

What do we understand when we say that an animal is "useful"? We certainly use animal energy for performing jobs and carrying us around, just as we use specialized animal talents for hunting, herding, exterminating vermin, detecting explosives and drugs, and finding truffles. The uses that come more readily to mind, however, involve the products of their bodies: milk, eggs, feathers, fur, wool, hides, meat, bones, horns, and hooves. I will call all of these unquestioned and unambiguous human employments of animals and animal products "material uses."

But isn't the companionship provided by a pet also a use? Or the uplifting song of a caged bird? Or the enchanting display of a golden carp, or of a peacock fanning its tail feathers? I will call these employments of animals "affective uses" because they involve our sensibilities—affection, aesthetic appreciation, spiritual aspiration—rather than the material betterment of human life.

Most discussions of the origins of domestication—taking "domestication" here in the conventional meaning of a purposeful human activity—focus on material uses. They ask the question: How did humans gain control of the animals whose products, labor, or abilities they wanted to make use of? But this question has hidden traps. As the general history of technology teaches us, the ultimate uses to which an invention or discovery may be put are not necessarily ones that were known to or visualized by the inventors or discoverers. Humans tamed fire, for example, never dreaming that it would someday be used to bake clay pots or extract metal from ores. They invented distillation with no anticipation that it would someday enable them to make vodka or turn sticky crude oil into gasoline.

The assumption that the desire to use animals in the material sense triggered domestication confronts the theorist with the problem of understanding how the people doing the domestication knew that they were going to benefit from one or another use once the process was complete. Wildness surely made some useful employments impossible. One can easily imagine, for example, that wild goats and cows would have energetically resisted people trying to milk them. So if it took the passage of many generations for a level of tameness to be achieved that would allow milking, who could have anticipated that outcome at the start of the domestication process? In *The Savage Mind,* Claude Lévi-Strauss considers this conundrum in connection with both animal domestication and an array of other Neolithic developments and comes to a radical conclusion.

> To transform . . . a wild beast into a domestic animal, to produce . . . nutritious or technologically useful properties which were originally completely absent or could only be guessed at . . . there is no doubt that [such] achievements required a genuinely scientific attitude, sustained and watchful interest and a desire for knowledge for its own sake. For only a small proportion of observations and experiments (which must be assumed to have been primarily inspired by a desire for knowledge) could have yielded practical and immediately useful results. . . .
>
> Neolithic, or early historical, man was therefore the heir of a long scientific tradition. However, had he, as well as his predecessors, been inspired by exactly the same spirit as that of our own time, it would be impossible to understand how he could have come to a halt and how several thousand years of stagnation have intervened between the neolithic revolution and modern science like a level plain between ascents.[1]

What prompts Lévi-Strauss to postulate early man engaging in a special type of long-term scientific thinking and experimentation is, in the specific case of animal domestication, his assumption that humans desired to derive material uses, "nutritious or technologically useful properties" in his words, from captive wild stock. Since these "properties" were not originally present in the wild stock and could only be achieved through prolonged experimentation and observation, an application of "scientific" thinking and a quest for "knowledge for its own sake" seems to be the only answer. But would this assumption of a brief but amazingly productive spurt of scientific thought in Neolithic times have been required if affective uses had been taken into account?

The history of canaries can tell us something about this. When the Norman adventurer Jean de Béthencourt initiated European settlement of the Canary Islands in 1402, he was probably too busy fighting the indigenous island dwellers, the previously unknown Guanches, to pay much attention to the small greenish-grayish-brownish finch we now call a canary. After his death in 1408, the rights to the islands granted to him by Henry III of Castile and León passed to a series of Spanish nobles who after much bloodshed finally managed to subdue the Guanches toward the end of the fifteenth century.

There is no record of the earliest export of the wild finches to Europe, but it happened quite soon. In his pioneering four-volume work on animals *Historia Animalium*, published in 1555, Konrad Gesner describes the canary in detail, and remarks: It is "the bird of sweetest song . . . brought from the Canary Islands, productive of sugar. . . . It is sold everywhere very dear, both for the sweetness of its singing, and also because it is brought from far places with great care and diligence, and but rarely, so that it is wont to be kept only by nobles and great men."[2]

The export of canaries seems to have been prompted solely by the enchantment of its song. But captive breeding soon led bird fanciers to select for distinctive traits and mutations, as they had been doing for centuries with pigeons. In 1709, Hervieux de Chanteloup, the "gouverneur des serins" (canary curator) of a French princess, published a treatise on canaries that listed twenty-nine varieties, including: (1) the common grey canary; (2) the slightly variegated frilled canary, with white feet; (5) the pale canary with pink eyes; (13) the lizard with pink eyes, showing cinnamon origin; and (15) the slightly variegated frilled lizard.

Canaries proved so easy to breed that by the mid-eighteenth century, Dutch East India Company ships were delivering them to Nagasaki to fill orders from Japanese noblemen. Subsequently, Japanese references to canaries diminish, apparently because local breeders learned how to supply the market. The wife of a British consul who was posted to Nagasaki in 1859 wrote of seeing "a great many canaries" including "snow white birds with pink beaks."[3]

By every criterion of domestication except material use—leaving aside those birds legendarily used in mines to detect lethal gas—canaries must be classed as domestic animals. European importers and breeders were drawn first to their song, and later to their color varieties. But why, out of all the world's songbirds, was this finch from a remote island in the Atlantic the only one to become a common domestic animal? The songs of the lark and the nightingale loom larger in European tradition, but history records no craze for caged larks and nightingales. As a bird-watcher friend put it to me, "A thrush in a cage does not sing."

Ease of captive reproduction along with a willingness to sing in a cage seems to have made this instance of domestication possible. The various nonwild color patterns, including "canary yellow," recorded within two centuries of the bird's first appearance as an exotic animal, could only have come about through captive breeding and the deliberate selection for color mutations. Other imported wild birds, of which many species are mentioned in historical records from the period of European exploration, seem not to have been bred so experimentally. Caged parrots, cockatoos, and macaws generally retain their wild coloration.

It is hard to argue that the singular success of the canary stemmed from uncommon human skills at managing bird breeding. If such skills had existed, more species would have become domestic. It is better that we should look at the Canary Island habitat. Located in the Atlantic Ocean almost seventy miles off the western extremity of the Sahara desert, the islands had no snakes, no birds likely to dine on canary eggs, and no native rats or other mammals, except for the domestic livestock of the Guanches. Following the ideas put forward in the preceding chapter, it seems likely that the Europeans encountered there a bird that had responded to a very low predatory environment by becoming tame in the wild, like the dodos of Mauritius and the blue-footed boobies of the Galapagos. Being genetically endowed with comparatively weak fight-or-flight responses, the canaries took well to living, breeding, and singing in cages.

We don't know precisely how the first canaries reached Europe, but we must suppose that European settlers quickly found out how easy it was to capture and breed them. The early reports attesting to the wild coloration pattern indicate that they had not already become domestic among the

Guanches. Someone enjoyed the song of the wild bird, captured it, put it in a cage, and discovered that it was perfectly happy to lay eggs and care for its young under those conditions. The motivation was purely aesthetic. No form of scientific thought was required. No one had to anticipate that captive breeding would eventually lead to domestication.

A cardinal difference between affective uses and material uses is immediate gratification. The warm feeling we get from playing with baby animals requires no time lapse and no quest for knowledge for its own sake. Nor does it require domestication. A baby wild animal is just as cuddly as a baby domestic animal. Similarly, an iridescent display of tail feathers delights the eye whether made by a domestic peacock or a wild bird-of-paradise. Historically, therefore, if immediately gratifying some sensibility played a significant role in prompting people to keep some specimens of a particular species captive over many generations, it might be possible to explain the eventual emergence of the genetic tameness in that species without recourse to theories of prehistoric scientific thought and a quest for knowledge for its own sake. In this scenario, the exploitation of products, talents, and labor would constitute subsequent discoveries arising well after the species had become genetically tractable.

Nevertheless, the dominant trend among scholars currently theorizing the origins of domestication attends primarily to the question of material uses, though it recognizes a distinction between primary uses and secondary uses. The former term essentially boils down to meat. The latter consists of uses that we closely associate with domestic animals today, but ones that could not plausibly have been part of the original process of domestication.[4] Secondary uses are ones that arose *after* the emergence of the domestic strain and must therefore be considered unanticipated consequences of domestication, rather than probable causes.

Wool affords the most obvious case.[5] Humans did not domesticate sheep to use their wool. The wild sheep from which domestic sheep genetically descend have a woolly undercoat that is seasonally shed, but their coat is mostly made up of long, stiff hairs that are not suitable for spinning into thread. Many breeds of domestic hair sheep are still raised in sub-Saharan Africa, some of them sporting distinctive black and white color patterns that fit well with a cross-species sub-Saharan preference for two-toned animals but are totally unsuited to utilization of the hair for fabrics.[6] Wool without the stiff hairs, like long tails, fat tails, and piebald coloration, developed only gradually among domestic flocks, presumably through selective breeding.

A discussion of other secondary uses will help to boil down the central questions surrounding the original domestication of sheep, goats, and cattle, the animals normally connected with the Neolithic revolution in the Fertile Crescent. I will first discuss milk and milk products and then draft harnessing and the placing of riders or burdens on animals' backs. This will eventually lead to a consideration of the thornier issue of meat, where questions of material uses and affective uses sometimes intersect.

Milk and Milk Products

Adult mammals do not commonly regard milk as a food for themselves. If they did, the risk would arise of adults competing with newborns for access to lactating females in periods of dearth. A powerful and universal mammalian instinct to protect the young of the species at all cost might seem to stand in the way of such disastrous competition, but this instinct is largely limited to mothers (and occasionally fathers) protecting their own particular offspring. A more practical restraint is the inability of most adult mammals to digest milk fully and a consequent absence of interest in it as a food. Lactose-tolerant adult humans are a Darwinian anomaly: we are animals that could conceivably destroy our own progeny by looking upon lactating females as food sources. In fact, however, we do not do so because of profound cultural taboos on adult consumption of human milk—not to mention butter, cheese, yogurt, or ice cream made from human milk. I have discovered that even mentioning such products gives rise in some people to instantaneous feelings of revulsion comparable to the feelings they have about cannibalism. I know of no ethnographic report of human milk ever being converted into such milk products. In all probability, therefore, those societies in which many or most adult humans are lactose tolerant evolved as a consequence of animal milk becoming abundant and available rather than as a continuation of a peculiar and nonuniform human genetic trait from the era of predomesticity. (This potentially opens the door to the question of whether humans too should be considered a domestic species, but the question is too semantically complex to attend to here.)

Under what circumstances did this abundance and availability of animal milk arise? It was once commonly asserted and many people still believe that access to milk was a primary motivation in the domestication of sheep, goats, and cows, and possibly camels and horses. No one, however, has made the same assertion regarding the milk of asses and llamas (not to mention pigs and dogs), though its nutritional quality differs little from that of those other species. It seems likely that the distinction Western society has inherited from earlier centuries between animals properly used for milk and animals never used for milk has influenced the popular notion that milk was the key to domestication. However, the general scholarly agreement, based on the natural range of the wild parent species, that China and Korea derived their use of cattle, sheep, and goats by way of inner Asia from presumed points of original domestication in the Middle East or North Africa makes it clear that patterns of milk consumption are subject to change over space and time. Prior to the twentieth century, those East Asian societies had effective taboos on the consumption of milk and milk products even though it is known that the Central Asian herders who first introduced the animals practiced milking.

Arguments in favor of milk as a rationale for animal domestication typically presume an awareness of milk products—butter, ghee, yogurt, cheese, and so on. Yet none of these products occurs naturally. All mammals deliver liquid milk directly from producer to consumer. Therefore, accumulations of liquid milk that might be observed to turn naturally into a consumable milk product do not occur in nature. By comparison, observation of ripe grain or fruit lying on the ground and naturally fermenting in a puddle of water might well have been the means by which humans first discovered alcoholic beverages. But no parallel observation of milk transformations could occur without there first being a deliberate collection of liquid milk in some sort of vessel. Only then could people discover the effects of churning, aging, boiling, evaporating, and colonizing with bacteria.

Why, then, might a society totally without knowledge of what milk might be turned into decide to collect liquid milk in a vessel, considering that wild female animals almost certainly objected strongly to any attempt to implement the decision? For adults to drink? Very unlikely. Milk is not a normal food for adult mammals, and Neolithic adults probably could not digest lactose. How about infants, then? A human infant deprived of milk by insufficient lactation or its mother's death might reasonably be considered a potential consumer of nonhuman milk. But there are reasons to be skeptical of this. First of all, pastoral peoples with abundant milk supplies commonly seek wet nurses for such children. Not only is the nutritional composition of human milk better for human babies, but it is far easier to feed an infant through suckling than through the administration of milk by some other means.

Moreover, milk drawn directly from a teat is essentially sterile, while unrefrigerated liquid milk in a vessel provides a good culture for dangerous bacteria. Studies of English nursing habits during the early Industrial Revolution have brought to light the plight of female factory workers who could not breast feed because of heavy work schedules and therefore left their infants in the care of other women. The infants that were put on a diet of cow's milk administered by some sort of sponge or funnel had a disastrously high mortality rate in comparison with those put with a wet nurse.[7]

Since humans reared their children for tens of thousands of years without milking domestic animals, it seems implausible that in Neolithic times people would have decided to maintain a herd of milk-producing animals solely for the feeding of the occasional needy infant for whom a wet nurse could not be found, given that the infant would probably die as a result. When animal milk *was* used as food for human infants prior to the evolution of a generalized culture of milking, it is more likely that the child was put to suckling the animal directly, as happens in the Roman legend of Romulus and Remus, the Muslim legend of Hayy ibn Yaqzan, and the passage from the epic of Gilgamesh quoted in chapter 3. After all, instances of women suckling piglets or puppies are well attested ethnographically. In the case of such direct suckling by another animal, of course, there again would have been no reason to collect liquid milk in a vessel, and hence no discovery of milk products.

Thus there is a serious problem in thinking about how human consumption of animal milk began. Rather than being a plausible rationale for domestication, it seems more likely to have developed slowly as an unanticipated benefit. Archaeologists deduce the presence of dairying from the preponderance of female cattle bones found in excavations. By this evidence, milking would appear to have spread to Europe around 4000 B.C.E., well after the domestication of cattle.[8] Images of cows being milked first appear in Egypt and Mesopotamia in the fourth millennium B.C.E., but these cannot be relied on to represent the beginnings of milking.

Chronology aside, human groups in the contiguous landmass of western Eurasia and northern Africa unquestionably did for some reason adopt the practice of collecting in vessels the milk of already domesticated cows, ewes, and nanny goats. There is no way of knowing what that reason was, but something other than consumption as a beverage or transformation into milk products would seem to have been involved.

Speculatively, and with the question of affective uses in mind, I would suggest that the people who first milked their animals might have used the milk for ceremonial purposes. Aside from an actual pregnant woman or newborn child, milk is the primary physical indicator of fecundity. Hence liquid milk in a vessel might originally have served in rituals for promoting fertility, a matter of constant concern for humanity since the first appearance of massive-breasted, pregnant-bellied "Venus" fig-urines in the early Paleolithic era. In Anatolia (modern Turkey), part of the supposed heartland of cattle, sheep, and goat domestication, a sym-bolic role for milk and lactation is well attested in historic times in the cult of multibreasted Cybele, a fertility goddess. It is conceivable, for example, that as an emblem of fertility milk was poured on an altar or on the ground in a libation to the gods or was used to lave the statue of a goddess. Farther to the east, the Vedic peoples of India, who were re-lated to some of the early Anatolian peoples, commonly offered the gods bright-burning clarified butter (ghee) in the sacrificial rituals, and Hindus wash statues of their paramount goddess with milk to the pres-ent day. Collecting milk in a bowl or skin bag for libations would have afforded the opportunity to discover milk products, which would quickly have become the primary object of milking. But genetically transmitted tameness must be considered a prerequisite for any such discovery.

The point of this speculation is not to propose some specific prehistoric ritual for which it is unlikely one could ever find concrete evidence. Ra-ther, it is to suggest a possible affective rationale for the collection of liquid milk in a vessel that is unrelated to the eventual exploitation of domestic animals as sources of milk and milk products for human nourishment.

Draft Harness

The use of domestic animals for draft purposes also has some appeal as a rationale for domestication. Economist Frederic L. Pryor, in an article devoted to the invention of plowing, makes the seemingly self-evident statement: "The most important prerequisite of the plow is the presence of large animals that can be domesticated to pull a plow."[9] But it is likely that there was a substantial time gap between the domestication of those large animals and the harnessing of them to plows.

The earliest depictions of animals being used for draft do show cattle as the primary pullers of plows and carts, but they date from well after the earliest evidence of cattle domestication. Depictions of yoked oxen appear around 3500 B.C.E., which is approximately when plow-made scratches, often both vertical and horizontal, have been uncovered on ground surfaces underlying datable European sites.[10] This evidence suggests that three thousand years may have intervened between cattle domestication and yoke harnessing.

Clearly there were many generations of cattle-herders, most of whom probably also consumed porridge or bread made from grain, who tended their livestock without giving any thought to utilizing them for draft purposes. The many rock paintings of domestic cattle dotted across the Sahara desert from Egypt to Mauritania, for example, never show animals harnessed to plows. These pictures are difficult to date, but they long precede 2500 B.C.E., when climatologists say the Sahara reached its current aridity, which is too extreme for cattle herding. Nor do depictions or figurines of yoked cattle show up at Çatal Hüyük, a seventh and eighth millennium B.C.E. site in Turkey where giant images of bulls along with long-horned cattle skulls adorn rooms of apparent ritual significance. Nor is there evidence of plowing at 'Ain Ghazal, a seventh and eighth millennium site in Jordan, where two dozen bull figurines and large numbers of cattle bones have been excavated. These examples, to which others could be added, are noteworthy inasmuch as Turkey, Jordan, and North Africa are among the regions proposed as the homeland(s) of cattle domestication.[11]

On the other hand, evidence of early ritual and symbolic roles for cattle, which would fall into the category of affective uses, are comparatively easy to find. The cattle figurines at 'Ain Ghazal are probably early examples of the myriad animal figurines from many later sites dedicated as symbolic offerings to gods. In Minoan culture, artists had no particular interest in the oxen plowing the Cretan landscape, but they painted many scenes of a game or ritual involving athletes vaulting over or being tossed by the horns of a bull. Whether or how this "sport" may have related to later bullfighting traditions is unknown, but scholars consider it a major feature of Minoan culture and religion. And in ancient Egypt, two anthropologists have proposed that images of a crook-topped, fork-footed, and eared wand commonly carried by gods and pharaohs reflect a custom of using a dried bull's penis as a sign of power.[12]

Thinking on the subject of cattle domestication runs along several lines. One school of thought sees the wild cow, *bos primigenius*, as a crop-raiding beast that gradually associated itself with human beings after they adopted grain agriculture. We might question, however, the wisdom of the Neolithic farmers who supposedly tolerated such a scourge. Early crop yields were very low, and wild cattle had big appetites.

Moreover, *bos primigenius* was a powerful and dangerous animal, much larger than the animals depicted in the earliest representations of domestic cattle. Archaeologists have found evidence in bone remains of a significant size differential between wild and domestic stock, both for cattle and for other animals. One theory used to explain this runs counter to the idea of cattle being attracted to the abundant food in cultivated fields. It maintains that the process of domestication, involving captivity and limited interbreeding with wild stock over a period of many generations, reduced the average size of the animals because the captive beasts had to subsist on a more meager diet than their wild cousins. (Food limitations are also used to explain the diminutive size of wild species on small islands in comparison to the same species on the mainland.)

Consideration of the energy budget of primitive agriculture may help explain the time gap between domestication and plowing. Maintaining a pair of adult oxen is not free of costs. Depending on the climate and the local terrain, the animals may have to be sheltered, led to more or less distant pastures, and fed during dry or cold seasons when no fresh grazing is available. Moreover, oxen die and need to be replaced with young animals. Every Neolithic farmer would not have needed to maintain his own breeding herd, but someone would have had to do so. So the cost of obtaining the animals in the first place has to be factored in. Then, too, there is the manufacturing and maintenance cost, in terms of time and labor, of the plow and yoke.

Planting without plowing, on the other hand, involves casting seed on unprepared soil by hand, or, more productively, scratching the soil or poking holes in it with a stick before sowing. The costs in this case are negligible in terms of materials, but substantial in terms of human labor. It is also not particularly productive. Casting seed on unprepared ground may yield scarcely more at harvest time than the amount of grain used as seed. Disturbing the soil gives seeds a much better chance of taking root, and rooting out competing weeds helps them even more. These considerations obviously led in time to some farmers recognizing plowing—either before sowing, like the Greeks, or after sowing, like the Egyptians—as a superior way of increasing the yield of certain crops. However, many Neolithic peoples drew other conclusions. Farmers continued to eschew plows and use hoes and digging sticks in most of Africa and southeastern Asia and in the entire Western Hemisphere until comparatively modern times.

The idea of yoking oxen to what probably started out as a sort of digging stick and exploiting their strength to gouge a furrow, freeing the farmer to guide both stick and animals, could not have occurred until grain yields reached a level sufficient to support the costs mentioned earlier. This probably involved further genetic changes in the domestic grain plants. The turning point would have come when the yield of the farmer's crop became great enough after seed for the next season's planting had been set aside to support not only the farmer's family, but also his oxen. Whenever this turning point was reached (some point well after the first domestication of wheat and barley), domestic cattle must already have been available. Wild or near-wild oxen, even when castrated, would scarcely have been tractable enough to work together under a yoke. This is not to say that wild animals can never be tamed and harnessed to a vehicle. Ancient times and modern experience demonstrates the contrary for certain species. But *bos primigenius* was a much larger animal than a reindeer or a zebra and it was not reluctant to use its horns.

The difficulties in visualizing plowing as a major rationale for the origin of cattle domestication hold true for pulling carts.[13] The earliest known wheels, those that have survived from the third millennium B.C.E. in Danish bogs, were made of solid wood. A circle of wood strong enough to bear substantial weight and to resist splitting when pulled over uneven ground must be thick and heavy. Four solid oak wheels of the Danish variety, for example, must have weighed around 600 pounds. A travois made of two flexible poles with a load fixed between them, after the style of the American Indians, would have been a more sensible means of carriage because it accommodates bumps and irregularities and weighs very little. Wheels only make sense economically when their weight can be reduced by more sophisticated construction, a course of development that can easily be reconstructed from ancient pictorial remains. In wood-poor regions like the Sahara desert, pack oxen and later pack camels were always more efficient.[14]

To compound the improbability of vehicle use as a rationale for domesticating cattle, the earliest depictions of vehicles, dating from the fourth millennium B.C.E., when cattle had already been domestic for several thousand years, often show four-wheeled wagons rather than two-wheeled carts. Four-wheeled vehicles have the virtue of a flat wagon-bed and provide more stability than a two-wheeled cart, but they had the disadvantage, at least prior to the popularization of the pivoting front axle in Renaissance Europe, of being extremely difficult to turn.

This raises the question of whether the uses to which the earliest vehicles were put were economic or ritual. A wagon that can keep a load upright might have been well suited to moving a statue, urn, or other ritual item a short distance along a level path with no curves. In these instances, problems with weight, speed, a wide turning radius, or the friction of wheel on axle and wheel on road could have been subordinated to achieving the ritual goal of the ceremony.

Evidence of ritual use of wheeled vehicles includes the first depictions of vehicles found anywhere. Mesopotamian images going back to the fourth millennium B.C.E. seem to show a shrine carried on sled runners evolving into a shrine (in some cases with a statue inside it) proceeding on four wheels. However, Mesopotamian images of war wagons, for which economic considerations may also have been secondary, are almost as old. In somewhat later times, after the development of light, spoked wheels, the ritual functions of wheeled vehicles remain apparent. Some of the most elaborate ancient European and Central Asian burial sites contain complete vehicles along with the skeletons of the horses that drew them. And archaeological sites in Europe have yielded models of wagons carrying large ritual items, such as an urn and a sundisk.

Riding and Pack Animals

Domestic riding animals at various times and places have included horses, asses (donkeys), onagers, one-humped camels, two-humped camels, reindeer, and cattle. However, neither concrete evidence nor strong argument supports the proposition that riding provided a rationale for domestication in the case of any species other than the horse. The ass became domestic in the Nile valley and the surrounding desert lands some five thousand years ago, but it never appears as a riding animal in early paintings and rock carvings from ancient Egypt. Nor is it shown pulling plows or carts. The onager, a relative of the horse and the donkey native to Iran, Iraq, and Syria, appears carrying burdens and pulling carts and wagons in Mesopotamian artwork from the fourth millennium B.C.E., and a figurine in the Bahrain Museum from around 600 B.C.E. seems to show a person riding on an onager. All told, however, the weight of the evidence, including the eventual replacement of domestic onagers by asses and horses brought into Mesopotamia from the west and north respectively, is strongly against the onager having been domesticated for riding. For two-humped camels, the earliest evidence for domestication comes from Central Asia and consists of clay models of four-wheeled wagons with the head of a camel at the front of the wagon-bed, presumably symbolic of the animal being used for pulling. There is no early evidence of riding. Early depictions of cattle being ridden are similarly rare, and it seems quite unlikely that reindeer were an early domesticate at all. Finally, the earliest saddles for one-humped camels appear to have been designed for tying on loads, not for carrying riders.[15]

Thus the debate on riding as a rationale for domestication comes down to the horse. Herds of prehistoric wild horses roamed the vast grasslands north of the Black and Caspian seas and provided early human groups in that region with meat. The abundance of horse bones at early archaeological sites establishes this fact. But sometime around 4000 B.C.E., certain horse bones and artifacts indicate a transition to domestication. One rear tooth, for example, has a groove worn in its forward surface that most likely came from friction with a bit lodged in the gap between the animal's front and rear teeth. It is debatable whether this use of a bit indicates someone riding a domestic horse, but it is hard to imagine a bit being used on a wild animal for a long enough time to wear a groove into a tooth.

Did the people who ate the horses decide they could herd and hunt them more effectively if they were mounted on horseback? If so, this would point to riding as a rationale for first domestication. But it would also raise the question of what prompted people who seem to have had no shortage of horse steaks drawn from wild herds to segregate a few animals and interbreed them long enough to establish tameness as a genetic trait, a process that might have taken a century or more, judging from the experiments with rats and foxes described in the last chapter.

Consider a comparison with bison in North America. Some Native Americans hunted bison before the first European explorers arrived in the Great Plains, but the pattern of tribes following the herds and living primarily from the products of their bison hunts only arose when horses became available from the Europeans. Horses made an intensification of bison exploitation possible by enabling the Indians to keep up with the herds and run down targeted animals. But the desire to hunt bison more effectively seems not to have prompted the Indian hunters to try domesticating bison or riding them. A similar case seems to obtain with reindeer herders in northern Asia. Domestic reindeer pull sleighs and provide mounts for people who gain an appreciable part of their sustenance from wild reindeer, but the use patterns of the domestic reindeer strongly suggest that these practices were borrowed from people to the south who utilized domestic horses.

The frequent mention of lassos in ancient legends emanating from Central Asia probably reflects the earliest method of capturing and subduing wild horses. However, while today we have inherited an image of cowboys lassoing mustangs and "breaking" them to take a rider, there is no way of telling how feasible this was in 4000 B.C.E., thousands of years before the invention of the saddle. After all, today's mustangs are not wild. They are feral, meaning that they descend from domestic animals that have been able, for one reason or another, to range freely. Under feral conditions, in which animals are deprived of the umbrella of human care and protection from predators, natural selection normally favors a return of "wild" characteristics. The low-adrenaline easy-breeders die young, and the more skittish and competitive survive to reproduce. (The feral camels of Australia provide an instructive comparison because the absence of predators in the outback makes them just about as docile as domestic camels.) But feral animals, whether horses, donkeys, pigeons, cats, dogs, or pigs, do not truly become wild. For example, they do not regain uniform wild coloration patterns. And they do not resist a return to conditions of domestic breeding control as strongly as wild species do.

Making guesses about how horse hunters might, after tens of thousands of years, have come up with the idea of riding leaves much to be desired in trying to explain the origins of horse domestication. A more fruitful approach may be to consider the general situation of the animals belonging to the group of late domesticates in western Asia and northeastern Africa. The horse, the donkey, the onager, the one-humped camel, and the two-humped camel all enter the ranks of the domestic animal between 4000 and 3000 B.C.E., when it is safe to assume that the human societies involved in their domestication were long familiar with domestic sheep, goats, cattle, and pigs. Clearly, what the new domesticates offered these societies was transportation. But if people had wanted transportation and had known how to domesticate animals, why would they have waited thousands of years until recollections of the earlier domestication episodes had certainly faded from human memory?

Cattle belong to the early group of domesticates, but as we have seen, evidence of their playing a role in transportation dates only to the same general period when the late domesticates first appear, 4000 to 3000 B.C.E.—a suggestive coincidence indeed. Except for the donkey, to be discussed later, all of these late domesticates might be regarded as replacements for cattle in their capacity as transport animals. Imagine the first experiments with putting a heavy load on the back of an ox or with fitting a yoke to its neck. One has to assume complete docility of the sort that the word "bovine" eventually comes to suggest, for wild cattle are ferocious horned beasts. Even then, getting the oxen to stop and start on cue, keeping them from trying to get free, and designing the linkage between the animals and a plow or sledge or cart must have been a challenge. Animal harnessing was a stunning technological breakthrough. And if the near simultaneity of early wheel remains from Denmark and vehicle images from lower Mesopotamia does not reflect two independent centers of invention, a likelihood specialists have been reluctant to entertain, then it would look like the new technology spread very quickly.

The horse is central to the transportation revolution of the fourth millennium B.C.E., if one may call it that. Whether this fact argues persuasively for transportation being the original rationale for domestication is debatable, however. Save for the worn tooth mentioned earlier, the bulk of the evidence for early horse use—pieces of draft harnesses, images of horses pulling vehicles, and inclusion of horses and vehicles in some 250 burials—points less to riding than to draft harnessing.[16] Packhorses do not show up in early depictions. Moreover, the type of harnessing originally used to attach a pair of horses to a cart or wagon was derived from the yoke harness used for oxen even though it is poorly adapted anatomically for use on equids. Yet the small size of the wild horses from which the domestic stock derived militated against their pulling carts or wagons with heavy, solid wheels. Horses eventually found their niche pulling chariots with light, spoked wheels. But it may well be that they were already domestic by the time wheelwright technology had reached this level of sophistication.

So did late domestication take place in reaction to the harnessing (draft or pack saddle) of cattle, when people went looking for other animals to use for transportation? The fact that the onager was used for transport for several centuries and then dropped as a domestic animal suggests either a failure to achieve full docility; an inability, for some unknown reason, to compete effectively with domestic donkeys and horses brought into the region from the west and north; or a limited agenda on the part of the people using them for transportation. Bone assemblages indicate that neither onagers nor camels (of either species) contributed much to the prehistoric diet. In the case of horses, however, hundreds of thousands of bones at Central Asian sites prove that horse flesh was commonly eaten both before and after domestication, and this opens up the question of whether domestic horses derive from wild horses kept for meat, with transport being developed only after domestication had occurred.

Meat

Milk and wool were secondary uses. Riding was probably a secondary use. Harnessing beasts to pull plows and carts was a secondary use for cattle but may have been a primary use for *some* late domesticates. Meat, however, always gets ranked as a primary use—the ultimate explanation of animal domestication.

There are various ways of thinking about this. One might imagine that grain agriculture led to a population increase that in turn led to a shortage of game. Tame animals would supply the dietary shortfall. Or one can imagine that grain agriculture compelled people to abandon migratory life and kept them from following the game animals as their foraging forefathers had. Again, tame animals would make up for reduced hunting opportunities. Or one could conjecture that certain animals were drawn to the fields planted by the early farmers, particularly if they were irrigated fields in semi-arid regions where lush grazing was scarce. With game so readily at hand, people might have given up true hunting in favor of slaughtering and eventually keeping the animals close at hand.

All of these scenarios leave something to be desired, however. Could population growth based on agriculture really have been substantial enough to strip the countryside of game? A shrinking ratio of wild bones to domestic bones in early agricultural sites is inconclusive. Agriculture might actually have increased the number of game animals. It is well established that in North America the forest clearance that accompanied the spread of European-style farming in the Midwest caused the population of deer, a prime meat animal, to soar. Deer prefer forest edges to deep forest, and the farmers' fields increased the area of this ecological niche.

A better indicator of the abundance of wild game than bone ratios may be the presence of large predators. If growing throngs of humans had reduced the game supply below a threshold that could sustain hunting, the lion population should have suffered. Meat may have amounted to as much as twenty percent of the human diet, but lions eat a lot more meat than that. Historical records from the Fertile Crescent, however, from the story of Samson and the bees making honey in the lion's head, to royal hunting scenes in the bas-reliefs covering the walls of Assyrian palaces, to the tale of Hercules and the Nemean lion, indicate a continuous presence of lions for thousands of years after the advent of agriculture.

The same objection holds for the idea of game being driven so far away from human settlement that hunters couldn't reach it easily. If so, the lions should have disappeared into the outback as well. As for animals being drawn to the human fields, even if this happened, it does not by itself explain how the farmers went from killing such crop raiders to keeping them and penning them up.

Taking into consideration our earlier discussion of the many generations of reproductive segregation from wild stock required to make the transition to inherited tameness, the core of the meat hypothesis boils down to the rate at which meat from captive animals could have been harvested. To illustrate, let us consider the case of a hunter killing a couple of wild ewes and bringing home four lambs, two male and two female. (Herding a whole flock of wild sheep into a pen is another possibility; but the larger the group, the slower the rate of genetic change.) The folks back at the campsite find the little ones cute and cuddly. They also know that they would be good to eat.

Suddenly some clever person has the bright idea that keeping the lambs until they grow up will increase the amount of meat, so the lambs are not killed immediately. We have to imagine his speech going something like this: "Let's hold on to these lambs long enough for them to produce lambs of their own. Then we can butcher and eat a few of those lambs but still keep enough to grow up and form a breeding herd. That way, maybe we can eventually live from herding and *give up hunting*." Not only is this highly Calvinist deferral-of-gustatory-satisfaction-to-some-later-date scenario implausible, but there is no evidence that human males have ever *wanted* to give up hunting.

Modern figures for domestic sheep show the four lambs reaching maturity about a year and a half after capture. The ewes then weigh perhaps 150 pounds and the rams over 200 pounds. To keep peace in the sheep pen, the people decide to kill one of the rams. This is the first meat harvested from the project. The ram carcass yields eighty pounds of meat.

How much each person gets depends on how many people there are in the camping group. Some surveys of modern foraging peoples suggest twenty-five as the optimum size of such a group. Though some situations permit large groupings, we can use twenty-five for our example and estimate that each person gets 3.2 pounds of meat. If the group is larger, the yield per person goes down. Farming villages of a traditional sort in northeastern Iran, where wild sheep may have first became domestic, average around 150 inhabitants. If we assume an agricultural setting for our thought experiment, the meat yield falls to about half a pound per person. This is all they get for a year and a half of keeping the sheep penned, protecting them from predators, and generally caring for them. It is hard to imagine even the unluckiest hunters failing to provide more meat than that over such a long period of time.

Now, however, the ewes get pregnant and after five months produce one lamb each. If one of the lambs is male, it might be eaten young, but the meat yield would be perhaps a quarter that of a grown ram. For a camping group of twenty-five, this means an additional three-quarters of a pound of meat by the end of the second year of the project. For·an agricultural settlement of 150, it means that everyone gets one skewer of kebabs. The group now waits a year and a half for the remaining female to reach maturity. Over that time, the first generation ewes each produce three more lambs, half of whom are males who are slaughtered and eaten: another 2.25 pounds of meat per person for the group of twenty-five. But three years have now elapsed and they still can't kill more than one or two animals every six months or so and still have a growing flock.

One can tweak the parameters of this experiment in various ways, but it always results in phenomenally low meat yields per capita over a period of years. The only way of increasing the yields substantially is to start with a much larger number of captured wild lambs, but the wait for a nutritional payoff is still long, the work of penning and caring for the flock increases greatly, and no one in the group knows enough about breeding to be encouraged that eventually, domestic tractability will make things easier. It is not hard to see why Lévi-Strauss thought there must have been an intense desire to accumulate knowledge for its own sake. Hunting couldn't have been bad enough to justify keeping wild stock captive for tens of generations on the basis of meat supply alone.

Up to now, I have suggested processes by which dogs, cats, and possibly pigs might have more or less domesticated themselves. And I have suggested that animals living in forbidding habitats, like camels, llamas, and possibly donkeys, may have been tame in the wild. And I have raised the possibility that the harnessing of cattle may have caused people to target some of the late domesticates, particularly onagers and camels, in their quest for draft, pack, and eventually riding animals. The animals remaining—cattle, sheep, and goats—present the toughest problem, however. If the initial idea of keeping them captive throughout their lifetimes cannot plausibly be ascribed to a desire for milk, wool, labor, or meat, what other alternatives are there?

7. From Mighty Hunter to Yajamana

Both sheep and goats became domestic somewhere in western Asia at roughly the same time. Cattle followed, at least some of them in the same general area and probably for similar reasons. I have excluded wool, milk, and labor as rationales for first domestication by reason of these being for the three species in question secondary uses. I have further proposed some back-of-the-envelope guesses that indicate ridiculously low meat yields from small numbers of captive stock, and further suggested that large numbers of captive animals present an unpromising scenario with respect to tameness becoming genetically established. So the question remains: Why were numbers of these wild species held captive and reproductively isolated long enough for domestication to occur?

Sacrifice, or, more broadly, sacralization of meat production, is the answer I will propose in this chapter. It is an answer that combines both material and affective uses. The meat from a sacrifice is eaten. The patron or sponsor of the sacrifice gives it away freely after special portions of the slaughtered animal have been offered to the gods, the officiating priests, or other specially entitled parties. Yet at the same time, the ritualized offering satisfies the spiritual and social needs of the patron of the sacrifice and of his community.

An inveterate materialist arguing against this proposition might maintain that the basic function of animal sacrifice is the distribution of meat, and the ritualistic element is secondary and ultimately trivial. I hope to show, however, that set in the broader context of the overall transition from predomesticity to domesticity, the ritual aspect of sacrifice takes on a greater importance and cannot be lightly dismissed, even if older hypotheses centering on domestication to service a specific cult of a mother goddess strain credulity.[1]

The Mighty Hunter of foraging times, I propose, became the Yajamana, or patron of the sacrifice, of early domesticity. The term "Mighty Hunter" I am taking from Genesis 10:8–9. In the Revised Standard Version this reads: "And Cush became the father of Nimrod; he was the first on earth to be a mighty man. He was a mighty hunter before the Lord; therefore it is said, 'Like Nimrod a mighty hunter before the Lord.' " In the lineages of Noah recorded in the Bible, Nimrod is the only figure between Noah's sons and Abraham to be so strongly and specifically characterized. Cush, the name of Nimrod's father, normally refers to Ethiopia in biblical usage, but here it is derived from the name of the Kassites, a people from the mountains of western Iran who ruled Mesopotamia from the eighteenth to the twelfth century B.C.E. The Bible vaguely credits Nimrod himself with founding Babylon and other great Mesopotamian cities.

The less familiar term in this chapter's title, Yajamana, literally means "sacrificer" in the Sanskrit language of ancient India. However, it is used exclusively for the patron or sponsor of the sacrifice, as opposed to the priest or priests who slaughter the animal, chant hymns, and so forth. The Yajamana is a silent presence at the sacrifice, an individual for whom "host" might be a suitable translation in English were it not so mundane. The Yajamana appears in commentaries on the Rig-Veda, the collection of hymns sung at sacrifices performed by Indo-Iranian priests dating back, like Nimrod the Mighty Hunter, to the second millennium B.C.E. In practical terms, the Yajamana was usually a king, chief, or community big shot—I'll call him a king for the sake of convenience—who ordered the sacrifices performed on behalf of his people. He generally also allowed his people to be present and share in the distribution of meat from the sacrificed animal.

Both of these terms, Mighty Hunter and Yajamana, bring the killing of animals, and consequently the distribution of meat, into conjunction with "royal" status and religious ritual. I take it as significant, in other words, that Nimrod was not just a mighty hunter, but "a mighty hunter *before the Lord*," understanding the last three words to imply if not sacrifice then at least a sacred ritualization or sacralization of meat distribution. With the transition to domesticity, what the predomestic Mighty Hunter presented to his community in the way of meat from the hunt becomes the living animal, first captive and eventually domestic, presented for sacrifice by the Yajamana. In both cases, the distribution of meat serves to elevate the social status of the meat provider by placing his action in a sacred setting and thus associating him with divinity. To the degree that the Mighty Hunter and the Yajamana gained or confirmed "royal" status in this way, one might look at meat distribution as a source of inequality dating back to the dawn of the Neolithic period in western Asia.

Philosophers have long associated inequality with profound changes in the social and political order. Jean Jacques Rousseau, in "A Discourse on the Origin of Inequality," wrote:

> The first man who, having enclosed a piece of ground, bethought himself of saying *This is mine*, and found people simple enough to believe him, was the real founder of civil society. From how many crimes, wars and murders, from how many horrors and misfortunes might not any one have saved mankind, by pulling up the stakes, or filling up the ditch, and crying to his fellows, "Beware of listening to this impostor; you are undone if you once forget that the fruits of the earth belong to us all, and the earth itself to nobody."[2]

Karl Marx distances himself from Rousseau by observing that the earliest communities, like those known to him in his own day in other parts of the world, probably labored in common on collectively owned property as they would within a family. Both thinkers, however, place agricultural life at the center of their thinking, thus reflecting the paramount role of land ownership and agricultural labor in European history. Though it is universally recognized that in many agricultural societies and in all pastoral societies ownership of domestic animals is of utmost economic importance, the idea that inequality may have roots in the ownership of animals has attracted less attention than it deserves.

Surveys of the ethnographic literature describing foraging societies of the last three centuries have identified in most of them a strong egalitarian predisposition:

> The term *egalitarian* does not mean that all members have the same amount of goods, food, prestige, or authority. Egalitarian societies are not those in which everyone is equal, or in which everyone has equal amounts of material goods, but those in which everyone has equal access to food, to the technology needed to

acquire resources, and to the paths leading to prestige. The critical element of egalitarianism, then, is *individual autonomy*.[3]

How do these societies deal with actual inequality resulting from variable prowess in hunting?

> In fact, there is always a tendency for some individuals to attempt to lord it over others. In response, egalitarian hunter-gatherers have developed a variety of ways to level individuals. . . . Humor is used to belittle the successful hunter . . . and gambling, accusations of stinginess, or demand sharing maintain a constant circulation of goods and prevent hoarding. . . . A hunter who acknowledges his worthlessness while dropping a fat antelope by the hearth relieves the tension created by sharing. The result is not a group of disgruntled would-be misers and dictators, but individuals who are assertively egalitarian, who live a life in which the open hoarding of goods or the imposition of one's will upon another is at odds with cultural norms.[4]

Not all foraging societies fit this pattern, however. Several, from regions as widely separated as the Pacific Northwest, southwestern Florida, and northern Japan, exhibited nonegalitarian features. These societies are typically distinguished by "high population densities, sedentism or substantially restricted residential mobility, occupational specialization, perimeter defense and resource ownership, focal exploitation of a particular resource (commonly fish), large resident group sizes, inherited status, ritual feasting complexes, standardized valuables, prestige goods or currencies, and food storage."[5]

Relating these firsthand observations of foraging groups in modern times to unknown prehistoric situations must obviously be inconclusive, but "on the strength of archaeological data it is reasonable to assume that nonegalitarian society developmentally succeeds egalitarian society. If this is true, then, evolutionarily speaking, what happens to a band of 'fiercely egalitarian' hunter-gatherers that makes them relinquish some of their autonomy?"[6] The answer put forward by the anthropologist and archaeologist Lawrence H. Keeley correlates population density with nonegalitarian sociopolitical organization. He concludes that "population pressure fits very well the expectations for a necessary and sufficient condition for and the efficient cause of complexity among hunter-gatherers."[7]

Returning to the Mighty Hunter and the Yajamana, imagine a pre-historic society somewhere in western Asia that is beginning to enjoy the benefits (more food) and burdens (more work) of augmenting their diet with deliberately planted wheat and barley. Families stay put for longer periods of time (if not permanently), storage of food makes nutrition more reliable the entire year round, and both factors contribute to a growth in population. But the foraging band, on its way to becoming agricultural and fully sedentary, still depends on hunters for meat. Since work in fields and gardens is seasonal, most men still hunt; but as always, some have more skill and luck than others. Nevertheless, the meat is shared by the group as a whole, and the tendency of the best hunters to pride themselves on their skill is deflated by various leveling behaviors.

Now imagine the same community two hundred years later. Farming and gardening take up larger amounts of time. The village is substantially more populous. Life in general is losing its pristine egalitarian character. Who benefits most from the growing inequality? Who emerges as the strong man or chief? Rousseau might answer, "the man who claims own-ership of the largest fields." Marx might answer, "the man who gains the power to direct the labor of others in producing commodities." But it is difficult to find historical examples of rulers known for their legendary prowess as farmers. The Prodigious Plowman? The Heroic Harvester? No. Rulers and aristocrats the world over have preferred to associate themselves with hunting rather than farming. This is attested in myriad ways, including tales of kings encountering wondrous animals while hunt-ing, portrayals of the king and his retinue at the hunt, myths of hunting in the afterlife, appropriation of wild animals as heraldic symbols, designa-tion of wilderness areas as royal or aristocratic hunting preserves, and the representation of wild game in pictures of royal feasts.

If population growth was, as Lawrence Keeley has argued, a sufficient cause of inequality appearing in previously egalitarian foraging commu-nities, it is not unreasonable to suppose that the successful hunters who had previously been the targets of humor, belittling, and other behaviors designed to keep the social playing field level would, as nonegalitarian practices made their appearance, have been among the first to seek spe-cial status. The characteristics of nonegalitarian foraging societies, one will recall, included "perimeter defense and resource ownership, focal exploitation of a particular resource (commonly fish), . . . inherited sta-tus, ritual feasting complexes, . . . and food storage." While dried fish may have been the particular resource exploited, stored, and feasted upon in the case studies on which these generalizations are based, proximity to rich fishing grounds being, like crop growing, a spur to sedentary life and population growth, the entire package of characteristics holds up well when applied to our hypothesized threshold farming community in western Asia.

"Perimeter defense and resource ownership" fits exactly a situation in which animals, either wild captives or domestic stock, are kept penned and protected. "Focal exploitation of a particular resource" describes well a concentration on keeping livestock. "Ritual feasting complexes" equate to animal sacrifice followed by distribution of the meat. "Food storage" can mean live storage, in the form of captive animals, as well as smoked fish. "Inherited status" follows from ownership of a valued resource, namely, a flock of animals that passes to the heirs of the owner.

So many examples of sacrifice known from historical sources involve domestic animals that at first blush it appears that wild animals were never sacrificed. If true, this might imply that animal sacrifice only arose after domestication. But the sacrifice of wild animals is not unheard of. The most important annual ritual of the Ainu of northern Japan, a foraging society classed as nonegalitarian, is the sacrifice of a bear cub as a spirit messenger to the gods. And in the Western Hemisphere, human sacrifice abounded in societies with no large domestic animals, like that of the Aztecs. Bear cubs and humans share a particular characteristic, however: they are comparatively easy to feed and control until the day of the sacrifice. By contrast, most wild game arrives at the campsite or the village already dead. A proclamation issued in Japan in 764, when the emperor was deathly ill, reflects this. Composed under the influence of newly circulating Buddhist doctrines, the proclamation declared a five-month moratorium on the killing of animals and on using deer and wild boar as sacrificial tributes. Neither swine nor deer ever became domestic in Japan, so the implication of the proclamation clearly indicates that meat from the hunt or possibly captured prey animals were customarily presented in sacrificial offerings.[8]

The transition from Mighty Hunter to Yajamana, then, mirrors the transition from game being distributed in a ritualized fashion—"before the lord"—to blood sacrifice of a living animal followed by the distribution of meat. Given the powerful effect on the human nervous system of watching blood being shed, as discussed earlier in connection with post-domesticity, it should not come as a surprise that some societies came to accord a special place to the blood sacrifice of a living victim, even while retaining, perhaps, dead meat offerings to the ancestors or other spirits.

Then again, human sacrifice may have pointed the way to the blood sacrifice of animals. One of the many possible ways of interpreting the story of Abraham's sacrifice of Isaac (for Muslims, Ibrahim's sacrifice of Isma'il) is as a symbol of the Israelite substitution of animal sacrifice for the child sacrifice practiced by their Canaanite kin. Biblical texts confirm the practice of child sacrifice among the Canaanites, and this is further supported with respect to Carthage, a Phoenician (that is, Canaanite) colony, by Roman reports and the archaeological discovery of children's bones in association with altars.

Like many other boys living in domesticity, the child Isaac was accustomed to seeing animals slaughtered on an altar. He asks his father where the lamb is. Abraham replies that the Lord will provide the lamb. But as the tale unfolds, the Lord provides not a lamb but a full-grown wild ram—that is, a ram that appears to have no owner. Substituting a ram for the conventional lamb signifies the greater importance of human sacrifice over ordinary sacrifice. In other settings, including the Andean region after the domestication of the llama, it would appear that blood sacrifice of domestic animals similarly superseded human sacrifice. Reports of human sacrifice in domestic societies die out early in the common era, but blood sacrifice of animals continues to the present day in a number of cultures.

Whether the transition that took place was from the Mighty Hunter offering dead meat on an altar to the Yajamana offering a live animal for sacrifice, or, in some settings perhaps, from human sacrifice to animal sacrifice, having an animal on hand when it was needed for sacrifice must have constituted a problem. A hunter might have gone out in search of game when a sacrifice situation arose, but a hunter cannot always count on returning with a living wild animal. Sacrifices may have been performed at regular intervals. Or they may have occurred only on special occasions, such as enthronements, burials of rulers, or a visit by an honored guest. Or emergency conditions may have demanded them, as, in the Iliad, the becalming of the sea so that the Achaean fleet could not sail required Agamemnon's sacrifice of his daughter Iphigenia. But regardless of the reason, sacrifice requires victims—and sacrificers cannot depend on whether or not the community's hunters happen to run across a wild lamb or, less likely, manage to net a wild boar and get it back to the village alive. Rituals requiring the slaughter of a living animal require the keep-ing of animals. The keeping can be short term, as with the Ainu bear cub, or it can be longer term, as with Aztec prisoners of war waiting their turn to ascend the pyramid and have their hearts cut out. But there is much to be said for bringing the entire operation in-house by raising victims from birth in captivity.

Hunters play a lead role in this scenario. When they come home with meat, egalitarian ways demand sharing with the entire group. But there is no way to share a living wild sheep. It can't be ignored because it will simply flee into the wild, but treating it as common property would make it available for slaughter by whoever feels hungry for a mutton chop. Cropland may be held collectively, but a captive wild animal must be owned. Only after domestication has occurred and hereditary tameness ensures the animals' continuing presence in the community can owner-ship become collective or be ignored with feral stock allowed to run free. Did the hunter himself care for the lambs and kids he brought back from the hunt? Perhaps not. But he is the person most likely to have deter-mined whether they should be killed or kept, and he is the person most likely to have owned them as property.

The transition I am hypothesizing from Mighty Hunter to Yajamana would have been gradual. Victims bred in captivity may initially have only supplemented wild game. The continuation of hunting might have been necessary, in fact, for the captive herds to multiply and not be con-sumed too rapidly. In time, captive flocks and herds grew to such a point that it was possible to sacrifice many animals simultaneously, a possibil-ity that would have been hard to realize in a purely hunting-based econ-omy (*hecatomb*, a common Greek word for sacrifice, literally means one hundred cattle: *hecaton* = "hundred" + *bos* = "cow"). More or larger ani-mals meant more blood, more meat, more favor with the gods, and more status for the Yajamana.

The case of the mithan, a domestic bovine species found only in the highlands of northeastern India and Burma, provides a suggestive illus-tration. The mithan appears to be the domestic form of the gaur, a type of wild ox found in the same region. Frederick J. Simoons, in *A Cere-monial Ox of India*, made a comprehensive study of the peoples who keep and esteem mithans and the uses to which they are put. With scarcely any exceptions, mithans are not used for milk, plowing, draft, or leather. Instead, they are used as sacrifices and as a form of wealth that can be used to pay a bride-price, ransom, fine, or any other weighty obli-

gation. The mithans are owned by individuals or groups but are not ordinarily penned or herded. Ownership may be indicated by ear-notching.
The sacrifice of a mithan enhances the social status of the Yajamana:

> The mithan sacrifice is by far the most important one for the Dafla
> [people of India's Northeast Frontier Agency]. It pleases every-
> one, the spirits to whom the mithan is offered, the feast giver [i.e.,
> the Yajamana] who hopes to achieve a specific end, and the rela-
> tives and guests who share the meat, which they relish. No other
> sacrifice is so effective and in no other are the rites so elaborate or
> carried out with such care.[9]

Among the Zahau Chin people of northern Burma, economic organization centers on Feasts of Merit that involve most Chin surplus goods
and give the Yajamana great psychological and spiritual satisfaction.
Different grades of feast call for the sacrifice of different numbers of pigs
and mithans—the highest feast requiring seven pigs, two mithan bulls,
and one mithan cow.

> The Chin feast giver [i.e., the Yajamana]...tries to gain the goodwill
> of various supernatural beings and thereby prosperity and well-
> being. The Chin believe that mithan ritually sacrificed go straight to
> the Land of the Dead; they are considered, in a sense, as obligatory
> gifts sent on ahead of the feast giver, which both please and impress
> the inhabitants, but which the feast giver expects to have again. He
> has thus established connections in the Land of the Dead which will
> assure his status and guarantee his wealth when he arrives.[10]

The fine line between Yajamana and Mighty Hunter appears among
the Falam Chin people. Sacrificing mithans and pigs and hosting a feast
is not the only route to social advancement. A feast can also be held in
celebration of a successful hunt. Killing a small game animal such as a
barking deer calls for the additional killing of a half-grown pig. Large
animals, such as a tiger, elephant, bear, wild boar, or gaur, require the
additional killing of a full-grown pig or, if the hunter is wealthy enough,
a mithan.

> When a Falam hunter kills an animal of the large game category
> he sings a song of triumph, joined in by others, to notify people,
> especially those of his village, of his kill. In addition, before he can
> eat again he must perform a special ritual to protect himself from

the evil results of the killing. He must also hold a Feast of Celebration, a certain number of which are necessary for a man to enter the Plain of Heaven. At the feast for big game animals and at the feast for tigers, beer is divided into five types; the best one of these, the *sia hau zu*, or "mithan kill beer," is distributed only to those who have already slaughtered a mithan at a big game celebration feast; the second category of beer is for those who have slaughtered a pig at such a feast. In drinking these categories of beer, moreover, a system of priorities is observed, with the greatest hunter and giver of Feasts of Celebration taking precedence over everyone else. The greatest hunter also has certain other benefits. Among them, he receives the choicest food at the feast, and his hunting skill and generosity are praised extravagantly by other men as well as by himself. In such affairs, he is given precedence over all others, including village headman and chief, if they happen to be there. . . .

The flesh of the mithan or pigs slaughtered and of the dead game animal is divided according to tradition. That of the game animal, for example, goes to satisfy various obligations incurred by the hunter: to headman, blacksmith, loaner of guns, beaters, and others. This division, in turn, places reciprocal obligations on the recipients. And the village as a whole benefits from the meat and beer provided at the feast.[11]

How and when the mithan came to be domestic remains a mystery. The peoples who sacrifice mithans practice agriculture and also keep pigs, dogs, and chickens, the customary mix of domestic animals in southeastern Asia. They only rarely own ordinary cattle or water buffalo, and when they do, they do not esteem them as they do a mithan. The difference in appearance between a wild gaur and a mithan, which is particularly evident in the curvature of the horns and the mithan's occasional and varied white markings, makes it evident that some genetic change occurred in the domestication process. This suggests that the practice of allowing most mithans to roam freely and of not subjecting them to human breeding control developed after the original domestication. Simoons disagrees and prefers a scenario that borders on self-domestication:

In the hypothesized case of salt being offered to a wild gaur, the less wild animals would be the most likely to approach man. This in itself would be a selective factor. Survival of their relatively gentle young that were not killed along with the parents might have been assisted by proximity of human settlements, which were avoided by wild dogs and tigers. When the young were old enough to browse in the forest, they might have been drawn back to the village by human urine, or men might have maintained the tie as they do now, periodically providing the animals with salt. The gentle offspring would remain and multiply, but those with inherited wildness would return to the deep forest and the wild state. Since mithan bulls are most commonly sacrificed, wilder bulls were probably dispatched young, and gentler ones survived to breed. This also contributed to development of a gentle quality. Though this is a process of selection that involves a vastly longer time span than the systems of close control envisaged by many theories of domestication, it does seem feasible.[12]

The feasibility of this scenario diminishes when genetic issues are taken into account. Even if only the most naturally tame gaurs proved willing to approach a salt lick provided by humans, and their offspring did prove to be comparatively gentle, there is no reason to think that these offspring would not have mated with fully wild gaurs while roaming freely in the bush, thus diluting any accumulating genetic tendency toward tameness. Simoons's scenario also fails to account for mithans becoming objects of individual ownership and does not explain how the mithan became so important as a sacrificial animal. On the other hand, in trying to explain the disinclination of the Dafla, Chin, and other mithan keepers to pen and control their animals, Simoons makes it clear that the route to mithan domestication probably did not depend on lessons learned from keeping other types of domestic animal.

The domestication of the mithan, probably centuries rather than millennia ago, seems to reflect a social and economic context similar to the one that gave rise to sheep and goat domestication ten thousand years earlier and more than a thousand miles to the west. Foraging peoples under the pressure, perhaps, of a population growth spurred by their adoption of agriculture, are forced to abandon their egalitarian ways. They develop a system of property ownership based (in part) on the possession of captive gaurs (or sheep, goats, or cattle), a choice quarry for hunters. Ritualized offerings of meat from the hunt and the celebration of the Mighty Hunter's prowess come to be supplemented by the slaughter of captive stock. As the generations pass, the herd of captive wild gaurs, from which the most intractable bulls are culled for sacrifice, turns into a herd of domestic mithans that are sufficiently tame genetically to be allowed to roam freely. At the same time, new rituals arise in which the mithan owner sacrifices his domestic stock in return for social and spiritual benefits. The feasts celebrating the hunt decline in importance or disappear, and the Yajamana takes the place of the Mighty Hunter of predomestic times.

In the one case cited by Simoons where the feast of hunting survives in parallel with the Yajamana's offering of his animals for sacrifice, the owner of domestic mithans ordinarily enjoys a higher status than the Mighty Hunter, except when a major kill temporarily elevates the hunter above the chief or headman. But even then the celebration of the kill calls for the sacrifice of living domestic animals, possibly because with population growth the amount of meat to be shared from a single game carcass has become too meager or because the people have come to look forward to the act of killing.

In some cases, the killing of the sacrificial mithan imitates a hunt:

[Among one clan of the Ao Naga in India,] it begins with the baiting of the mithan by a warrior who crashes his shield against the mithan and hits it with a stick. Then the animal is smeared with lather to make it slippery and difficult to grasp. Later young men march around it in procession and then attack it. They throw it to the ground, hold it so that it cannot rise, and some of them jump and dance on it until it is exhausted. Then it is released and permitted to get up. After a little while it is again thrown to the ground and danced on, the entire process being repeated three times. The third day, after more ceremony, the mithan is finally dispatched by an old man who spears it behind the right shoulder. This thrust does not kill the beast, and the young men then cut the knee tendons, hamstringing the animal, and drag it alive to the sacrificer's house. There a puppy is dashed against its forehead. The mithan, whether dead or not, is then cut open and disemboweled, and left thus until morning.[13]

Though patently disgusting to our postdomestic sensibility, this grisly procedure serves as a reminder that sacrifice and hunting are both about killing. Fanciful biblical illustrations of a trussed sheep on an altar, a white-bearded Abraham looking up to heaven with a knife in his hands, and a total absence of blood—the illustrators prefer to show the sacrifice just before the killing—convey a sanitized notion of sacrifice designed to spare the reader any thought of actual killing. Reflecting a similar squeamishness, some modern Muslims fulfill their ritual obligation of sacrificing an animal during the annual Feast of Sacrifice by paying a butcher to slaughter an animal on their behalf—and out of their sight—and distribute the meat to the poor.

In their earliest manifestations, however, sacrifices did not hide the killing and the butchering of the carcass. Not only was everyone accustomed to the shedding of blood and the killing of animals, but the particulars of the animal's death were closely observed. One remnant of this earlier sensibility that has survived is the Moroccan practice of televising the king's slaughter of a ram on the Feast of Sacrifice and commenting on whether the ram tries to rise after its throat is cut. A strong ram that tries to rise signals a strong king.

For the most part, however, the most grisly aspects of sacrifice have diminished over the centuries. The animal sacrifices of ancient India over which the Yajamana presided survive today as Vedic ritual ceremonies that involve a great deal of chanting but call for nothing but ghee to be thrown on the sacrificial fire. Christianity definitively replaces the animal sacrifices practiced at the Jewish temple in Jerusalem with the metaphorical sacrifice of Christ, the Lamb of God, on the cross, and the subsequent symbolic consumption of the blood and flesh from the sacrifice in the rite of Holy Communion. And so long as the Temple Mount remains in Muslim hands, Judaism is spared the problem of reinstituting animal sacrifice in a rebuilt temple and countering the inevitable public revulsion.

The slight vestiges of the sacrifice of game animals in nonegalitarian foraging societies and the antiquity and diminishing prominence of blood sacrifice in agricultural societies point to sacrifice being, in general, a phenomenon of early domesticity. We are perhaps disinclined to ask why blood sacrifice declined because we find it appalling that it ever existed in the first place. However, we cannot escape the fact that the slaughter of animals increased even as sacrifice declined. In ancient Greece and Rome, virtually the only meat available came from temple sacrifices, but the end of paganism did not mean the end of meat eating. Slaughter simply became desacralized, as it is in most societies today. So the decline in blood sacrifice does not equate to a rise in the humane treatment of animals.

What disappears with the demise of blood sacrifice is the belief that animals afford some sort of contact with the unseen world of divinities and spirits. The popular culture of domesticity preserves recollections of such beliefs in tales of witches using cats as familiars, and domestic high culture occasionally resurrects them for artistic purposes, as when Wagner has Siegfried understand the songs of a bird after he tastes the blood of a slain dragon. But on the whole, the idea of animals as intermediaries with an unseen spirit world ceases over time to resonate with cultures whose attitudes toward animals become overwhelmingly use oriented. European farming people of, say, the sixteenth century, who used oxen for plowing, consumed smoked ham and salted herring as their main meat sources, spun wool, and prided themselves on their cheeses, preserved any number of curious animal-related customs that they little understood. But they did not believe, as the ancient Greeks, Romans, and Mesopotamians did, that the state of the world or future events could be determined by examining the entrails of sheep or observing the flight of birds. As domestic animals became more useful, they became more commonplace and less mysterious.

In China, evidence of this evolution can be traced from the time of the late Shang dynasty (circa 1200–1045 B.C.E.). Divination was one of the main functions of the Shang kings. They practiced it by applying a hot point to a specially prepared tortoise shell or cow shoulder blade and reading the message from the unseen world from the cracks produced by the heat. In some instances the questions asked, answer divined, and ultimate results were written on these "oracle bones," which consequently became the earliest evidence of Chinese writing. In addition to the spiritual implications of using the bones of cattle, the inscriptions often mention blood sacrifice: "Crack-making on *dingchou* (day 14), Bin divined: 'In praying for harvest to Shang Jia (the predynastic founder of the royal lineage) we offer in holocaust [i.e., burnt offering] three small penned lambs and split open three cattle.'" And, "On *xinsi* (day 18) divined: '(We) will pray for a child to [female ancestors] Mother Geng and Mother Bing and offer a bull, a ram, and a white boar.'"[14] The Shang practiced human sacrifice as well.

Seven centuries later, animal sacrifice still played a key role in the rituals that formed, along with humaneness, one of the foundations of proper human life in the thinking of Confucius (551–479 B.C.E.). A generation or so later, however, the thinker Mozi held that Confucius placed too much emphasis on such rituals. Mozi granted the role of sacrifice in honoring the ancestors but saw only the most general connection with the unseen world:

> How do we know that Heaven loves the people of this world? Because it enlightens them universally. How do we know that it enlightens them universally? Because it possesses them universally. How do we know that it possesses them universally? Because it accepts sacrifices from them universally. Because within the four seas, among all the people who live on grain, there are none who do not feed their sacrificial oxen and sheep, fatten their dogs and pigs, prepare clean offerings of millet and wine, and sacrifice to the Lord-on-High and the spirits.[15]

Not long after Mozi, Mencius (385?–312? B.C.E.), a forceful exponent of Confucian views, nevertheless expressed a much more mundane view of animal sacrifice in a parable designed to promote humane thinking:

> While the king was seated in the upper part of the hall, someone led an ox through the lower part. Upon seeing this the king asked where the ox was going and was told that it was being taken to serve as a blood sacrifice in the consecration of a bell. The king said, "Spare it. I cannot bear its trembling, like one who, though blameless, is being led to the execution ground." Asked whether in that case the consecration of the bell should be dispensed with, the king said, "How can it be dispensed with? Substitute a sheep instead. . . ."
>
> Though the people all thought it was because the king grudged the ox, the minister certainly knows that it was because the king could not bear to see its suffering.
>
> The king said, "That is so. The people must truly have thought this, but, although the state of Qi is small and narrow, how could I grudge a single ox?". . . .
>
> Mencius said, "The king should not think it strange that the people assumed that he grudged the ox. How could they know why he substituted the smaller thing for the larger one? Had the king been grieving over its being led, blameless, to the execution ground, then what was there to choose between an ox and a sheep?"
>
> The king smiled and said, "What kind of mind was this, after all? It was not that I grudged the expense, and yet I did exchange the ox for a sheep. No wonder the people said that I grudged it."

Mencius said, "There is no harm in this. This was after all the working of humaneness—a matter of having seen the ox but not the sheep. This is the way of the noble person in regard to animals: if he sees them alive, then he cannot bear to see them die, and if he hears their cries, then he cannot bear to eat their flesh. And so the noble person stays far away from the kitchen."[16]

Not surprisingly, when the Han Chinese of the north expanded southward in the following millennium and became familiar with wet rice agriculture and the use of water buffalo for plowing, the buffalo, a late domesticate, did not get added to the list of animals eligible for sacrifice. The Chinese word *chu* signifying the "six domestic animals" encompasses horses, cattle, sheep and goats together—all animals that reached northern China already domesticated via Central Asia—and pigs, dogs, and chickens—animals that probably reached northern China from southeastern Asia. It would appear that these were the animals thought worthy of sacrifice. A parallel development in early India recognizes a distinctive class of five animals suitable for sacrifice—humans, horses, cattle, sheep, and goats—but excludes the water buffalo and camels that became an important part of the post-Vedic Indian agricultural economy but were probably unknown as domestic animals to the Indians of Vedic times.[17]

The most plausible measure of this steady decline in the mystery of animals is the duration of elapsed time from the era of predomesticity. As discussed earlier, the art, myth, and folklore of late predomesticity portray a world in which human-animal relations are deeply imbued with spiritual and aesthetic sensibility. Every foraging society that survived into modern times long enough to be described ethnographically abounds in animal mysteries and uncertain boundaries between what is human, what is divine, and what is animal. Many of them preserve divination practices using animals and conceive of certain animals as emissaries to or from the unseen world. But these things all disappear or become submerged as domesticity progresses.

While our postdomestic mentality considers the domestication of animals a marvelous if inexplicable act of human genius, it probably attracted little notice when it was occurring. When the first wild animals were being penned or tolerated as they skulked around the campsite catching mice or scavenging garbage, no one knew that ox-drawn plows, horse-drawn chariots, pinstriped wool suits, frozen yogurt, and Kentucky Fried Chicken were looming in the distant future. What they did know was that omens could be read in the flight of birds, that shamans could communicate through animals with the unseen world, that killing animals involved the hunter with their spirits, that animal combat made an awesome spectacle, and that every sort of human experience or thought could be recounted in the form of stories about animals. Domestication took place on the margins of this world, and survivals of predomestic beliefs persisted long into the era of domesticity, finally to be obliterated by the overwhelming weight of material usefulness.

There is limit to how much we can find out from archaeology. Excavations at the Pakistani site of Mehrgarh between 1974 and 1997 uncovered evidence of people settling down and gradually concentrating their energies on growing plants and herding domestic animals.[18] The level just above virgin soil dating to 6500 to 6000 B.C.E. contained animal bones, stone blades that retained a vegetable gloss from cutting wild grasses or domestic wheat and barley, and traces of mud-brick houses. Simple pottery appears a bit later. Most of the animal bones in the earliest levels reflect a hunting economy. They include gazelle, deer, pig, sheep, goat, cattle, nilgai (a large antelope), water buffalo, and onager. Bone measurements indicate that a few of the goats may have been domestic, and two burials from the earliest level included five young goats presumably sacrificed on behalf of the deceased.

By 5500 B.C.E., bones from wild animals become comparatively few, and bones from sheep, goats, and cattle increase. Measurements of bones from the humped zebu (*bos indicus*), the most prevalent variety of cattle, show a progressive diminution in size that has led archaeologist Richard Meadow to conclude that domestication of this subspecies took place locally. By 4500 B.C.E., local potters are ornamenting their wares with images of zebu bulls with huge horns, and eventually an image of a cattle-horned deity makes its appearance in the same general area.

Did Mighty Hunters metamorphose into Yajamanas during the process of zebu domestication at Mehrgarh? Did the community interact with captive and eventually domestic zebus the way the mithan keepers of northeastern India and Burma do with their livestock today? No milk, no plowing, no ox-carts? Just blood and sacrifice? There is no way of telling archaeologically. But the frequency with which animal sacrifice appears in early domestic cultures around the world and the regularity with which its importance diminishes over time suggest not so much a common root as a recurrent process.

There would be no reason to single out the particular scenario of human-animal interaction advanced in this chapter were it not for the likelihood that keeping animals for sacrifice occasionally led to an unanticipated result: domestication. A further implication of this sacrifice-centered scenario, however, is that sheep and goats probably became domestic in several places—possibly many places—within a cultural area stretching from Afghanistan to the Red Sea. The same thing probably happened with cattle, with the added fillip of people being fascinated by their dangerous horns and massive power. For cattle, four different regions of possible original domestication have been mentioned: northeastern Africa, Anatolia, Pakistan, and the mithan country of northeastern India and Burma, but there is no absolute necessity to postulate the diffusion of the practice from any one of these regions to the others.

Hunters in any part of the world could have entertained thoughts that made them want to keep captive some of the animals they hunted—or the humans they warred against. They might have thought that preserving captives of selected species from immediate slaughter, while continuing to fill the ordinary larder by hunting, would mean always having an animal available when worldly or otherworldly conditions called for sacrifice. Or that captured stock would enable them to address the spirit world not with a carcass brought in from the hunt, but with fresh blood dripping on an altar or with a newly slaughtered victim's fat throwing off bright yellow flames and a pungent odor in the sacrificial fire. Or that making the wealth of the Yajamana in animal (or human slave) property the only limit to the number of sacrificial victims, and thus freeing sacred rituals from the luck of the hunt, would both please the gods and elevate the status of the Yajamana.

But nothing obliged hunters to think these thoughts. Hunters in western Europe, for example, where Stone Age art attests to an array of rich and complex views about herd animals, may never have felt that keeping animals captive would be a good way of expressing those views. No animal becomes domestic in western Europe. And hunters in the Western Hemisphere continued for the most part to satisfy their need for sacred killing with human victims down to the period of European contact. The misleading notions that domestication was a deliberate process with a known outcome and that all large species susceptible of domestication were brought under human control by 2500 B.C.E. not only defy plausibility, for reasons already discussed, but reduce the rich complexity of human-animal relations in the predomestic era. The fact that some groups chose to keep animals captive, and thereby inadvertently inaugurated the era of domesticity, does not make their choice more intelligent or more interesting than the alternative strategies for relating to animals developed by groups that continued to live by foraging.[19]

Late domesticates like the horse, donkey, one- and two-humped camel, and water buffalo put into relief the peculiar circumstances that prevailed at the dawn of domestication, before people had gained familiarity with domesticates by observing or borrowing from their neighbors. All became domestic within societies that already practiced agriculture and husbanded a variety of domestic animals, including ones long used for sacrifice. All except the donkey seem to have served, to some extent, as surrogates for cattle, whose capacity for laboring under harness had only recently been realized. None but the horse became extensively used for sacrifice, and the evidence for horse sacrifice, coming mainly from burials of horses with their owners and with the carts or chariots they pulled, points to the importance of harnessing.

Yet the most important descriptions of horse sacrifice, coming from Vedic texts dating to the second millennium B.C.E., point in a different direction. The ritual was the exclusive prerogative of a married king. The king began the ritual by setting one horse free to roam at will for a year, followed by four hundred men from the king's army. All lands traversed by the horse became the domain of the king. At the end of the year, the horse was ceremonially killed, after which the queen got under a linen sheet with the dead horse and performed an act—symbolic, one hopes— of sexual intercourse. As strange as the climax of the year-long ritual may seem, it was mirrored thousands of miles away in pagan Ireland— like India a culture with roots in the Proto-Indo-European traditions of Central Asia—where upon his coronation a king ritually had sexual intercourse with a mare.

It seems apparent that the two royal horse rituals stem from a common origin. Horses were phenomenally popular as subjects of Paleolithic cave painting in France and Spain. Wild horses were the most popular predomestic game animal in eastern Europe and Central Asia after climate changes brought forests to the cave country and moved Europe's grasslands farther to the east. And it is generally accepted that both the Vedic Indians and the Celtic Irish, whose languages stem from the same Proto-Indo-European tongue, migrated to their historically attested territories from an ancient homeland in those grasslands. Moreover, it is possible that the royal horse sacrifice dates back to the very beginnings of horse domestication, if not earlier. A domestic horse wandering freely for a year would normally stay close to its accustomed home, but the sacrificial horse was expected to roam far and wide, a behavior more appropriate for a wild animal. As for the acts of intercourse that seem to symbolize a transference of one or another of the horse's potencies to the king or his queen, they also fit better with the notion that the sacrificial horse was originally wild, since the domestic mentality rarely imagines symbolic sexual liaisons with domestic animals. Finally, the fact that rituals for the sacrifice of cattle, sheep, and goats among the same peoples are more or less conventional and do not normally include horses points as well to a different origin.

It would appear, therefore, that when the development of secondary uses for cattle—primarily milk and yoked labor—prompted people living in wild horse country to try capturing some of the animals they normally hunted and treating them as surrogate cattle, some of the reverence those people had for the wild horse gave rise to a type of sacrifice entirely unknown among cattle, sheep, and goat herders. Too little information remains to establish firmly that the first kings to consolidate their royal status through sacrificing and symbolically mating with a wild horse were Mighty Hunters on their way to becoming Yajamanas in a society that was moving from group predation on wild herds to nonegalitarian ownership of domestic herds. But if so, it would be but another example of a pattern of domestication that combined material uses with affective uses.

I argued earlier that no single strategy of domestication ever existed. Each occasion of domestication, therefore, should be viewed in terms of the human-animal relations existing at the time. Moreover, most domestication took place very slowly and within communities that had little possibility of anticipating its outcome, either physically or in terms of animal usefulness. Hence, no one would have been capable of analyzing the emergence of a distinctive domestic species in terms of a human-controlled process. And no one could have thought of replicating such a process with another species. Consequently, it is likely that some species became domestic on numerous occasions.

Nevertheless, instances of animal domestication do appear to have clustered. The cluster I have been considering in this chapter involves sheep, goats, and cattle. A later cluster in areas bordering on this one (though not bordering on each other) involves horses and two-humped camels in Central Asia, one-humped camels and onagers on the desert frontiers of Arabia, and donkeys in northeastern Africa. A third cluster identified by Carl O. Sauer in southeastern Asia involves dogs, pigs, and chickens. Yet all bovine domestication cannot be fit into the first cluster. Water buffalo, yaks, and mithans became domestic in other places at other times. Nor can Sauer's pattern of dog and pig domestication, focusing heavily on sacrifice, possibly account for the great variety in domestic attitudes toward dogs and pigs around the world. There is no room for easy compromise between eating dogs (much of eastern Asia and pre-Columbian America) and shunning dog meat (the rest of the world), or between considering pigs too filthy to consume (Jews and Muslims) and relishing ham, bacon, and fresh pork (the rest of Europe and Asia). As for reindeer, rabbits, cats, pigeons, canaries, peacocks, turkeys, ducks, geese, llamas, and guinea pigs, no geographic, chronological, or social pattern relates more than a couple of these to each other, or to the three other clusters.

The contention of Jared Diamond that all domesticatable species were domesticated in prehistoric times and that the most important ones just happened to live in more or less the same region provided him with an explanation for the later appearance of material inequality among human societies. But the inequality in animal domesticatability on which he bases his uplifting celebration of universal human equality accords poorly with the actual processes of domestication. Animals have become domestic at different times and in many parts of the world. The clustering of domestication incidents that has occasionally occurred has arisen from area-wide social and economic developments in predomestic foraging societies and from their spiritual and aesthetic attitudes toward particular wild species. The social organization of the animals may explain why goats became domestic in western Asia and gazelles, a favorite quarry for hunters, did not (though individual tame gazelles are known in Bedouin society). But overall, differences in human-animal relations depended more on the humans than on the animals.

Because animal domestication proved in time to be of such momentous consequence for human society, there is a temptation to attribute uncommon acumen—Lévi-Strauss's hypothesized search for knowledge for its own sake—to the peoples among whom domestic species emerged. The mentality of early domesticity, however, looked back, often with deep emotional feeling, toward predomestic interrelationships between humans and animals. The case of the mithan gives us a glimpse of what that mentality was like. For the most part, material usefulness lay hidden in the future. If a person from the dawn of domesticity could observe our contemporary patterns of human-animal relations, he or she would undoubtedly be more saddened by the spiritual and imaginative impoverishment of our outlook on the animal world than impressed by our industrialization of animal exploitation, our pet cemeteries, and Mickey Mouse. We must keep this in mind when looking at the subsequent history of domesticity.

8. Early Domesticity
My Ass and Yours

Predomestic societies are also prehistoric. Lacking the sedentary life and social complexity made possible by agriculture and animal husbandry, they do not leave written remains, except insofar as they are described by outsiders, whether ancient chroniclers or modern ethnographers. With the era of domesticity, however, information on animals becomes so abundant as to make a general history of human-animal relations impossible. That these relations change over the course of the domestic era is beyond question. I have already introduced one important trajectory of change, namely, a gradual disappearance of animal sacrifice. There are many others. For the purposes of this book, however, the types of change that are most significant are the ones that culminate in the end of domesticity and the rise of postdomesticity.

The simplest way to visualize long-term change of this sort is to think of a graph. One curve on the graph starts low and heads upward while a second starts high and heads downward. The curve representing the exploitation of animals for material purposes is the one that steadily rises from a very low point at the beginning of domestication, while the curve representing the weight of animals in human spiritual and imaginative life steadily declines from its very high level at the point of transition from predomesticity.

Once it is recognized that a substantial period of time separates the most common material uses of animals—the so-called secondary uses—from the onset of domesticity, the upward trending curve becomes more or less self-evident. To be sure, different societies use animals in different ways. Large areas of East Asia shun milk. Sub-Saharan Africans do not use their cattle for plowing. Jews and Muslims do not eat pigs. But these cultural differences are well known and do not, on the whole, change markedly over time or stand in the way of other types of material exploitation. Nor do they explain why postdomesticity eventually develops in Britain, North America, and Australia in a more precocious way than in France, Russia, or Argentina.

The downward trending curve similarly varies from animal to animal and from culture to culture. Gods in animal forms or with animal heads generally disappear, though elephant-headed Ganesha remains one of the most popular gods in India. Muslims resist the trend away from animal sacrifice, which they still perform during the pilgrimage month of Dhu al-Hijja. Spectators who want to watch animals fight have largely retreated to the back alley, but the elaborate ceremonies of bullfighting remain a popular spectacle in some Hispanic societies.

The purpose of this chapter is to illustrate the survival of the imaginative and spiritual uses of animals into the era of domesticity, and their eventual decline as the moment of domestication recedes ever further into the past. Of the many ways of doing this, I have chosen to explore the history of a single animal, the ass. Equivalent histories could be written for almost any other domestic animal, and some have been. *A Singular Beast: Jews, Christians, and the Pig* by Claudine Fabre-Vassas is an exemplary and provocative study along these lines, though it does not extend back all the way to the period of domestication.[1]

In choosing the ass, however, I am also self-indulgently fulfilling a long-held desire. The seed from which the ideas in this book grew was my curiosity about the religious and sexual symbolism of donkeys, which first struck me over twenty-five years ago. I had finished my book on camels, which was devoted almost entirely to material uses, and had begun to look at the role of donkeys in camel-using economies. However, I quickly discovered that donkeys were much more interesting as symbolic animals than as beasts of burden. I soon decided to write a book on donkey symbolism. As my research progressed, however, I found that it was much harder to visualize the spiritual conditions that led ancient peoples to revere donkeys than it had been, for my work with the camel, to imagine the early transportation economy of the Middle East. Why did the donkey weigh so heavily as a religious symbol, seemingly from the very moment of domestication? Why did its symbolism persist for thousands of years, even after all understanding of its connection with divinity had faded? Why was the donkey a symbol both of the devil and of the messiah? Why did the donkey eventually become a symbol of stupidity?

It was my search for answers to these and related questions that prompted me to look more broadly at the affective uses of domestic animals, and ultimately to question received opinions about how animals became domestic. It also convinced me that what I have come to call "early domesticity" differed greatly from the later stages of domesticity, when secondary uses became predominant and the ever greater preoccupation with material exploitation led to a steady attenuation of the spiritual significance of animals, particularly domestic animals, which early domesticity had inherited from late predomesticity. The story of the donkey as symbol thus became exemplary of the early domestic stage in human-animal relations rather than a topic in its own right. Other animals suffered a similar erosion of their early symbolic character, but their stories must await other historians.

I am devoting this chapter to the history of the donkey as symbol as a case study in how early human affective attitudes toward one domestic animal persisted through the centuries, though with steadily diminishing salience, and how they remain subliminally with us even today. To show how the broad context of human-animal relations proposed in this book can change the point of view of the historian, I will begin with an episode in the history of donkey symbolism that I wrote several years ago, before I had grasped that I was dealing not just with a scholarly mystery, but with a tiny scene from the epic story of humanity's attempts to come to terms with the animals it shares the planet with.

Ass-Man: God of the Christians

Carthage was never a city of refinement.[2] The Phoenician seafarers who settled the region of Tunis on the southern Mediterranean coast built a trading center that in time developed into the capital of a commercial empire. This Punic Empire, as its Roman rivals called it, extended to Spain and Sicily and encompassed most of Tunisia and adjoining parts of Algeria and Libya. But it died on the sword points of Roman legionnaires after three brutal wars between 264 and 146 B.C.E. The city of Carthage was destroyed and its religious rites, including the sacrifice of children, were abolished. Nevertheless, Phoenician speech and popular beliefs survived in the countryside for several centuries.

Though a momentous event in the history of Rome, the destruction of Carthage marked no great loss for the world of arts and letters. Punic Carthage had never been much more than a rough and brutal outpost of the more sophisticated Phoenician cities of Sidon and Tyre in Lebanon. Archaeologists have confirmed the comparatively low quality of Carthaginian art and architecture and the dominating role of religion and violence in their culture.

So when after a suitable period Carthage was rebuilt as the provincial capital of the Roman territories in North Africa, it is hardly surprising that its rough edges and zealous temperament reappeared. Retired legionnaires who received land grants in Africa provided the city with a Roman core, though hardly of the most sophisticated sort. Yet much of the region's population descended from the Phoenicians or belonged to local Berber-speaking tribes that had largely been excluded from Punic society. Though the revived city's official cult centered on the gods of the Romans, Semitic cults, Judaic and Christian as well as Phoenician, appealed to many, as did indigenous beliefs in magic and in the sanctity and power of holy men that continued even beyond the grave. Latin was the language of government and literature in Roman Carthage. Greek, which was cultivated extensively in Rome itself as the vehicle of a superior culture, was little taught.

Though the fifth-century c.e. St. Augustine ultimately became the most famous thinker and writer of Roman Africa, the best-known pagan author was a mid-second-century writer named Apuleius. His novel *The Golden Ass*, a version of a fable that also survives in Greek, entertained and scandalized its readers with the adventures of a young Greek whose dabbling in magic inadvertently transforms him into an ass.[3] The asinine adventures of the hero Lucius climax in a scene that illustrates the vulgar tenor of popular entertainment at the time, not just in Carthage but in the Roman Empire at large.

The discovery that Lucius, as an ass, still enjoys eating human food and drinking wine amuses the jaded, hedonistic patron of the high-end caterers who come to own Lucius. The patron is even more titillated when Lucius enters into a torrid love affair with a beautiful woman. He decides the situation is so entertaining as to be worth exposure in a public spectacle, so he proposes to exhibit in the arena Lucius copulating with a condemned female criminal—and then put them both to death. Fortunately for Lucius, as the moment of public humiliation and death draws near, he finds the magic antidote and returns to human form during a carnivalesque travesty of a religious procession parading into the arena.

Though copulation between donkeys and humans was surely not a common public entertainment—then as now it was probably reserved for shady sideshows—the citizens of Roman Carthage loved the bizarre and bloody games in the amphitheater and were probably highly amused by the thought of such a display. They were accustomed to seeing gladiators fight to the death, watching hunters kill wild animals brought in from the mountains, and, at the bottom of the entertainment heap, laughing at those pathetic individuals who made a living by letting themselves be mauled by animals and priding themselves on the resulting scars. As a special treat, when an emperor ordered a persecution of Christians, individuals who refused to forswear their faith were sacrificed to the hungry beasts.

The people of Rome itself enjoyed the same entertainments, of course, but the Carthaginians seem to have taken special delight in them. Since many of North Africa's Christian leaders were strong advocates of martyrdom, there was an ample supply of pious victims. However, Christian martyrdom did not imbue these bloody events with an aura of holiness, at least in the minds of the non-Christian audience. On the contrary, before the main event it was common for performers to present ribald tableaus and pantomimes depicting gods and goddesses, not excluding their divine nudity.

Apuleius describes Venus in the procession that saved Lucius's life: "She was rather unclad, and the grace that her nakedness uttered had no flaw. Unclad she was, save for a gauzy silken scarf which shadowed her admirable loins, and which sometimes lifted at the gay twitch of the lascivious wind to show how truly young she was, and sometimes clung the closer to delineate more deliciously the moving contours of her body."[4] At other times, the audience watched victims being castrated in imitation of the god Attis or burned alive in an effigy of Hercules.

Given the well-known linkage between sexual arousal and scenes of violence, the overall tone of the story of Lucius the Ass coupling publicly with a condemned woman prior to execution does not seem far-fetched. People fuelled their imaginations with such lubricious pleasures and became excited by their mere suggestion. An admixture of religion simply sweetened the enjoyment.

This same mix of passions is revealed in an anecdote related by another Carthaginian, Quintus Septimus Florens Tertullianus, better known to the history of Christianity as the Church Father Tertullian. Tertullian was born to the wife of a Roman army officer around the time that Apuleius's *Golden Ass* was becoming known. After converting to Christianity, he became an avid and eloquent defender of his new faith, believing strongly in the power of the Holy Spirit to descend upon and inspire individual believers and praising the holy sacrifice of martyrs. "The blood of martyrs," he wrote, "is the seed of the church."

In two separate works written in the early third century, Tertullian relates this peculiar anecdote, which took place in Carthage. An apostate Jew who was also a lowlife arena employee—one of those who allowed themselves to be mauled by wild animals—publicly paraded a picture of a man dressed in a toga and carrying a book but with the head and long ears of an ass. The hoof of an ass protruded from the toga. Beneath the picture was the following label:

DEUS CHRISTIANORUM ONOCOETES
[God of the Christians *Onocoetes*]

Astonishingly, Tertullian writes, "*risimus et nomen et formam* [we laughed at both the label and the image]." Not only did he find it funny to see the God he believed in so brazenly depicted with a donkey's head, but he found the scandalous joke so memorable that he wrote about it in two separate books.

The third word on the sign, *onocoetes*—alternative spellings are given in different manuscripts—never occurs elsewhere in Latin literature. Nor is it quite certain what it means. The several scholars who have studied the matter concur that the first two syllables, *ono-*, represent the Greek word *onos*, meaning "ass," and agree that the remainder of the word has something to do with sex. One view is that it means something like "born from copulation with an ass."

A more intricate argument, that of the Belgian scholar Jean Préaux, starts from the premise that the meaning of the unusual word must have been immediately apparent to Tertullian and other bystanders and within the plausible vocabulary of an arena lout. Comparing the word with vulgar sexual terms used by other Roman authors of the period, he comes to the conclusion that the onlookers probably understood the label to be a play on the word *embasicoetas*, a synonym, more or less, for the words *cinaedus* and *asellus*. All three words refer to male prostitutes or libertines who offer their services to women and men. The special denotation of the unique term *onocoetes*, in Préaux's view, would have been a male prostitute equipped like a donkey, that is, with a thick penis a couple of feet long.

Whether the cartoonist who created the sign wanted the people of Carthage to think that the Christians worshipped the son of an ass or simply a stud with a penis the size of a donkey's cannot be resolved, but related visual images from roughly the same period confirm the sexual overtone of the anecdote. One small carving depicting an ass in a toga shows the hoof protruding from the garment in a fashion suggestive of a large penis, while another depicts a monkey-like member of an ass-man's audience with an erect penis.

"We laughed at both the label and the image," says Tertullian. Was it just the depiction of his God as an ass-man, presumably in the context of the bawdy religious satires and parades connected with arena entertainments, that tickled the churchman's fancy? Or was there more?

In the eleventh book of Tertullian's *Ad Nationes*, in a passage entirely unrelated to the ass-man anecdote, he remarks that the enemies of Christianity have spread the story that the Christians worship the head of a donkey. This calumny, he maintains, derives from an earlier belief that the Jews worship the head of an ass, which they preserve in their temple in Jerusalem. Though these charges seem bizarre today, there is abundant testimony to their popularity in Roman times. One eloquent example is a figure scratched on the wall of what may once have been a schoolroom in Rome. It shows a man with a donkey's head crucified on a T-shaped cross beside the awkwardly written words in Greek: "Alexamenos worships God."[5]

Tertullian himself dismisses what scholars call "the donkey libel" somewhat jokingly, saying that at least the Christians are only accused of worshipping part of an animal instead of the whole menagerie of domestic and wild beasts associated with the pagan gods. However, a contemporary Christian writer, Marcus Minucius Felix, responded to the charge in a more frustrated tone: "Who is so stupid as to worship such a thing? And who is even stupider in that he believes such worship occurs?"

Not surprisingly, Christian and Jewish scholars have written extensively on the donkey-libel question, analyzing every text and nuance. Their findings, published for the most part in European scholarly journals and for a purely scholarly audience, provide extensive evidence of donkey veneration in the ancient world and numerous clues to the peculiar association of the ass with Judaism and Christianity. Some note the fact that the two donkey stories in Tertullian are not connected to make the point that the charge of worshipping a donkey's head is quite differ-ent from the charge of worshipping a god sired by a donkey and bearing elements of his paternal attributes.

Yet the literature on ass worship and donkey libel almost entirely avoids discussion of the ass itself. Moreover, it seldom strays past the Roman period, except in mentioning the possible survival of donkey veneration in certain medieval Christian church celebrations, and men-tion is rarely made of parallel examples of the religious symbolism of donkeys in Islamic culture.

The Red God of the Desert

Absent a suitable theoretical context, Tertullian's story of the donkey libel against the Christians is little more than a whimsical example of the strange lore one encounters when doing research on animals. However, in light of the likelihood that affective uses played a major part in the domestication of some species, an idea that had not occurred to me when I wrote the preceding account, the image of an ass-headed Christ sug-gests some sort of link with the original domestication of the donkey.

Though related to the zebras of sub-Saharan Africa and the wild horses and half-asses (onagers) of western and central Asia, the ancestor of the domestic ass or donkey is the Nubian wild ass, an animal native to the desert regions of northeastern Africa. We have already noted that the donkey is one of the later domesticates, one of the group of animals that became domestic between 4000 and 3000 B.C.E., in areas adjoining the zone of domestication of cattle, sheep, and goats. Thus we can assume that the Africans who originally decided to keep some wild asses captive were familiar with other domestic animals. We have also noted that unlike the horse and the two-humped camel, the donkey seems not to have been used as a substitute ox. Ancient Egypt has bequeathed us no images of donkeys plowing or pulling carts. Nor, for that matter, does the donkey appear frequently as a riding animal. Its primary material use, judging from Egyptian art, was as a beast of burden, but that is most likely a secondary use that developed after domestication had rendered the ani-mal reliably docile. Tying your worldly belongings to the back of a wild animal would have been a good way to lose them. Ancient descriptions of Egyptian customs also make only scant mention of donkey meat or don-key milk. If the first donkey-keepers owned domestic sheep, goats, or cat-tle, they wouldn't have needed an additional meat or milk animal.

The prominence of animal-headed gods in ancient Egypt and early Egyptian images of wild animals including hyenas and baboons being led on leashes hint strongly that religious beliefs helped inspire keeping wild asses captive. In later Egyptian history, the ass is unequivocally identified as the animal of the god Set, a red god associated with the desert and depicted with a donkey's head. The earliest representations of Set's animal, however, do not look all that asinine. The slightly built four-footed beast has a long, somewhat pointed snout that droops slightly. Its ears are long, erect, and squared off, but not obviously donkey-like. And its tail sticks straight up, making a long, perfectly vertical line with a fork or division at its end. Some scholars are satisfied that the Set animal, which appears in predynastic times as early as 3500 to 4000 b.c.e., is a donkey. Many others remain skeptical and suggest alternatives that resemble the image no more closely than a donkey does, or consider the animal entirely imaginary, which seems improbable, given that real animals represent the other gods.

The perfectly straight vertical tail is particularly curious. Since mammalian backbones do not make right-angle turns, it cannot be taken as realistic. Its configuration is evidently symbolic and of a piece with the long ears and snout. All three, I propose, are symbols of or homologues for the donkey's penis—a "homologue" being something that has the same relative position, value, or structure as something else. This may seem a wild assertion, but sexual potency, represented by the markedly oversized penis of the donkey and by its homologues, is the thread that runs consistently through the history of donkey symbolism from the worship of a sexually potent god in ancient Egypt to the unconsciously phallic children's game of pin-the-tail-on-the-donkey.

The penis played a central role in the ancient cultural practices of the peoples of northeastern Africa. The ritual circumcision of men in Judaism and Islam finds its origins in this region, or just across the Red Sea, as does the genital mutilation of women. Reference was made earlier to the hypothesis that the hooked staff with a forked bottom carried by gods and rulers in ancient Egyptian art was actually a dried bull's penis, but regardless of whether that can be verified, some of the central myths of Egyptian religion—the search for the missing penis of Osiris, the erect penis of the fertility god Min—focused on the penis. In ritual, symbolic phalluses were also offered by devotees of another fertility deity, Hathor, who was represented by a cow.[6] And many scholars have suggested that the famous obelisks of Egypt are phallic symbols.

The donkey's penis impressed not only the Egyptians. An Indian legend preserved from the Vedic period tells of a divine chariot race run to celebrate the wedding of Surya (the divinized sun) and Soma (a divinely intoxicating drink and object of sacrifice). Each chariot was drawn by a different animal. The Açvins, the Vedic equivalent of Castor and Pollux, won, their chariot pulled by a team of asses. "In that the Açvins won, the Açvins attained, therefore is his [i.e., the donkey's] speed outworn, his energy spent; he is here the least swift of all beasts of burden; but they did not take the strength of his seed; therefore he has virility and possesses a double seed."[7] This high potency of the lowly ass was signaled in practical terms by the requirement that a student of the sacred scriptures (*brahmanas*) who violates his vow of celibacy must sacrifice an ass, eat a portion of its penis as his share of the sacrifice, and wear the ass's skin for a year. Normally, the Vedic Indians did not consider the ass a sacrificial animal, but the spending of semen that inevitably accompanied a lapse from celibacy called for special measures to recoup the lost virility.

Of course, Set was not the only Egyptian god to be identified with an animal. Among domestic animals, a bull represented Amon, a ram Khnum, and a cat the goddess Bast. Other divinities were identified with wild animals. Both the ibis and the baboon represented Thoth, for example. Since it is known that domestic animals sacred to specific gods were kept in temples of those gods, the images that show leashed wild animals suggest that many species were thus kept captive for ritual purposes. Of these wild African animals, only the donkey became domestic. This probably reflects the tame-in-the-wild phenomenon discussed in chapter 5. Few predators threatened the Nubian wild ass in its natural desert habitat, and later interbreeding between domestic and wild stock was not uncommon.

Originally one of the foremost gods, Set became transformed, for reasons that are now obscure, into a figure of evil early in the third millennium B.C.E. When the Greeks learned about him many centuries later, they equated him with an evil, monstrous figure from their own mythology: Gaea's son Typhon, whom Zeus flattened beneath Mt. Etna. Set remained in myth the brother of Osiris, the most beneficent of gods, but the same myths recounted his murder and dismemberment of Osiris—this is how Osiris's penis was lost—and his eventual defeat at the hands of Horus, Osiris's son. As a consequence of his demonization, Set's name was effaced in inscriptions, statues of Set were decapitated, the eating of donkeys and pigs (an animal later associated with Set) became taboo, and the faces of donkeys in paintings of farming scenes were sometimes scratched out. However, Set's sexual potency remained. One of the most powerful curses recorded in Egyptian writing consisted of calling upon Set to penetrate with his penis the female relatives of the person being cursed. By Greco-Roman times after 300 B.C.E., the red-eyed, red-skinned, ass-headed former god became a demon to conjure with. A magician wishing to punish his enemies would place the head of an ass between his feet and cover his hands and mouth with ass's blood. Then he would summon the demon: "I call on you, Typhon Seth; I conjure you, for I call you by your true names, which you cannot refuse to hear: Jo-erbeth, Jo-pak-erbeth, Jo-bolcho-seth . . ."[8] *Jo* was the Egyptian word for "ass."

This does not mean that the Egyptians did not make full use of the donkey as a beast of burden nor that the worship of Set entirely disappeared. Some Egyptians continued to sacrifice to him and many Egyptians believed that he remained the chief god of the nomads who herded donkeys in the deserts bordering the Nile valley. Among those nomads were the ancestors of the Israelites and related tribes speaking northwestern Semitic languages, generally known as the Canaanites. As for the Israelites themselves, it is certain that they did not worship Set or sacrifice his animals. They not only adopted the Egyptian taboo on eating pigs and donkeys—these two animals were the only common domestic animals put off limits by kosher law—but an exception to the requirement of sacrificing first-born domestic animals was made for the ass. A lamb had to be sacrificed in place of the young ass, or else the ass had to be strangled.[9] This rule most likely prevented the Israelites from imitating a ritual followed by neighboring Canaanites who did sacrifice donkeys, just as the substitution of the ram for Isaac in the story of Abraham symbolized Israelite rejection of the child sacrifice practiced by some of their cousins. A cuneiform tablet from Mari in Mesopotamia equating "donkey killing" with "forming an alliance" attests to the importance of donkey sacrifice among other northwestern Semites and even uses the Biblical phrase, "an ass, the foal of an ass."[10]

The Israelites, like all the northwestern Semitic nomads, herded many thousands of asses nevertheless. They were valuable riding animals and beasts of burden, but the numbers mentioned in the Bible go far beyond the needs of transport. Rather, they attest to the value as property of a domestic animal that was not normally consumed.[11] Biblical stories also reflect a belief that asses had a special connection with the unseen spirit world that ordinary domestic animals did not have. Among the peoples related to the Israelites, if not among the Israelites themselves, a donkey could serve as a spiritual contact for a priest or seer, the donkey's voice often signifying the contact. An Israeli Arab friend informed me that in his home village the sound of a donkey's bray during a funeral procession was a bad omen because it was considered a response to the donkey hearing the screams of souls in Hell, the realm, needless to add, of the ancient god Set.[12]

The biblical story of Balaam and his ass attests to this affective employment of donkeys. After their exodus from Egypt and during their wanderings before entering the Promised Land, the Israelites encroach on the territory of the Moabites. The king of Moab reacts by summoning a foreign prophet named Balaam, asking him to curse the Israelites. Balaam initially refuses, having been told not to cooperate by Yahweh, but he eventually complies with the king's request.

> So Balaam rose in the morning, and saddled his ass, and went with the princes of Moab. But God's anger was kindled because he went; and the angel of the Lord took his stand in the way as his adversary. Now he was riding on the ass, and his two servants were with him. And the ass saw the angel of the Lord standing in the road with a drawn sword in his hand; and the ass turned aside out of the road, and went into the field; and Balaam struck the ass, to turn her into the road. Then the angel of the Lord stood in a narrow path between the vineyards, with a wall on either side. And when the ass saw the angel of the Lord, she pushed against the wall, and pressed Balaam's foot against the wall; so he struck her again. Then the angel of the Lord went ahead, and stood in a narrow place, where there was no way to turn either to the right or to the left. When the ass saw the angel of the Lord, she lay down under Balaam; and Balaam's anger was kindled, and he struck the ass with his staff. Then the Lord opened the mouth of the ass, and she said to Balaam, "What have I done to you, that you have struck me these three times?" And Balaam said to the ass, "Because you have made sport of me. I wish I had a sword in my hand, for then I would kill you." And the ass said to Balaam, "Am I not your ass, upon which you have ridden all your life long to this day? Was I ever accustomed to do so to you?" And he said, "No."

Then the Lord opened the eyes of Balaam, and he saw the angel of the Lord standing in the way, with his drawn sword in his hand; and he bowed his head, and fell on his face.[13]

Other than the serpent in the Garden of Eden, Balaam's ass is the only animal in the Bible that speaks. It is evident, however, that the prophet Balaam should have divined the presence of the angel of the Lord from the behavior of his donkey, which, by the donkey's own testimony, he had ridden every day of his life without being led astray. Being subjects of divination, like birds in flight, was part of the role donkeys played as mediators with the unseen world on behalf of a seer. The Hebrew Bible mentions a number of lesser prophets riding on donkeys, but later Jewish religion was not entirely comfortable with the idea. The rabbinical midrash went so far as to assert that Balaam's ass was specially created between sunset and nightfall of the sixth day of creation.[14]

Nevertheless, the voice of the prophetic ass lurks in the background of the story of Samson. An angel of the Lord came to a barren woman and told her she would conceive a son who would be a Nazirite, that is, a person separated from the community for service to the Lord. He foretold that "he shall begin to deliver Israel from the hands of the Philistines."[15] In due course, Samson embarked on his career of slaying Philistines, wearing his hair uncut as a condition of being a Nazirite. However, his violent acts endangered the people of Judah, who persuaded Samson to allow them to bind him and hand him over to the Philistines. As this was being done,

the Spirit of the Lord came mightily upon him, and the ropes which were on his arms became as flax that has caught fire, and his bonds melted off his hands. And he found a fresh jawbone of an ass, and put out his hand and seized it, and with it he slew a thousand men. And Samson said,
"With the jawbone of an ass, heaps upon heaps,
With the jawbone of an ass have I slain a thousand men."
When he had finished speaking, he threw away the jawbone out of his hand; and that place was called Ramath-lehi [the height of the jawbone].[16]

The Protestant commentary of *The Interpreter's Bible* offers the opinion that "a fresh jawbone would be heavier, less fragile, and therefore a better weapon than the ordinary jawbone."[17] Such feeble exegesis only serves to emphasize the magical power that the voice of the donkey, symbolized by its jawbone, conferred on the chosen agent of the Lord.

Religious writings outside the Israelite orbit preserve much stronger evidence of the donkey-prophet connection. The seers or *kahins* of the Arabian desert in the time before Muhammad were often associated with asses, and Muhammad himself rode both an ass and a mule.[18] According to later lore, the ass, which came to him from a Jewish source, was given to conversing with Muhammad. In one story, he claimed to come from a line of sixty asses ridden by prophets, and in another he relates a story about Noah that was transmitted to him through a string of donkey fore-fathers. When Muhammad died, being the last of God's messengers according to Islamic belief, his ass ran to a well and dove in head-first to commit suicide, thus ending the hereditary line of prophet's asses that had previously served Jesus, Moses, and Abraham, among others.

Returning to the Bible, this association between a donkey or mule— originally, perhaps, a cross between an ass and an onager rather than an ass and a horse—and prophetic or sacred leadership appears again at the time of King David's death.[19] The dying ruler instructs Zadok the priest and Nathan the prophet to put his son Solomon on David's own mule and take him to be anointed. The story, repeated three times, with Solomon riding on his father's mule being specified each time, is remi-niscent of the Muslim traditions of successive prophets riding donkeys from the same lineage.

There is no way of telling whether the prophet Zechariah had this specific royal mule ride in mind when he proclaimed his well-known vision of the coming of the Messiah: "Rejoice greatly, O daughter of Zion; shout, O daughter of Jerusalem: behold, thy King cometh unto thee: he is just, and having salvation; lowly, and riding upon an ass, and upon a colt the foal of an ass."[20] But his words reflected what everyone in the Semitic world knew. Messiahs or sacred kings ride on donkeys.

This universal belief explains a lot of things:

- Why a "false prophet" who appeared in Yemen after the death of Muhammad was known simply as *Sahib al-Himar*, the "Master of the Ass," an epithet also used for Muhammad himself.
- Why the strongman who usurped control of the Umayyad ca-liphate in the 740s was nicknamed *al-Himar*, "the Ass."
- Why some early Shi'ite extremists believed that the Mahdi—the Islamic messiah—would come in the company of Ya'fur and Dul-dul, Muhammad's ass and mule respectively.

- Why other Shi'ites paraded before the leader of a chiliastic upris-
  ing a gray mule—Duldul was gray—bearing on its back an empty
  chair for the Mahdi.
- Why the religious rebel who almost overthrew the fledgling Fa-
  timid dynasty in Tunisia in the early tenth century C.E. was known
  as the "Man on the Donkey."
- Why Ibn Tumart, the Muslim Mahdi of twelfth-century Morocco,
  insisted on riding a donkey, while giving a horse to the military dis-
  ciple who would ultimately establish the Almohad empire on his
  teachings.
- And beyond the Islamic world, why there was such an uproar in
  Cromwell's England in 1656 when James Nayler, one of the first
  Quaker leaders, rode into Bristol on the back of a donkey with
  admirers singing "holy, holy, holy" and spreading scarves in his
  path.[21]

The case of Nayler, who received 311 lashes, had his tongue bored
with a hot poker, and his forehead branded with a B for blasphemer,
indicates the enduring symbolic power of the donkey-messiah affinity in
a Christian tradition rooted in the words of the gospel writers. The
gospel accounts of Jesus' entry into Jerusalem use this symbolism to represent Jesus as the sacred king and messiah of the lineage of King David.
The Gospel of Luke has Jesus saying to his disciples as he prepares for
the ride that Christians ever after commemorate on Palm Sunday:

> "Go into the village opposite, where upon entering you will find a
> colt tied, on which no one has ever yet sat; untie it and bring it
> here. If anyone asks you, 'Why are you untying it?' you shall say
> this, 'the Lord has need of it.'" So those who were sent went away
> and found it as he had told them. And as they were untying the
> colt, its owners said to them, "Why are you untying the colt?" And
> they said, "The Lord has need of it." And they brought it to Jesus,
> and throwing their garments on the colt they set Jesus upon it.
> And as he rode along, they spread their garments on the road.[22]

The Gospel of John is more explicit:

> And Jesus found a young ass and sat upon it; as it is written, "Fear
> not, daughter of Zion; behold, thy King is coming, sitting on an
> ass's colt." His disciples did not understand this at first; but when
> Jesus was glorified, then they remembered that this had been writ-
> ten of him and had been done to him.[23]

Zechariah's invocation of the ass as a lowly creature provides a fig leaf to disguise the pre-Abrahamic Semitic association between donkey and prophet. But lowliness and humility play no part in the parallel Muslim traditions about predictions of Muhammad's coming. In one, a Jew says that the Torah tells of a prophet who will be "a man neither short nor tall, wrapped in a cloak, and riding an ass."[24] He will also have red eyes—the consonantal root *h-m-r* in Arabic that yields the word *himar* ("ass") also yields *ahmar*, meaning "red"—a detail that recalls an enigmatic image of messianic import in Genesis.

> The scepter shall not depart from Judah, nor the ruler's staff from between his feet, until he comes to whom it belongs; and to him shall be the obedience of the peoples. Binding his foal to the vine, and his ass's colt to the choice vine, he washes his garments in wine and his vesture in the blood of grapes; his eyes shall be red with wine, and his teeth white with milk.[25]

Another Muslim tradition attributes to a Jew of Medina this report of the prophet who is to come: "A man who is neither short nor tall, has redness in his eyes, wears a cloak, rides an ass, his sword is on his shoulder and this town is his place of *hijra*. [Muhammad and his community made an emigration or *hijra* to Medina in 622 C.E.]"[26] Other versions of these traditions substitute a camel—sometimes a red camel—for the ass.

Humility is also absent from the story related by a man remembering how as a boy he was standing in front of a church or synagogue (*kanisa*) in the Iraqi city of Kufa circa 660 C.E. A stately man rode by on a gray mule. The boy asked his uncle who the man was. His uncle said that the mule's name was Duldul, and the man was Ali ibn Abi Talib, "*Shahanshah al-Arab* [King of Kings of the Arabs]."[27] Since the Persian imperial title Shahanshah was then taboo in Muslim usage, it being a time when the son of the last Sasanid shah was still alive in China waiting for an opportunity to regain his throne, the story is obviously spurious. Duldul, however, was Muhammad's mule—the prophetic steed that did not commit suicide—which passed by Muhammad's bequest to his cousin and son-in-law Ali ibn Abi Talib, the man in whose cause the Shi'ite branch of Islam later developed. The only way to make sense of Ali's title in the story is to recognize in it an Islamized Arabic form of "Jesus of Nazareth, King of the Jews," the inscription, according to the Gospel of John, placed by Pontius Pilate over Jesus's head at the crucifixion. In other words, Ali riding Muhammad's mule is here being identified as a messiah through symbols borrowed from the Christian culture of seventh-century Iraq. The subsequent emergence of Duldul as a revered animal in some Shi'ite milieus confirms the messianic implications of Ali inheriting Muhammad's mule.[28]

Paradoxically, al-Dajjal, the evil, red-complexioned anti-Messiah of Muslim popular belief, also will come in the final days riding on a giant white donkey, and a widely reported saying of Muhammad reflects fear of the donkey's voice: "When you hear the bray of an ass, seek refuge with God from the devil."[29]

The Maiden and the Ass

The Egyptian demonization of Set and his animals, the sacred role accorded the ass of a prophet among the Canaanite donkey herders who may have been the first to bring the animal from Egypt to western Asia, and the Jewish and then Christian and Muslim efforts to fit popular beliefs about donkeys into their respective theologies and prophetic traditions all stem from the donkey's great symbolic weight at the time of first domestication. Though slightly paralleled by Arabian traditions concerning the one-humped camel, the sacred aura surrounding the donkey far exceeded that of any other domestic animal in the region.

If sheep, goats, and cattle became domestic in a manner at all similar to the meat and sacrifice model hypothesized in chapter 7, the donkey obviously entered the ranks of domestic animals by a dramatically different route. The specifically sexual aspect of the donkey's symbolic role, which is essential for understanding the donkey libel of the Christians described by Tertullian, can best be seen from a perspective that was neither Egyptian nor Semitic.

Donkey-headed demons, or priests impersonating them with donkey masks and pelts, show up frequently in the Minoan art of Crete. Since donkeys are not native to Crete and Egyptian influences in Minoan culture are common, it is reasonable to guess that these images are a borrowing from Egypt, in all likelihood a reflection of the role that Set had assumed there by the second millennium B.C.E. They appear most often holding jugs, a signal, perhaps, of the sort of association of donkeys with grapes and wine that appeared in the messianic verses from Genesis cited earlier.

The Greeks, who borrowed extensively from Minoan culture, also believed in half-donkey, half-human beings. They called them *silenoi*.

The word seemingly comes from an Anatolian (Thraco-Phrygian) language and means "he-ass." Unlike the other cross-species beings that the Greeks fancied, like the centaurs, fauns, and satyrs, the silenoi faded away and were replaced by a single minor god named Silenus. Silenus is usually represented as a fat, drunk, rubicund old man riding on a donkey in the retinue of a much greater god, Dionysus or Bacchus. As the aged mentor of Dionysus, Silenus has an honored place—but he is too drunk to do much of anything by himself.

Legend sometimes conflates Silenus with a *silen* (a singular form of *silenoi*) named Marsyas, the inventor of the flute, whom King Midas of Phrygia lured into his garden with wine and then, taking advantage of his pixilated state, persuaded to grant the hollow boon of the golden touch. Legend maintains that Midas always wore a peaked Phrygian hat to hide the fact that he had the ears of a donkey. Some Phrygians eventually crossed into Europe and settled in Macedonia near Mount Bora. These Hyperboreans—that is, the "people from beyond Mt. Bora,"—reputedly sacrificed large numbers of asses.

The Greeks became familiar with Dionysus as a foreign god, also originally from Anatolia (modern Turkey). His devotees disported themselves in drunken and lascivious revels, and his festivals in Athens nurtured the first blooms of Greek drama. When Dionysus is depicted, he is commonly riding an ithyphallic ass—that is, one with an erect penis. His satyr followers sometimes ride ithyphallic asses as well.

Though the first home of the domestic grape was probably a cooler, more elevated land than Egypt—Armenia has been suggested—grape pips have been found in Egypt dating to the fourth millennium B.C.E., and winemaking was known by the time of the First Dynasty (circa 3000 B.C.E.). It seems likely that an association between winemaking and donkeys began in Egypt and spread from there throughout the Mediterranean. For the donkey-herding Canaanites, whose views of the donkey as a sacred animal were rooted in the era of the animal's domestication, the image of donkeys working in vineyards may not have been as compelling symbolically as donkeys speaking to prophets. Anatolian culture, however, took the Semitic notion of the sacred donkey and emphasized the overtones of inebriation, sexual excess, and the redness of wine foreshadowed in the passage from Genesis. That this occurred at the popular level and not just in mythology is evident from a small terracotta image from Hellenistic times of a man furtively having intercourse with a donkey laden with baskets of grapes.[30] The popular notion survives to this day in Turkey, where ten copies of the lewd but very funny satirical cartoon magazine *Le Man* yielded four images of men sexually engaged with donkeys—and one involved with a sheep.[31]

With this in mind, let us return to *The Golden Ass*, in which Apuleius wove together the basic transformation narrative and a series of unrelated tales to comment satirically on the moral, religious, and social conditions of the second century C.E. The scene, you will recall, is set in Greece. Lucius, a young man of noble family traveling the country to improve his education, gets into his asinine predicament by seducing a lady's maid named Fotis, who unwisely allows him to witness the transformation of her witch mistress into an owl. Apuleius promptly introduces themes of wine, drunkenness, red roses (!), and animalistic sex.

> No sooner was I laid in bed than lo! Fotis. Her mistress had now retired for the night; and the girl had come to me gaily garlanded with roses and with one rose in full blossom opening between her breasts. She embraced me with fast kisses, and tied a wreath about my head, and strewed flowers over me; and then she snatched a cup, and pouring warm water into it [to mix with the wine] she proffered me a draught; and before I had finished, she indulgently took the cup away from my lips, and sipped the remainder of the wine with little dainty birdlike sips, keeping her eyes intently upon me all the while . . . she leaped into bed, and saddling and bridling me she rode agilely into pleasure.[32]

Sneaking into the witch's room, Lucius drinks the magic potion but is transformed into an ass instead of an owl. Before he can eat the rose petals that he knows will reverse the transformation, bandits attack the house, kill everyone in it, and commandeer him to carry away their loot. On their next outing, the robbers return with no booty "except a lonely girl—a lady by her figure and the cut of her dress—belonging to one of the best families roundabout—by God, a girl not beyond the love of an ass (such an ass as I was, anyway)."[33]

When the opportunity arises, Lucius kicks the old woman who keeps the robbers' house and escapes with the maiden on his back. As they race along, she says:

> And you, the engine of my life and liberty, O bear me homeward safe. Restore me to my parents and my beautiful lover [i.e., fiancé]; and you will find what thanks will be yours, what honour you will

earn, what food I shall shower upon you. First, I shall finely comb your mane and adorn it with my maiden necklets. Next, I shall elegantly part and curl the rough and matted bristles of your tail till they are soft enough to dress. . . . I shall perpetuate the memory of my present calamity and of divine providence by dedicating in the vestibule of my house a tablet carved with the Story of our Flight. There the eyes will see it, and the ears will hear it, told for all time in learned narratives, simple as it is, under the title: The Royal Virgin Fleeing Captivity on Ass-back. You will be enlisted among the miracles of antiquity.[34]

Since Apuleius, like any educated Carthaginian, was well familiar with Christianity, it must be assumed that this scene resonated maliciously with the image, quite popular in early Christian times, of the Virgin Mary and the infant Jesus escaping into Egypt riding on an ass.

Apuleius's scathing opinion of popular cults shows up more openly after Lucius, who is represented as an ass from Cappadocia, a part of Anatolia known for its religious excesses, is purchased by a eunuch who turns out to be a priest of Cybele, the Great Mother goddess of Anatolia. The priest intends to use Lucius to carry the statue of the goddess from village to village, but he intends to use him sexually as well.

As soon as he reached the threshold, he cried out, "Girlies, troop up and spy the darling slavelet I've bought you."

The girls, however, turned out to be a band of eunuchs, who at once began squeaking for delight in their splintering harsh womanish voices, thinking that it was really a man brought home trussed to do them good service. When they saw their mistake . . . they turned up their noses and sneered at their chief, saying that this isn't a servant for them but a husband for himself. "But mind," they ended, "don't keep the pretty chickabud all to yourself. Don't forget that your dovie-wovies want a look-in sometimes." . . .

Next day the priesthood went out in a body, gowned in all the colours under the sun and hideously bedizened. Their faces were ruddied with cosmetics and their eyes ringed darkly; they wore little turbans; their linen was saffron-hued; and they were surpliced with silk. Some had donned white tunics covered with purple stripes pointing out every way spear-wise; and the whole mob displayed girdles and yellow shoes. They dressed the [statue of the] Goddess in a silk-vestment, and placed her on my back. Then swinging oversized swords and axes, with their arms bared shoulder-high, they frolicked and bounded in maddened ritual-dance to the inciting flute-accompaniment.

After performing before several cottages, they arrived at a rich man's villa; and screeching their tuneless threnes from the moment they saw the gates, they rushed frantically inside. Bending their heads, they twisted, writhed, and rolled their necks to and fro, while their long hair swung round in circles. Every now and then they dug their teeth into their own flesh; and as a finishing effect each man slashed his arms with the two-edged sword that he flourished.[35]

The wild begging antics of the priests, which seem quite realistically observed, arouse nothing but contempt in Apuleius. He has Lucius escape their clutches by braying inconveniently in his alarm at a homosexual orgy they engage in after their day of taking advantage of the piety of the rustics. His greatest contempt, however, he reserves for the wife of a baker who subsequently buys Lucius and puts him to work turning a mill. Though he does not explicitly label her a Christian, readers then and now needed no label:

For there wasn't any known fault lacking from this woman's composition; every kind of vice had flowed into her heart as if that were a general cesspool of devilry. She was lewd and crude, a toper and a groper, a nagging hag of a fool of a mule. She was grasping in mean thefts, riotous in vicious living, an inveterate liar and whore. She scorned and spurned the gods of heaven; and in the place of true religion she professed some fantastic blasphemous creed of a God whom she named the One and Only God. But she used her deluded and ridiculous observances chiefly to deceive her wretched husband; for she spent the morning in boozing, and leased out her body in perpetual prostitution.

This woman persecuted me with a curious malice. As she lay in her bed before dawnlight she would call out and bid the men yoke the new ass to the mill; then, as soon as she had risen and come out, she would insist that I should be whacked unmercifully before her eyes.[36]

Lucius, or The Ass, a much briefer version of *The Golden Ass* written by the Greek writer Lucian,[37] a contemporary of Apuleius, contains the episode of Lucius working the baker's mill but makes no mention of the baker's wife, just as it contains the story of the young girl's escape from the robbers but makes no mention of her promise to immortalize the event as "The Royal Virgin Fleeing Captivity on Ass-back." Both associations of the ass with a woman in contexts that have Christian overtones are inventions of Apuleius.

In the case of the escaping girl, the ass simply carries the virgin, just as he later bears the statue of the Goddess. In the case of the baker's wife, on the other hand, the Carthaginian readership would have seen sexual overtones that are lost on us today. Historians of ancient technology use a scene on a Greek vase as a unique illustration of an early form of hand mill. In addition to the mill, however, the scene depicts a donkey, along with men with erect penises. The sexual meaning of the scene is confirmed by the word *cinaedus*, one of the two words for a professional stud that Jean Préaux used to explain the meaning of *onocoetes*. Just as for contemporary readers "grinding" has a slang meaning of sexual intercourse—witness Memphis Slim's "Grinder Man Blues" or Helen Humes's singing "he grinds my coffee" in "Kitchen Man Blues"—so it did in Apuleius's day, but with the added fillip of the one doing the grinding having the penile equipment of a donkey. Therefore, when he writes "As she lay in her bed before dawnlight she would call out and bid the men yoke the new ass to the mill," he intends the reader to read it partly as applied to Lucius hard at work and partly as a continuation of the immediately preceding description of the woman being engaged in "perpetual prostitution."

All of these episodes prefigure the climactic relationship that almost costs Lucius his life. His final owner, a man who had climbed the social ladder, become a magistrate, and bought him after witnessing his consumption of wine and delicacies, charges admission for the privilege of gawking at Lucius carrying on.

> He taught me to recline at table, leaning on my elbows; to wrestle and dance with lifted forefeet; and (a specially admired attainment) to converse by raising my head as a sign of yes and by lowering it as a sign of no. . . .
>
> Among the visitors there was a rich and respected lady who after once paying for a view was so tickled by my manifold gambols that her flustered wonder drifted into a wondrous lust. Unable to cool her turbulent blood, she took heart at the example of

Pasiphae [who bore the Minotaur to a bull lover] and decided to act the she-ass. . . .

Good gods! how lordly were the preparations. Four eunuchs strewed the ground with mattresses of down and air-filled bolsters. The coverlet was of cloth-of-gold and broideries of Tyrian dye; and the pillows were small but wide enough for their purpose, and soft like those on which delicate ladies lay their lazy cheeks or necks. The eunuchs, anxious not to delay the pleasures of their mistress a moment longer, closed the bedroom doors and went away. . . .

She gave me a lingering kiss; not the kind that you met in the stews, in the whore-shops and the open markets of venery. No, it was a sisterly and sincere salutation, accompanied with such remarks as "I love you," "I want you," "You're the only one in the world," "I can't live without you," and other phrases of the kind that women use to lead-on their lovers and to express their emotions. Then she took me by the neck-rope and placed me on the bed; and as she was a very beautiful woman, and as I was flushed with excellent wine and soused in fragrant ointments, I had no difficulty meeting her half-way.[38]

Once the secret amour between the ass and the woman becomes known, Lucius sees his fate change quickly from bedded bliss to humiliation and death in the arena. Apuleius chooses to save him through a vision of the goddess Isis, who is presented as a true divinity, unlike the degraded statue of Cybele. Isis tells Lucius that one of her priests will be bearing a crown of roses in the procession preceding the scheduled entertainment. The story ends when Lucius eats the roses, resumes his human form, and becomes a priest of Isis.

Lucian's Greek version ends differently. Lucius is in the arena and on the bed with the woman condemned to be his final companion when an attendant walks by carrying roses. Lucius eats them and is instantly transformed into a naked youth. A portion of the audience still wants to see him die as a practitioner of black magic, but he pleads his case to the governor of the province, who turns out to be one of his father's noblest friends. Freed at last of his asinine form, Lucius pays a call on the woman who had been his lover. All goes well until they go to bed:

I jumped up and, with the idea of giving her a treat, took off all my clothes and displayed myself in the nude, fondly imagining that compared with a donkey I should be quite irresistible. But she was so disappointed to find that I was in every respect a normal human being, that she actually spat in my face.

"Get to hell out of my house!" she screamed. "Go and sleep somewhere else!"

"Why, what on earth have I done?" I asked.

"Oh, for God's sake, don't you understand?" she exclaimed. "It was the donkey I fell in love with, not you! And I did so hope that there'd be one thing left, at least, to remind me of that splendid great animal—but just look at you—you're nothing but a wretched little monkey!"

She then called her servants and told them to throw me out of the house.[39]

We now know most of the story of why Tertullian and his Christian friends laughed at both the cartoon of a donkey-headed Christ and its "Ass-man" caption. Though nothing was more humble or commonplace in Roman Carthage than a donkey with a load of goods on its back, the slightest reference was sufficient to trigger a torrent of religious and sexual associations, dating from the time of the animal's domestication. The Carthaginians who saw the apostate Jew carrying the sign retained a vague notion of a donkey-headed god and of an association between a prophet and a donkey as part of their Semitic Phoenician heritage. But they also knew the stories told by Apuleius. Those who thought that *onocoetes* meant the offspring of a donkey doubtless conjured up a ribald image of the Virgin Mary misbehaving, or even of Christ as the son of a red, asinine Set/Satan—a sort of *Rosemary's Baby* scenario. Those who thought it referred to the god's sexual appetite and masculine endowment doubtless had the notion of Set somewhere in the back of their minds.

Confirmation that the climate of the times inclined toward a melding of Greek and Semitic ass stories comes from a passage in an apocryphal book of the New Testament that might be entitled: "The Flight into Egypt Encounters the Golden Ass." Known as "The Arabic Gospel of the Infancy of the Saviour," the book was apparently composed between the fourth and sixth centuries c.e. and then translated from Aramaic into Arabic.[40] One of numerous miracles performed by the infant Jesus during the period of his flight with his mother into Egypt to escape Herod's persecution is narrated as follows:[41]

They set out, therefore, on the following day; and as they came near another city, they saw three women weeping as they came out of a cemetery. And when the Lady Mary beheld them, she said to the girl who accompanied her: Ask them what is the matter with them, or what calamity has befallen them. And to the girl's questions they made no reply, but asked in their turn: Whence are you, and whither are you going? for the day is already past, and night is coming on apace. We are travelers, said the girl, and are seeking a house of entertainment in which we may pass the night. They said: Go with us, and spend the night with us. They followed them, therefore, and were brought into a new house with splendid decorations and furniture. Now it was winter; and the girl, going into the chamber of these women, found them again weeping and lamenting. There stood beside them a mule, covered with housings of cloth of gold, and sesame was put before him; and the women were kissing him, and giving him food. And the girl said: What is all the ado, my ladies, about this mule? They answered her with tears, and said: This mule, which thou seest, was our brother, born of the same mother with ourselves. And when our father died, and left us great wealth, and this only brother, we did our best to get him married, and were preparing his nuptials for him, after the manner of men. But some women, moved by mutual jealousy, bewitched him unknown to us; and one night, a little before daybreak, when the door of our house was shut, we saw that this our brother had been turned into a mule, as thou now beholdest him. And we are sorrowful, as thou seest, having no father to comfort us: there is no wise man, or magician, or enchanter in the world that we have omitted to send for; but nothing has done us any good. And as often as our hearts are overwhelmed with grief, we rise and go away with our mother here, and weep at our father's grave, and come back again.

And when the girl heard these things, Be of good courage, said she, and weep not: for the cure of your calamity is near; yea, it is beside you, and in the middle of your own house. For I also was a leper; but when I saw that woman, and along with her that young child, whose name is Jesus, I sprinkled my body with the water with which His mother had washed Him, and I was cured. And I know that He can cure your affliction also. But rise, go to Mary my mistress; bring her into your house, and tell her your secret; and entreat and supplicate her to have pity upon you. After the woman had heard the girl's words, they went in haste to the Lady Mary, and brought her into their chamber, and sat down before her weeping, and saying: O our mistress, Lady Mary, have pity on thy hand-maidens; for no one older than ourselves, and no head of the family, is left—neither father nor brother—to live with us; but this mule which thou seest was our brother, and women have made him such as thou seest by witchcraft. We beseech thee, therefore, to have pity upon us. Then, grieving at their lot, the Lady Mary took up the Lord Jesus, and put Him on the mule's back; and she wept as well as the women, and said to Jesus Christ: Alas! my son, heal this mule by Thy mighty power, and make him a man endowed with reason as he was before. And when these words were uttered by the Lady Mary, his form was changed, and the mule became a young man, free from every defect. Then he and his mother and his sisters adored the Lady Mary, and lifted the boy above their heads, and began to kiss Him, saying: Blessed is she that bore Thee, O Jesus, O Saviour of the world; blessed are the eyes which enjoy the felicity of seeing Thee.

Dumb Ass

The remaining part of the Tertullian story that has not been accounted for is one that survives to this day but seems not to date back to predomesticity. The donkey-headed figure that Tertullian laughed at was carrying a book and wearing a toga. In other images of the same period, the *asinus togatus*, as Latinists call it, appears in front of a class or audience. The derisive Arabic proverb "an ass is carrying a scripture [*himarun yahmilu sifran*]"[42] derives from the same image. What could be funnier, you might think, than a donkey, the personification of stupidity, posing as a teacher? If such is your view, you share a sense of the humorous that is universal in the popular culture of the Arabic, Persian, and Turkish-speaking worlds. Simply mentioning the word *himar*, *khar*, or *eshek* in a classroom of Arab, Iranian, or Turkish students respectively is guaranteed to draw gales of laughter. Yet the slightest amount of rural experience will convince anyone that the dumbest donkey in the world is a whole lot smarter than the smartest sheep.

When and why did the ass become primarily a humorous symbol of stupidity? The when evidently falls between Apuleius in the second cen-

tury C.E. and Shakespeare in the sixteenth. The funniest and most memorable scene from *A Midsummer Night's Dream* reworks the story of
Lucius the Ass and his lady fair, but with the notable change that the
transformed hero is no longer a handsome young man of excellent family but a ludicrously foolish weaver named Nick Bottom. Titania, Queen
of the Fairies, falls victim to an enchantment that makes her fall in love
with Bottom, whom the same enchanter has given the head of an ass.
When the enchantment is reversed, she passes it off as a dream: "My
Oberon! What visions have I seen! Methought I was enamour'd of an
ass." During the enchantment, however, her infatuation mirrors, in a
tasteful way, that of the rich woman who conceived a passion for Lucius:

Come, sit thee down upon this flowery bed,
While I thy amiable cheeks do coy,
And stick musk-roses in thy sleek smooth head,
And kiss thy fair large ears, my gentle joy.[43]

The ostensible joke is the misalliance between the most refined of
females and the crudest and stupidest of males, but directors have readily found ways of tapping the sexual humor behind this front, something
Shakespeare himself may well have intended by choosing the name Bottom. The ass is the common Shakespearean symbol of stupidity, to be
sure, but mention of Bottom's homologous "fair large ears" indicates
which part of the donkey is responsible both for its stupidity and for
Titania's attentions.[44]

The donkey's penis—or its ears or tail as homologues of its penis—
becomes a mark of shame and a signifier of foolishness and stupidity. In
old-fashioned schoolrooms in France, teachers made misbehaving students sit in the corner wearing a sign saying *Âne*, or ass, and a cap with
donkey's ears, recalling a jester's or fool's cap, which was sometimes
conical and sometimes had donkey's ears. Their naughty British and
American counterparts wore a tall conical dunce cap, a term probably
borrowed from French "*cap d'âne*," which means "ass's head." The ears
here are clearly homologous with the conical phallic symbol.

A more sinister lineage of shameful conical hats goes back to the
Spanish Inquisition, which condemned heretics to don one before being
burned at the stake. Parading a heretic on an ass, often with the condemned seated backwards and sometimes holding the tail, compounded
the shame. As Christian practices, these shaming rituals seem to have
spread from Spain.[45] It is not unlikely, however, that they originated dur-

ing the period of Muslim rule and reflect punishments known in North Africa and the Middle East. Stipulations in market inspectors' manuals and reports of actual incidents confirm that wrongdoers in medieval Egypt were often paraded in public on a donkey while wearing a conical hat.[46] The hat was called a *turtur*, a derivation apparently from the verb *tarita*, meaning "to be stupid." A hat of the same name was later worn by Turkish troops called *deli*, or "madman." In Muslim society, shaming people by parading them seated backwards on an ass was most recently reported from northern Afghanistan in the 1990s.[47]

These symbols still held meaning in Spain in the 1790s, when Francisco Goya produced *Los Caprichos*, the strange series of etchings that made him famous outside his homeland.[48] Caprichos 23 and 24 show a condemned woman wearing a conical hat first hearing her sentence read out and then being paraded through the streets on a donkey. The powdered wigs of the officials make it clear that this is intended as a contemporary rather than a historical scene. Caprichos 37 through 42 ridicule pretence by showing a donkey teacher with donkey pupils, a donkey as a connoisseur of music, a donkey studying his genealogy, a donkey as a doctor, and a donkey sitting for his portrait. Capricho 42 features two cavalrymen being ridden by donkeys. Goya has drawn the leg of one of the donkeys dangling like a giant penis between the legs of the man he is riding. Finally, two monstrous witches appear in Capricho 63, riding on donkey-headed demons.

In more recent times, the venerable tradition of the dumb ass—and its ironic cousin the wise ass—has come to a peculiar end. "Ass" and "jackass" (that is, a male ass) provided English speakers with useful insults for hundreds of years. The word "arse," on the other hand, referred to a person's backside and was too vulgar for polite usage. Shakespeare never used it. By the vagaries of linguistic change, however, the distinction in pronunciation between "ass" and "arse" became lost in the United States, a land in which the common words for ass were "burro" and "donkey." (The latter, pronounced originally to rhyme with "monkey" and sometimes used in the form "donkey dick," dates only to the eighteenth century, when it denoted the male ass in particular.) By the end of the nineteenth century, the humor in this confusion of meanings was already apparent. A cartoon from the Spanish-American War showing Uncle Sam punching a diminutive Spaniard carries the caption: "Uncle Sam to Spain—The only way you can lick me is to lick My" followed by a picture of a donkey.[49] In the twentieth century, American pronunciation and diminishing familiarity with "ass" as a synonym for "donkey" led to the bizarre coinage of the literally disgusting slang word "asshole," which has taken the place of "jackass" as the epithet of choice when one is confronted with stupid or rude behavior. The British, who still use "arse," remain uncomfortable with this word born of a vulgar misunderstanding of the word "ass," but it seems destined to become one of modern America's gifts to the world of language.

The Spanish Inquisition and its Muslim antecedents aside, the dumb asses who preceded Shakespeare's Bottom most often symbolized an overturning of official values. Fauvel the Ass appears in a fourteenth-century French poem as a king under whose chaotic rule vice replaces virtue in positions of authority.[50] Nigel Longchamp's story of Burnel the Ass, cited in Chaucer's "The Nun's Priest's Tale" in *The Canterbury Tales*, is entitled "A Mirror for Fools."[51] Even the church succumbed to the popular appreciation of the donkey as a source of mirth. The *Festum Asinorum*, or Feast of Asses, began in the eleventh century as a dramatization of a sixth-century sermon extolling the prophets who foretold Christ's coming. One of the prophets was Balaam, who duly appeared in church riding on a wooden ass—and sometimes cruelly spurring the man inside it. In time, the other prophets were dropped from the spectacle so the audience could focus its revel on Balaam alone. In Beauvais, a town that celebrated the feast, the ass also appeared on January 14, in a tableau commemorating the flight into Egypt. The prettiest woman in town, with a darling child in her arms, played the Virgin Mary and rode a richly caparisoned donkey to the church, where a mass was held. At the end of the mass, the transgressive burlesque underlying the entire ceremony came out. The medieval manuscript source stipulates that, "the priest, having turned to the people, in lieu of saying the 'Ite, Missa est,' will bray thrice; the people instead of replying 'Deo Gratias' say, 'Hinham, hinham, hinham.' "[52]

The last thinker to ponder seriously the paradox of the bivalent foolish/messianic ass was the sixteenth-century Dominican philosopher Giordano Bruno (1548–1600), building on Heinrich Cornelius Agrippa von Nettesheim's "Digression in Praise of Asses" (1530), which was contained in an attack on contemporary astrologers and magicians. Bruno's elevation of *asinatá* (asinicity) to the level of a philosophical principle is murky, to say the least. As guides, the two figures (Onorio the Ass and the Cyllenian Ass) are united. Bruno's love of *coincidentia oppositorum*, however, complicates the matter. Onorio and the Cyllenian Ass are also complementary opposites. Whereas Onorio is a source of revelations to be believed, the Cyllenian Ass's tale is undermined by irony, so that ultimately he is rendered ridiculous. His desperation to enter into an academy, where he is finally accepted, marks him as a pedantic version of Onorio.[53]

In contrast with late antiquity's invocation of the donkey as either messianic or demonic, Bruno falls in with the transformation of (demonic) sexual potency into stupidity exemplified by his contemporary William Shakespeare. And soon the prophetic ass would become but a quaint notion. G. K. Chesterton's poem "The Donkey" (1900) is a rare sad reminder of lost spiritual resonance:

> When fishes flew and forests walk'd
> And figs grew upon thorn,
> Some moment when the moon was blood
> Then surely I was born;
>
> With monstrous head and sickening cry
> And ears like errant wings,
> The devil's walking parody
> On all four-footed things.
>
> The tatter'd outlaw of the earth,
> Of ancient crooked will;
> Starve, scourge, deride me: I am dumb,
> I keep my secret still.
>
> Fools! For I also had my hour;
> One far fierce hour and sweet:
> There was a shout above my ears,
> And palms before my feet.

What became of the spiritual donkey, the prophetic donkey, the messianic donkey? Did the lowering of the status of domestic animals that accompanied their increasing exploitation turn the oversized penis that had once connoted divine sexual potency into an emblem of a new cliché: the larger the penis, the smaller the brain? Possibly. Evidence for such a stereotype certainly exists. Or did the donkey simply sink so low as a domestic beast of burden that no one could make sense any longer of the symbolic weight it had once seemed to have?

The mule Duldul inherited from Muhammad by his son-in-law Ali may still be a religious symbol in some Shi'ite circles, but the same word, from an Arabic verb being "to dangle," has come to mean penis in Persian slang. In all likelihood, the same association lies in the origin of the word "dildo," meaning "artificial penis" and also "a stupid person," which is attested only in English and Dutch. "Dildo" first appears in English, with a precise description, in a poem by Thomas Nashe (1567–1601), "The Choise of Valentines or the Merie Ballad of Nash his Dildo." Since the letter *o* at the end suggests a borrowing from a Romance language, and both England and the Netherlands were in contact and conflict with Spain at that time, a Spanish origin seems plausible. A century later, the second English poem to celebrate a dildo, "Signior Dildo" by John Wilmot, the second Earl of Rochester (1647–1680), makes the lady's companion an Italian. Since the Christian Spaniards seem to have borrowed from their Muslim compatriots a form of shaming by using the donkey's penis as symbolic headgear, could they not also have borrowed an Arabic word that signified both a sacred mule and a penis? The best one can say for this etymological whimsy is that it is no worse than any other explanation of the word "dildo." I offer it not as a specimen of philological erudition so much as an example of the extremes to which an effort to find survivals in modern times of the original symbolic donkey can drive one.

Woozy from coping with too much donkey trivia? My apologies. The point of this chapter might have been made more briefly, but the unusual byways of asinine research may haply have served to make it more memorable. The normal perspective from which domesticity is viewed is backward. With the passage of time, appreciation of material usefulness overcomes whatever other sentiments were in play at the outset of domesticity. However, at the point when the domestic varieties of different species first came into being, material uses were mostly unforeseeable, and those other sentiments were all-powerful.

The effort in this chapter to chronicle the evolution and gradual decay of the affective sentiments that brought donkeys into the orbit of domestication could be paralleled for other species. Some lost their magic more quickly than others, but all follow the same trajectory. As material usefulness increases, affective usefulness retreats, until a point is reached where domestic animals become mere objects. Objectification thus becomes a defining characteristic of late domesticity and forms the lens through which the earlier histories of domestic species are viewed.

9. Late Domestic Divergences

From the standpoint of postdomesticity, the culture of domesticity, for all of its great diversity around the world, was of a piece in several ways. First, fully elaborated domestic societies viewed domestic animals as objects of exploitation, and distanced themselves from wild animals. Second, most individuals grew up in the company of tame animals and considered them normal parts of both their visual and imaginative landscapes. And third, domestic animals and their products were integral to the economic and social system as objects of exchange and consumption. These characteristics did not diminish over time in the way that affective characteristics like animal sacrifice and belief in animal spirits did.

Yet the postdomestic mentality described at the outset of this book has so far developed in only a few late domestic societies and still does not affect their entire populations. Its appearance does not correlate closely with either industrialization or sophistication of scientific thought. If it did, France and Germany would be in the forefront and Australia well to the rear. Britain played a pioneering role and British colonies in North America and Australia followed her lead. But other British colonies, including those with substantial settler populations, such as South Africa, Kenya, and Rhodesia (now Zimbabwe), did not. Nor does religion correlate with the transition to postdomesticity. Animal-revering Hindu vegetarians are as much immersed in the mentality of domesticity—India has the world's largest cattle population—as animal-sacrificing Muslims, and the secular Japanese do not share the postdomestic moral anxieties of secular Americans.

In this chapter, I propose to investigate the roots of the divergence among late domestic societies that led certain of them to be in the forefront in embracing postdomesticity. I shall start by discussing the social and economic factors associated with pastoralism, on the one hand, and colonial ranching economies, on the other. I shall then address the rise of new attitudes toward animals in Britain in particular.

Pastoralism

Postdomestic societies arise in countries that do not have and perhaps never have had a pastoral nomadic sector, whether composed of full nomads who travel more or less constantly with their herds or transhumant pastoralists who travel only twice a year between summer pastures in the highlands and winter pastures in the lowlands. As the most intensive form of animal husbandry prior to the application of modern industrial methods, pastoralism has contributed disproportionately to shaping the attitudes toward animals of entire countries. In societies that do include a pastoral sector, people in the nonpastoral sectors acquire both live animals and animal products from pastoralists in exchange for agricultural or manufactured goods, and consequently think of pastoralism as the dominant form of domestic human-animal relations. Plow oxen and cavalry mounts, cart-horses and pack mules, butter and cheese, hides and fleeces, animal fat and protein all come, to a greater or lesser degree, from the pastoral sector.

Pastoralism is a low-cost mode of land and animal exploitation. A free-ranging beef steer converts no more than one-twentieth of the food it eats into meat; a pig converts as much as one-fifth. These low levels of conversion of vegetable calories into animal calories fall still more if the foods the animals consume could have been used for humans. A pig cannot digest grass, so its diet overlaps a human diet more than a cow or sheep diet does. However, the traditional European practice of letting pigs gobble up acorns and hazelnuts in forests that would otherwise have yielded negligible amounts of human food made efficient use of the pig as a harvester of otherwise wasted calories. Grazing cattle and horses on grasslands that for one reason or another—too dry, too steep, too insecure—cannot be used for agriculture achieves the same purpose. Donkeys and camels thrive in arid wastelands. Sheep and goats do well in grasslands, deserts, mountains, and even, in the case of some goats, treetops.

Pastoralism keeps animals away from agricultural land but allows farming communities to benefit from animal products. Mobility is the key. To have enough space to graze, during at least part of the year the animals must be led or driven to pastures in places that are remote from agricultural lands. Yet exchange with agricultural settlements is difficult if the animals are not nearby. Seasonal migration may solve this problem. During propitious parts of the year, the nomads camp near the farming villages and offer to exchange animals, animal products, and transport services. Middlemen who go out to where the nomads are, buy surplus animals, and drive them to market afford another solution. Both the Sudan and Arabia have long histories of itinerant buyers supplying tens of thousands of animals to the camel markets of Cairo, Basra, and Damascus. Accumulating durable commodities like hides, cheeses, wool, and camel's hair and transporting them to market by pack animal is a third solution.

Much of the pastoralist's life, however, is spent far from permanent human settlement, in the company of animals. More importantly, within pastoral groups, many day-to-day transactions are based on the societal convention that animals have value as living beings regardless of the products their bodies might yield. Animals can be used to pay bride-prices, ransoms, and fines. They can be slaughtered for a feast to demonstrate a herder's generosity. They can signify a person's wealth and constitute a person's inheritance. Stealing them can start feuds but can also usefully redistribute wealth. Domestic animals generally do not lack for ownership in pastoral societies (that is, few of them become feral) and do not need to be rendered into salable products for their value to be realized.

Modern governments around the world have more often than not looked upon their pastoral sectors as a problem. Pastoralists are too unsettled, too independent, and sometimes too well armed to fit easily into centralized systems of taxation, control, and government services. Furthermore, they cannot easily be converted into modern meat and milk producers for urban markets. Using pickup trucks to haul sheep from water hole to pasture and then to market helps, but such practices fall far short of modern industrial methods of animal exploitation. Though the low material standard of living of pastoral nomads has always kept the cost of their animal products down, modern animal management in an industrial mode achieves greater economies through scale, centralization, efficiency, selective breeding, and transportation systems that prevent the animals from wasting calories by extensive grazing. Rather than forming the nucleus of modernized meat industries, pastoralists in developing countries have more often found themselves subject to forced settlement and pauperization. Ironically, as economic development spurs higher levels of meat consumption, these traditional meat-producing sectors gradually disappear.

To the degree, then, that the transition to postdomesticity involves treating animal products as industrial commodities and the live animals as raw materials to be processed in the most efficient way possible, a pastoral sector in a society is more of an obstacle than a goal. Pastoralists appreciate living animals as objects of tangible value, an outlook that stands in the way of seeing them as raw materials whose value can only be realized through the sale of their products. And roaming pastoralist lifestyles do not fit the needs of industrial centralization and economies of scale. Thus modern industrial approaches to animal husbandry and meat processing must compete, at least initially, with an animal husbandry sector that has deep social and historical roots.

Prior to the twentieth century, pastoralism played a significant role in the economies of most African and Asian countries. Even in Europe, the domain of mixed farming from which the United States derived many of its agricultural practices, many countries had transhumant pastoralists who took seasonal advantage of highland pastures, whether to graze goats in Switzerland or pigs in Spain. European colonial rule did not, for the most part, seek to change pastoral traditions. European imperialists did not compete with colonial pastoralists through the export of European animal products in the way they used industrial exports to compete with local crafts.

Even after refrigeration and canning, by supplementing salting, gave greater scope to exports of meat and milk products in the second half of the nineteenth century, the rising levels of consumption that accompanied industrialization and urbanization in Europe created a demand for meat imports rather than exports. However, addressing this need by fostering export-oriented animal husbandry in colonies that were already satisfying their local markets through inefficient pastoralism was not a promising endeavor, especially when efficient suppliers were already available in countries that did not have competing pastoral traditions, notably Argentina, the United States, and Australia.

Ranching

The invasion of Australia and the Americas by European domestic animals had a long-term effect on the indigenous societies as great as that of the invasion of the Europeans themselves.[1] Cattle, horses, donkeys, sheep, and goats flourished spectacularly in the grasslands and deserts of Argentina, Mexico, and the United States, as did pigs in more forested areas like the Appalachians. The onslaught began when Columbus and subsequent Spanish adventurers imported horses for military purposes and other livestock for meat and wool. Unlike the European human population, which grew slowly, the animals multiplied so rapidly in ecological niches that presented few competitors that in some regions large numbers escaped human control and became feral.

The phenomenon of thousands of feral and sometimes unowned animals living on their own on thousands of square miles of unsettled rangeland was unprecedented in the domestic era. (Islands where Europeans released domestic stock for later hunting by sailors from passing ships constitute an exception, but the areas involved were quite limited.) Pastoralism had historically kept pace with the growth of animal herds because most domestic animals were recognized as a source of wealth. Ratios of human to animal populations remained fairly stable, and pastoral tribes frequently fought to protect claims to rangelands, even if actual ownership of land was not recognized. Pastoralist animal management could not entirely prevent escape into a feral lifestyle, but there were strong incentives for recapture, so large feral populations seldom developed. Only animals that did not constitute objects of wealth, such as dogs, cats, and pigeons, successfully established extensive feral populations.

By 1700, the Argentine pampas were teeming with feral cattle, New Mexico was overrun by sheep, and pigs abounded in the hillier parts of the Old South. It was not difficult for Native Americans in some areas to acquire them and create their own forms of pastoralism. Wool came to be used locally, but transportation costs militated against centralized marketing for export on the model of the Mesta, the sheep-raising organization that dominated the Spanish countryside. Sparse populations limited the demand for meat, though in some parts of California, tallow (rendered fat from cattle and sheep) could be sold in seaports as a naval supply. In Argentina, gauchos similar to the *vaqueros* of Spain followed an independent and semi-wild style of life, hunting and skinning feral cattle and exporting the hides to Europe. In North America, hunters did the same with the wild bison, but the cowboy lifestyle based on that of the gaucho did not appear until the nineteenth century.

The growth of African slavery changed the pattern of exploitation. Owners of sugar plantations in Brazil and the Caribbean islands and of cotton plantations in the American South had a vested interest in keeping their slaves healthy enough to work, but they did not want them spending their time growing food crops and raising animals. The per capita consumption of animal protein and fat by these slave populations may not have been great, but the aggregate demand for animal products purchasable on the open market was substantial. By comparison, the mixed farming pattern typical of the northern United States saw farm families fulfilling most of their needs for animal products from their own stock. Argentine cattlemen exported large quantities of salted beef (that is, corned beef) to Brazil. Corned beef also became a staple in the Caribbean. In the United States, pig drovers, mostly Irish, herded immense numbers of swine down from the mountains to the plantation belt, which became noted for its hams, bacon, pork sausage, and use of lard as a cooking fat. Feral roaming increasingly gave way to more formal animal ownership under conditions that recognized the value of animals solely in terms of the products derived from their bodies. No Irish pig-drover bought his bride for twenty sows and a boar. No Argentine gaucho sacrificed a bull to his god. Slave consumers also attracted the attention of mixed farmers. The cheese industry of upstate New York, based on the skills of hundreds of farm wives, sold much of its production to southern slaveowners.[2]

This was the background from which modern ranching emerged in the second half of the nineteenth century. Small numbers of people pastured enormous numbers of livestock on immense tracts of land. Unlike Old World pastoralists, the gauchos, cowboys, and shepherds worked for wages and prided themselves on their independence. "Get along little dogie" was as close as they came to expressing elevated feelings about animals destined for slaughter. As for the ranchers, they saw the value of their animals primarily in terms of the cash they received for delivering them to a slaughterhouse, or later, a feedlot. No ideological obstacles stood in the way of maximizing the efficiency of rendering animals into commodities.

A consortium of nine railroad companies bought 320 acres of Chicago swamp in 1864. The Union Stock Yard and Transit Company officially opened the next year, and in 1867, Philip Armour expanded his Milwaukee hog operation into the new meatpacking metropolis. Meatpackers Gustavus Franklin Swift, Nelson Morris, and George H. Hammond soon followed Armour's lead. Swift's development of refrigerated railroad cars in 1882 made possible the transport of fresh meat to eastern population centers, and by the turn of the century, Chicago was processing 82 percent of the nation's meat. Industrial-scale meatpacking then spread to Argentina. Berisso, a town near the seaport of La Plata, started as a meat-salting center in 1871, with England the prime export market. Swift in 1904, followed by Armour in 1915, brought refrigeration and industrial efficiency to Berisso and soon bought out the old salting businesses.

Australia and New Zealand underwent a parallel but later development. Today, Australia has hundreds of thousands of feral horses, water buffalo, donkeys, and camels descended from stock released into the wild when no longer needed for labor, as well as several million feral pigs, a million or so feral goats, and feral rabbits in the hundreds of millions. Sheep and cattle, however, the mainstays of the livestock industry, have always been more closely watched over.

Eleven ships full of prospective colonists, 736 of them convicts, left England in 1787, bound for Australia. The commander, Captain Arthur Phillip, made a port call at the Cape of Good Hope Colony of southern Africa, where he purchased what were to be Australia's first sheep, a meat variety with fat tails and much hair in their coat. A decade later, two other captains on a stock-purchasing expedition to the Cape of Good Hope Colony discovered twenty-six merino sheep for sale, descendants of animals given to the Dutch government eight years earlier by the king of Spain. These excellent wool providers, later crossbred with stock imported from elsewhere, became the nucleus of the Australian sheep ranching industry. By the second decade of the nineteenth century, the first shiploads of wool were making their way to England's textile mills. By the late 1830s, sheep were being raised in every part of the country. Australia was well on its way to becoming the world's greatest wool producer. Meat exports developed only with refrigeration, but eventually Australia became the world's largest exporter of lamb and a major exporter of beef.

The world's premier meatpackers are also the world's premier meat eaters. Seven of the top eight beef exporters in 1999 were Australia; the United States; Canada, which developed a meat industry following the

American example; Brazil, where ranchers were able to buy up large tracts of Amazon rainforest after 1973 and convert them to pasture; Argentina; New Zealand, with a history like Australia's; and Uruguay, with a history like Argentina's. India was the eighth, just before Uruguay. The top seven countries in beef consumption per capita in that the same year were Argentina, Uruguay, the United States, Australia, Brazil, New Zealand, and Canada. Australians eat only 78.5 pounds of beef per capita per year, as compared to 149 pounds in the United States and 190 pounds in Argentina, but they consume much more lamb, 28 pounds as opposed to 1 pound in the United States and 3.5 pounds in Argentina. Rounding out the picture, poultry adds 108.5 pounds per year to the diet in the United States, 55 pounds in Argentina, and 71.5 pounds in Australia, while pork accounts for 67.5 pounds, 42 pounds, and 2 pounds respectively. Total consumption of these four meats comes to 327 pounds in the United States, 251 pounds in Argentina, and 219.5 pounds in Australia.

By way of comparison, Japan in 1995 consumed 67.5 pounds of meat per capita from land animals, including 25 pounds of pork, 24 pounds of poultry, and 18.5 pounds of beef. Thirty years earlier, before the Japanese industrial miracle caused personal incomes to skyrocket, total annual meat consumption per capita was 14 pounds, less than one-tenth of the American consumption of beef alone in that year. Total meat consumption per capita in South Africa, a former British colony with a long tradition of pastoralism, is 75 pounds, divided into 23 pounds of beef, 39.5 pounds of poultry, 6 pounds of pork, and 6.5 pounds of lamb. Nigerians consume 14 pounds of meat annually and Chinese approximately 48.5 pounds.

The pattern is clear. When European colonists imported European domestic animals to lands suitable for stock raising and devoid of any indigenous pastoral traditions, the imported stock multiplied to form large herds of grazing animals, many of them feral. Those who sought to exploit these herds thought only in terms of selling animal products: wool, meat, and hides. The resulting ranching-meatpacking industry employed wage laborers who had no reason to value live animals as anything other than market commodities. The animal products industries and the transport lines that facilitated them concentrated on centralizing the processing of livestock, achieving efficiencies of scale in huge packing plants (and dairies) and distributing the products to consumers in distant places. It is well known that Henry Ford took the disassembly line of the slaughterhouse, where carcasses on hooks move by conveyor belt from work station to work station, as the model for his automobile assembly lines. The resulting abundance and low costs stimulated high rates of consumption.

To a surprising extent, the countries that manifest this pattern are the countries where the postdomestic mentality is most strongly in evidence. The correlation is greatest for Australia and the United States, with New Zealand and Canada in parallel but lesser positions. Brazil, where the boom in the animal industry is quite recent, fits least well. But what can be said of Argentina and Uruguay, its neighbor across the Rio de la Plata, the route by which most of the two countries' meat products head for world markets?

One index might be bullfighting, part of the Spanish and Portuguese heritage of Latin America. Bullfighting deeply embodies the idea of the animal having a worth that is more than the sum of its rendered parts. Only four Latin American countries have banned the sport: Argentina, Uruguay, Chile, and Cuba. The last vestige in Argentina is the annual "Toreo de la Vincha" in the village of Casabindo, where young men vie to tear a red ribbon, the "Vincha," from the animal's horns. Neighboring Brazil, on the other hand, retains the "Farra do Boi," an entertainment staged during Holy Week and in celebration of weddings and other special events. Villagers chase an ox through the streets and stab and beat it with sticks, knives, stones, and bamboo lances. Sometimes the animal's tail is pulled off.

Certain postdomestic philosophical viewpoints are also in evidence. The Uruguayan Alberto Villarreal is prominent in the world environmentalist movement, and a philosophy student in Buenos Aires maintains an online Peter Singer Web site. On the other hand, according to one online business source: "Until the 1990s, vegetarianism was virtually unheard of in beef-producing nations like Argentina and Uruguay."[3]

In fact, the late twentieth century saw a divergence between animal industry developments in the United States and those in Argentina. The Union Stock Yard in Chicago closed down in 1971, as fattening and meatpacking operations shifted to regional centers remote from large cities. Slaughterhouse jobs went increasingly to new immigrants, mostly Hispanic, as the occupation became stigmatized. A human-resources director for a slaughterhouse remarked:

We're just desperate for workers. Last month, I hired eighty-five people and ninety-two left. That's not uncommon. . . . The biggest problem is the simple fact that nobody wants to kill cows. The recruitment—boy, I use every tactic to get people to work in this place. I've made these clever little ads with cows. I use the job service, the social services. I go to jails and halfway houses. . . . A lot of what I end up doing is kind of like social work. I've arranged childcare for these people so they could come in to work. I've talked to Immigration about their green cards. Sometimes, if they get drunk and don't come in, I'll go try and pick them up.[4]

By contrast, Liniers Terminal, within the city limits of Buenos Aires, Argentina's biggest consumer market, continued to be the center of the Argentine meatpacking industry, particularly with respect to hogs. Most cattle were fattened within 350 miles of the city. Moreover, while meat processing for the export market is dominated by five large meatpacking companies, those same companies handle only a small percentage of the cattle slaughtered for domestic consumption. (In the United States, the five largest slaughterhouses account for 75 percent of total beef production.) This lack of industrial concentration accounts for the fact that in the late 1980s Argentina had 35,000 retail butcher shops. As late as the mid-1990s, retail butchers satisfied 60 percent of the demand for beef, while supermarkets accounted for only 28 percent.[5] In sum, the removal of live animals destined for slaughter from the sight of city-dwellers that occurred in the United States took place more slowly in Argentina, as did the psychological distancing brought about by substituting film-wrapped supermarket packages for meat selection in a retail butcher shop.

England

The quasi-correlation between colonial ranching and postdomesticity takes us only so far. We are left with a paradox. The four countries where colonial ranching correlates best with postdomesticity, the United States, Australia, New Zealand, and Canada, are all English-speaking; but even though parts of the British Isles have a long history of intensive animal husbandry, ranching of the colonial sort is unknown, and the United Kingdom has relied for the past 150 years on imports of animal products like meat and wool, rather than on domestic production. Whatever led to the birth of the postdomestic mentality in England is clearly unrelated to the culture of meatpacking and the extreme objectification of animals characteristic of colonial ranching. Yet the new outlook on human-animal relations moved much more readily to English-speaking countries thousands of miles away than it did to continental Europe.

Hundreds of historians, of course, have asked why England's eighteenth century witnessed the onset of the Industrial Revolution while continental Europe's eighteenth century did not. There are numerous answers, but most synopses of the subject see a close connection with an antecedent agricultural revolution whose high points are generally agreed upon. The century began with Jethro Tull (1674–1741) inventing a seed drill and a horse-drawn hoe. Then Charles "Turnip" Townsend (1674–1738) pioneered planting soil-restoring crops—guess which he favored most—in place of letting fields lie fallow for a season, and Robert Bakewell (1725–1795) used inbreeding to develop specialized traits in sheep and cattle. Thomas William Coke (1752–1842) carried on further breeding experiments and hosted an annual agricultural show called a "sheepshearing" to promote advances in farming. James Small (1730–1793) invented the cast iron plow and Andrew Meikle (1719–1811) the threshing machine.

Behind these activities by prosperous farmers was enclosure, a formal delimitation of property that gradually eliminated large tracts of common woodland and pasture and gave private farmers complete control of their lands. Prior to the eighteenth century, bounding fields with fences and hedges was not unknown, but the practice greatly intensified. Between 1750 and 1810, Parliament passed over a thousand acts authorizing such enclosures. One result, combined with the technical improvements of the agricultural revolution, was a great increase in food production, mirroring a great increase in population. England's population almost doubled in the eighteenth century. Another result was the dislocation of many peasants who were forced to seek jobs in factories because they no longer had access to common land. By 1870, only 14 percent of the laboring population was working in agriculture, compared with almost 50 percent in the United States.

Though poverty was often the lot of the new class of industrial worker, per capita meat consumption rose. Well into the nineteenth century, boasts were made that the average Englishman ate six times as much meat as the average Frenchman. In the first decades of the century, breeding oversized cattle became a passion, particularly among farmer aristocrats. Privately sponsored "sheepshearings" where fat cows were shown, and to a lesser degree fat sheep and fat pigs, became prestigious social events, and societies formed to institutionalize such spectacles. The most prominent centered on London's huge Smithfield market.

> The Smithfield Society (the name was changed to Smithfield Club in 1802) . . . first met on December 17, 1798, under the chairman-ship of Francis Russell, the fifth duke of Bedford, with most of the aristocratic stars of livestock husbandry in attendance. . . . All these gentlemen were on the spot because the pre-Christmas sea-son at Smithfield was a busy time; club legend credited the crowds that flocked to see "some extraordinary fat beasts" sent by the duke of Bedford to a butcher named Giblett with providing the immediate inspiration for the annual livestock exhibitions that were to be its major activity.[6]

The rage for livestock breeding for immediate market consumption bears comparison with the transformation of ranching into a meat-centered industry in Argentina, the United States, and Australia in the late nineteenth century. Any heritage in England of pastoralism as a form of social organization did not survive enclosure. Under the pre-dominant pattern of mixed farming, farmers counted their plow oxen and cart horses as capital assets and thought of their pigs and sheep as potential hams and fleeces. Simply owning a huge herd of animals did not make one either wealthy or noble. As horses increasingly replaced oxen for draft purposes, the way was open to view cattle exclusively in terms of meat and hides. The problem the eighteenth-century colonial rancher had in getting animals raised on remote grazing lands to urban consumers loomed less large for England's aristocratic cattle breeders, who effectively anticipated the later development of ranching in assess-ing their livestock value in terms of marketable products.

Industrialization and demographic growth combined to increase England's degree of urbanization at a time when the United States, Au-stralia, and Argentina were still heavily rural. As a consequence, Eng-land had a slightly earlier start on the path toward separating city dwellers from domestic animals used for production. When in the 1840s Charles Dickens was warning his readers about the free-ranging, garbage-eating hogs of New York City, London's hogs had mostly been relocated to the vicinity of suburban garbage dumps. Many American cities relied on roaming pigs for processing garbage into the twentieth century.

Thus despite the absence of a fully developed ranching and meat-packing economy, England's experience of late domesticity resembled in some particulars those later experiences in the United States, Australia, and Argentina. Population growth and urbanization created large consumer markets for animal products analogous to those of the slave-holding regions of the New World. As a consequence, stock-breeders intensified their interest in marketable products. For colonial ranchers, this meant searching for ways to transport animals, concentrate meat-packing, and distribute the resulting products. Somewhat earlier in England it took the form of scientific breeding for improved meat and fat yields. In the one situation, ranching and meatpacking proved an avenue to wealth and prestige. In the other, wealth and aristocratic rank saw livestock improvement as a worthy calling.

These comparisons, however, do not distinguish Spanish-speaking Argentina from English-speaking Australia and America. Changing economic conditions concerning animal husbandry and meat consumption provided a soil in which a postdomestic mentality might take root and grow, but in and of themselves, material circumstances did not necessitate a move in this direction. Elite sentiment provided the fertilizer that enabled the seeds of change to sprout and then be transmitted to the social strata in the United States and Australia that emulated the attitudes of the British upper class. The London Zoological Society was founded in 1826 and two years later opened the gates of its animal garden to scientifically inclined members only. The Zoological Society of Philadelphia was chartered in 1859 with similar scientific objectives, though the Civil War delayed the actual zoo opening until 1874. In Australia, the Royal Melbourne Zoological Society, which opened the first zoo, was founded in 1857. Argentina had to wait until 1907 for a zoo to open in Buenos Aires. At a more popular level, the craze for dog shows that was sparked by the first show in Newcastle, England in 1859 reached Hobart, Australia in 1862 and New York City in 1876. And the world's first cat show, held in the Crystal Palace in London in 1871, was the model for the first American cat show in 1881.

A key source of the new British sensibility about animals was revulsion against animal blood sports, which were uncommonly prevalent in eighteenth-century England. Judging from the frequency with which images of animal combat appear in ancient artistic traditions around the world, the spectacle of male animals of the same or different species fighting one another has fascinated male humans since predomestic times. It is doubtless part of our genetic legacy as a hunting species. In today's postdomestic society the voice of a television announcer reading a script about the natural hunting habits or mating practices of this or that species confers educational respectability on real-life footage of territorial combat and pursuit of prey, disguising the fact that the viewers of the nature documentary are viscerally stirred by the spectacle. Staged animal combat is anathema and generally banned. Such was not the case in earlier domestic times. Staged animal combat, and less frequently fights between humans and animals, took place in every part of the world. Different societies had different preferences. In Spain, bullfighting expanded from being a wedding entertainment to being a highly ritualized spectacle in its own right. Turkic-speaking peoples in many countries took an interest in wrestling matches between rutting male camels, which try to force their opponent to the ground. In Iran, historical chronicles tell of staged fights involving rams, buffaloes, camels, guard dogs, cocks, spiders, and scorpions. And cockfighting is so widely spread that it seems likely that the mating combat of the ancestral jungle fowl of southeastern Asia is what originally attracted human interest to the species. After all, eggs could be gathered in the wild, and wild birds were easily snared for meat.

Though far from unique in their love of blood sports, Englishmen relished them to an extraordinary degree. Bull-baiting and bear-baiting, in which the animals were tied to a brass ring and harassed by bulldogs and mastiffs, had been common entertainments for centuries. Many people believed that a bull yielded better meat after an hour or so defending itself from vicious dogs. Badger-baiting, cockfighting, dog fights, and ratting, in which terrier dogs killed rats by the hundreds, had their aficionados as well. However, as early as 1743, a glimmer of moral revulsion at the unstaunched flow of blood appeared in the form of Jack Broughton's "London Prize Ring Rules," which were designed to lessen the brutality of bareknuckle boxing. Rule Seven stipulated, "That no person is to hit his adversary when he is down, or seize him by the hair, the breeches, or any part below the waist; a man on his knees to be reckoned down."[7] Concerns about brutality toward animals followed with a parliamentary bill, introduced in 1802, to ban bull-baiting. It was defeated by thirteen votes, but a contemporary observer of English entertainments commented that "bull and bear-baiting is not encouraged by persons of rank and opulence in the present day; and when practiced . . . it is attended only by the lowest and most despicable part of the people."[8] The Society for the Prevention of Cruelty to Animals came into being in 1824, and in 1835 finally persuaded Parliament to ban animal fights of all kinds by criminalizing the keeping of a premises for staging such spectacles.

Historians of religion and philosophy may have good answers to the question of why leading elements in English society developed such sensitivity to the gruesome violence toward animals that their forefathers reveled in. I would simply observe that their kindhearted feelings coincided with an increasing focus on raising more productive meat animals and a proliferation of breeding experiments on domestic animals of all kinds. The breeders were certainly not philosophers, but it is hard to resist the thought that in the background of their efforts lay Descartes' notion that animals are simply organic automata not substantially different from the products of a factory. Regardless of its spiritual or philosophical roots, however, the spark of humane feeling toward animals that was kindled at the start of the nineteenth century fired many an English heart as the century progressed. As new ideas about animals proliferated, they were quickly transferred to English-speaking populations abroad—but they were most enthusiastically received in those lands that were not encumbered by indigenous pastoral traditions and that were developing their own forms of extreme animal commodification.

10. Toward Postdomesticity

The economic developments that foreshadowed the end of the domestic era were paralleled by equally striking changes in how people felt about and imagined animals, particularly in Britain and the United States. Institutionally, as we shall see later in this chapter, the United States followed Britain in forming humane societies, creating zoos, and staging cat and dog shows. In the realm of imagination, the two countries also followed similar paths. Authors, cartoonists, and filmmakers gave individual animals names and costumes and made them the protagonists in their stories. But creative imaginations diverged somewhat on opposite sides of the Atlantic. British tastes inclined toward wild beasts and the animalization of humans—that is, portraying humanlike animal characters according to their roles in nature. Americans, on the other hand, inclined toward the humanization of animals. Unlike Peter Rabbit, Donald Duck and his nephews converse, travel, and adventure as humans, not as ducks. Both tracks contributed to the emergence of postdomesticity in the second half of the twentieth century, but they also flavored the national forms that postdomesticity would take.

Fictional Beasts in Late Domesticity

As he spoke, a tall gaitered man with weather-beaten face, strong, lean, austere, and the blue-gray eyes of the hill-country, came striding into the yard. And trotting soberly at his heels, with the gravest, saddest eyes ever you saw, a sheep-dog puppy.

A rare dark gray he was, his long coat, dashed here and there with lighter touches, like a stormy sea moonlit. Upon his chest an escutcheon of purest white, and the dome of his head showered, as it were, with a sprinkling of snow. Perfectly compact, utterly lithe, inimitably graceful with his airy-fairy action; a gentleman every inch, you could not help but stare at him—Owd Bob o' Ken-muir.

At the foot of the ladder the two stopped. And the young dog, placing his forepaws on a lower rung, looked up, slowly waving his silvery brush.

"A proper Gray Dog!" mused Tammas, gazing down into the dark face beneath him. "Small, yet big; light to get about on backs o' his sheep, yet not too light. Wi' a coat hard a-top to keep oot Daleland weather, soft as sealskin beneath. And wi' them sorrerful eyes on him as niver goes but wi' a good un. Amaist he minds me o' Rex son o' Rally."[1]

Thus is the reader introduced to the title character of Alfred Ollivant's *Bob, Son of Battle*, published in 1898, the first novel to take the real life of a dog as its subject matter.[2] This highly popular Victorian story is laid in the Cumberland district of northern England. Bob does not speak and is not humanized. He herds sheep with prizewinning skill and is owned by a calm, firm, gentle-hearted farmer named James Moore. But is he also guilty of the horrible crime of killing sheep? Or is the culprit his rival, Red Wullie, also known as "the Tailless Tyke," owned by the blasphemous little Adam McAdams? I won't spoil the story.

Ollivant's was not the first novel to make realistic animal biography its central theme. Anna Sewall's *Black Beauty, His Grooms and Companions*, published in 1877, met with great success in both England and the United States. However, it was essentially a tract arguing for the humane treatment of horses disguised as the autobiography of a well-bred horse who is injured by a groom and consequently sinks to being a cab-horse and a cart-horse before being nursed back to health by a kindly farmer and finding a happy home.

By contrast, *Bob, Son of Battle* is pure story, and other dog sagas soon followed. Jack London came out with *The Call of the Wild* in 1903. Departing slightly from Ollivant's model, London tells much of the story from the point of view of his hero, a dog named Buck. Yet he does not attempt to take the reader deeply into Buck's mind as if he were a human in dog's clothing. *White Fang* followed in 1906 and *Michael,*

Brother of Jerry in 1917, the latter title obviously a tip of London's cap to Ollivant. Two years after London's last dog book, the American writer Albert Payson Terhune published *Lad: A Dog*, the first of his popular dog novels. Terhune would write over twenty of these dog novels, mostly about collies. In 1938, Eric Knight, an Englishman who came to the United States at age fifteen, penned the most popular dog story ever, *Lassie Come Home*, which first appeared as a short story in *The Saturday Evening Post*. In the subsequent movies and television series, Lassie repeatedly shows a feeling for the humans around her that is far less canine than what Ollivant and London allowed Bob and Buck to feel. Though much loved by a generation of young American readers, these stories by Terhune and Knight were not as popular in Britain.

A more extensive survey of early twentieth-century literature might pinpoint more precisely the evolution of the dog biography, but the broad outline seems clear. Dog stories find their most enthusiastic markets in the United States, and the animal protagonists move from being the objects of the narrative to having individual subjective points of view. Moreover, their subjective viewpoint evolves from a concern with sheep, wolves, or other dogs to a complex emotional involvement with human beings.

Horses proved less malleable as subjects. Mary O'Hara's *My Friend Flicka*, about a boy taming a wild mare in turn-of-the-century Wyoming, appeared in 1941 and spawned a sequel, two movies, and a television series, but the human point of view is the dominating one. A fully humanized if farcical equine point of view appears only with *Francis, the Talking Mule* (1949), the first of a series of hit comedy movies based on a novel published in 1946 by David Stern III. Two years after Francis appeared, H. Allen Smith's satirical novel *Rhubarb*, about a cat that inherits a baseball team, followed him to the silver screen. Other species trailed far behind. When sheep, goats, cattle, and pigs finally did appear, they were thoroughly humanized, like Munro Leaf's softhearted bull in *The Story of Ferdinand* (1935) or the naïve young piggy in E. B. White's *Charlotte's Web* (1952).

These early attempts to think about individual animals in human terms seem unadventurous compared with the fictional animals that spring from today's full-blown postdomestic imagination: In the American trend of humanizing animals, think of the wise-ass Donkey in the movies *Shrek* (2001) and *Shrek 2* (2004); and in the British trend of animalizing humans, consider the trekking rabbits with their elaborate cultures and institutions in Richard Adams's *Watership Down* (1972). However, all of these fictional animals represent a startling break with the conventional presentation of fictional animals inherited from earlier in the domestic era.

In the area of illustrated books and cartoons for very young children, British authors created a winning menagerie of humanized animals. Beatrix Potter's cuddly and well-dressed rabbits, squirrels, and mice, whose stories were related in the dozen books that followed *The Tale of Peter Rabbit* in 1902, found well-conceived successors in Little Grey Rabbit, Little Red Fox, and Sam Pig, some of the characters in stories penned by Alison Uttley from 1929 on. These were accompanied by the still-popular cartoon character (with his animal friends) Rupert Bear, who began to appear in the *Daily Express* in 1920 and gained wider popularity in the form of annual collections, when Alfred Bestall succeeded Mary Tourtel as storyteller and draftsman in 1936.

For older readers, however, the boundary between humanized animals and animalized humans blurred. The difference between Walt Disney's early cartoon characters, whose animality is limited to their physical features, and those of Kenneth Grahame, who was a secretary of the Bank of England when he published *The Wind in the Willows* in 1908, illustrates the British willingness to disguise social commentary with fur and paws. Grahame contrasts a noisy and common way of life, represented by the stoats and weasels of the Wild Wood, with the preferred gentility of the River-Bankers: Badger, Mole, Rat, and Toad.

More dramatically, George Orwell used animal protagonists to satirize the horrors of Stalinism in *Animal Farm*, published in 1945. He made pigs greedy and horses noble. In 1986, Art Spiegelman used the same device in *Maus*. He rendered predatory Nazis as cats and victimized Jews as mice. In using animal stereotypes to convey moral messages, however, both authors were reverting to a much older tradition of animal tales, rooted in early domestic if not predomestic times. Antiquity gives us Aesop's fables in Greek and the parallel Sanskrit collection *The Panchatantra*, which was rendered into Arabic in Islamic times as *Kalila wa Dimna*. Both works reflect similar roots and share a didactic purpose. The animals talk, think, and act like human beings, though certain species have stereotyped characters. The situations they confront mimic human situations, and each fable carries an explicit or implicit moral lesson. Similar lessons may be found in animal tales from sub-Saharan Africa and from Buddhist *ongaeshi* tales in East Asia.

The paucity of domestic animals other than the cat and the dog in these animal fables reflects the disappearance of these species from the moral universe of domestic society and the difficulty of fitting owned animals into this type of narrative. One survey of the versified fables of Jean de La Fontaine (1621–1695), which were mostly borrowed from Aesop, noted twenty-one appearances for Renard the Fox, seventeen for the lion, and sixteen for the wolf, as opposed to four for the horse, two for the sheep, and two for the cow. Cats and dogs figured in twelve fables each. The noteworthy exception to this undervaluing of domestic species was, not surprisingly, the ass, which figured in thirteen fables—plus two more for the mule.

Using animals to teach morals or to typify human character carried over into caricature—Goya's etchings satirizing human pretensions by showing doctors, teachers, and other honored professional men as donkeys in human clothes have already been mentioned—and into verbal abuse. Calling another person an animal—jackass, bitch, snake, worm, pig, wolf—with the intent of demeaning the person in some way connected with that particular animal seems to be a universal practice.

Animals abound in folktales and nursery rhymes as well. Some of these have deep roots in ancient fears of bears and wolves. Others are of more recent invention and are believed by some scholars to embody social or political commentary in a disguised form. Like the fables, however, they are episodic and do not purport to tell an animal's life story. Despite being gifted with speech, the sheep that reports on its wool output in "Baa, Baa, Black Sheep" makes no claim of individual identity.

Prior to the twentieth century, artists were ambivalent about clothing animals. The wolf in "Little Red Riding Hood," for example, is shown as a full-size, dangerous carnivore in fourteen out of seventeen editions from 1729 to 1916. But he appears dressed as a country squire in 1823 and he wears a sheepskin in 1875 and 1888. The Grimm brothers' Goldilocks similarly faces real bears in nineteenth-century illustrations. But the brothers' three little pigs are more commonly granted human dress, as is Br'er Rabbit in the African animal tales that Joel Chandler Harris (1848–1908) drew from African-American sources for his Uncle Remus stories. The determining factor appears to be whether the illustrator felt the animals functioned in the story as animals or as exemplars of human behavior. The "Three Little Pigs," for example, can easily be seen as a moral tale about human improvidence—hence the human clothes. But no illustrator had a mind to put costumes on the cacophonous ass, dog, cat, and cock who made up the Bremen town musicians, because the story has them acting in a thoroughly animal fashion. John Tenniel put clothes on the fuss-budget White Rabbit and the wacky March Hare when he illustrated *Alice in Wonderland* in 1895, but he left unclothed the Dormouse and the Cheshire Cat, who play less human roles in the story.

The new genre of dog and horse biography unequivocally presented its protagonists as animals, and usually as animals with owners, interacting on a daily basis with humans. Unlike the moral actors in Aesop's fables or fully developed postdomestic animal heroes like Richard Bach's *Jonathan Livingston Seagull* (1970), whose aspiration to fly freely had a liberating influence on many readers, the protagonist of a late domestic dog or horse story is not normally a stand-in for a human being or an exemplar of human virtue or vice. The authors grant their heroes full subjectivity as animals, and in so doing, despite the views articulated by Descartes and followed by most of his philosopher successors, they successfully persuade the reader that their fictional beasts think, feel, scheme, suffer, and rejoice. Peter Singer's liberationist proposition of the 1970s, which states that animals suffer just as humans do, is already present in *Black Beauty* and *Bob, Son of Battle*, but suffering has little resonance in the preceding centuries of animal fables, fairy tales, and nursery rhymes. The wolf whom the woodcutter dispatches with an ax in "Little Red Riding Hood" and his cousin who comes down the chimney of the sturdy brick house and falls into the boiling water in the "Three Little Pigs" excite in the reader no more sympathy than does Wile E. Coyote noticing that he has run off a cliff and waving good-bye as he plummets to the ground.

Animal-Related Institutions in Late Domesticity

The revulsion of cultivated English men and women against blood sports was the first step on the path that led to the attribution of full moral subjectivity to fictional animals à la *Black Beauty* and was what subsequently evolved into the postdomestic attribution of such moral subjectivity to all animals. However, there were many sights to see along the way. Harriet Ritvo recounts several significant episodes:

> If keeping a well-bred dog metonymically allied its owner with the upper ranges of society, then the elaborate structure of pedigree registration and show judging metaphorically equated owner with

elite pet. The institutions that defined the dog fancy projected an obsessively detailed vision of a stratified order which sorted animals and, by implication, people into snug and appropriate niches. Dog breeds were split and split again to produce categories in which competitive excellence could be determined. Aficionados of each breed developed a set of points prescribing the ideal toward which breeders should direct their efforts, and these ideals were publicly ratified and enforced in dog shows.[3]

The first dog show with over a thousand entries took place in Chelsea in 1863, only four years after the inaugural affair in Newcastle. (Earlier British get-togethers that focused on comparing ratters or other single breeds were too déclassé to count.)[4] Scotland's first shows were in Edinburgh and Glasgow in 1871. The number of shows of all sizes reached 217 in 1892 and 380 in 1899. Cat shows followed the same trajectory of growing enthusiasm. The Crystal Palace show of 1896, twenty-five years after the first such event, drew 740 entries. Closely specifying the physical characteristics of different breeds doubtless contributed to the "personification" of dogs and cats by breed, but shows based on looks diminished the earlier concern with a dog's ability to perform tasks like shepherding and game retrieving. Purebred dogs that conformed perfectly to the set standards won prizes and prestige for their owners. But the brave and resourceful dog of mixed breed retained its place in dog fiction.

A campaign for the humane treatment of animals anticipated the purebred pet craze. The Society for the Prevention of Cruelty to Animals received permission to prefix the term "Royal" to its name in 1840. The RSPCA's annual reports show that most prosecutions involved horses, donkeys, and (until 1854) dogs pulling carts in city streets, or abuses by butchers and drovers servicing city markets. Though mistreatment of cats and dogs amounted to only 2 percent of the cases, the reports signaled the growing separation of "companion animals" from other domestic beasts by devoting to these cases a disproportionate number (13 percent) of detailed descriptions. Refined society generally believed that the mistreatment of animals was a characteristic of the lower classes, without noticing that people of their own rank never worked as drovers, butchers, carriage-drivers, or carters.

Animal vivisection, increasingly seen by the medical community in the 1860s as a promising research tool, posed a difficult challenge to the RSPCA. The perpetrators of the vivisections were respected doctors

196 / Toward Postdomesticity

and physiologists, not lowly drovers, and the claim of great ultimate benefit to humanity could not easily be refuted. The society supported the Cruelty to Animals Act of 1876, but the act only required vivisectionists to apply for licenses, which were not difficult to get. That same year Frances Power Cobbe, a outspoken advocate of women's suffrage, established the Victoria Street Society for the Protection of Animals from Vivisection (now the National Anti-Vivisection Society), with Henry Edward Manning, a Roman Catholic cardinal and advocate of workers' rights, as her vice president. The issue of dogs, rabbits, and rats being tortured in scientific and medical experiments loomed less large then than it does now in comparison to mistreating cart-horses, because most animals have disappeared from view on city streets. But Cobbe's advocacy rested on moral grounds that went well beyond the laboratory:

> There is no argument in favor of Vivisection which does not apply more completely, more forcibly, to men than to animals. If the inferior is justly sacrificed to the higher, the legality of the surrender to scientific torture of idiots, criminals, those incurably diseased, and, indeed, all ignorant and brutalized men, including vivisectors, is beyond question.[5]

Cobbe wrote these words, which anticipate today's postdomestic militancy, in 1889 in *Vivisection in America*.[6] Five years later, the New England Antivivisection Society was formed. Once again, the United States followed the British lead on animal matters.

In considering these manifestations of new feelings about animals, it is important to keep in mind the lively public debate that followed upon the publication of Charles Darwin's *On the Origin of Species* in 1859. The challenge Darwinism presented to believers in the literal truth of the Bible in England is well known. In a United States soon to be immersed in civil war and reconstruction, however, Darwinism had a less immediate effect. To be sure, Harvard's Asa Gray, Darwin's strongest supporter, clashed with his faculty colleague, Louis Agassiz, who bitterly opposed him. Other scientists took their time in assessing the new theory, and theologians lagged still further behind.

> The majority of America's leading zoologists, botanists, geologists, and anthropologists within fifteen years or so embraced some kind of evolution, though few attached as much weight to natural selection as Darwin did.

Even Darwin's closest ally in North America, the Harvard botanist Asa Gray, who described himself as "one who is scientifically, and in his own fashion, a Darwinian," disagreed with Darwin on several key points. He not only questioned the ability of natural selection "to account for the formation of organs, the making of eyes, &c.," but appealed to a "special origination" in explaining the appearance of the first humans. He also urged Darwin, without success, to attribute to divine providence the inexplicable organic variations on which natural selection worked.

While naturalists debated the merits of evolution and the efficacy of natural selection, religious leaders typically sat on the sidelines, many of them doubting that evolution would ever be accepted as serious science. By the mid-1870s, however, American naturalists were becoming evolutionists in such large numbers that theologians could scarcely continue to ignore the issue. Some liberal Protestants, such as James McCosh, the president of Princeton University, sought ways to harmonize their doctrinal beliefs and their understanding of the Bible with evolution, often viewing evolution as simply God's method of creation. Most theologians and clergy, however, rejected evolution, especially of humans, or remained silent on the subject.[7]

Yet ideas like evolution and natural selection could not help but influence the thinking of people who were otherwise deeply involved with the humane movement or, in other cases, with defining the characteristics of different breeds of dogs and cats. Darwin drew much of the evidence he used to support his theory from domestic animal breeders. It stood to reason, therefore, that if humans and animals evolved according to the same natural process, as Darwin's supporters believed, and animal breeders in their selection for desirable traits were essentially imitating that process, then the distinction between humans and animals must simply be a matter of degree, and selective breeding of humans a feasible undertaking. Proponents of Social Darwinism, the doctrine stating that differences among human groups in power and prosperity result from natural selection, as embodied in the phrase "survival of the fittest," and of eugenics, the proposed science of selectively breeding superior humans, found audiences on both sides of the Atlantic. But the American response was more muted. Still a rural nation with strong religious roots and only a fledgling scientific community, the United States was more inclined to humanize animals, as writers of fiction were soon to do, than to animalize humans, as was implied by the new doctrine of considering humans to be but one among a myriad of animal species.

In 1896, a Dr. Samuel Johnson donated his orchard in Hartsdale, New York, for the first American pet cemetery. To date, more than 70,000 pets have been interred there, and some 600 currently active pet cemeteries answer the needs of grief-stricken pet owners. Pet cemeteries have enjoyed a similar level of popularity in Canada.[8] In Britain and Europe, however, such institutions are uncommon. Feminist Marguerite Durand founded Le Cimetière des Chiens at Asnières-sur-Seine just outside Paris in 1899. The World War I canine hero Rin-Tin-Tin is buried there. However, pet cemeteries are few and far between elsewhere in France.[9] As for Britain, though the royal family from Queen Victoria onward has made much of its affection for dogs, to the extent of memorializing some of them with stone monuments, and London's upper crust laid 300 pet dogs to rest in a Hyde Park cemetery between 1880 and its closing in 1915, elaborate memorializing of deceased pets has never become as institutionalized as in the United States. Britain's Association of Private Pet Cemeteries and Crematoria has only twenty to thirty members, each of which takes in an estimated twenty-five animals per year. The cemeteries are licensed as landfill sites under the Environment Protection Act.

In recent decades, the legend of Rainbow Bridge and the practice of pet-loss counseling have added a new dimension to American grieving over the loss of an animal friend. The text of the legend is anonymous and ubiquitous, but is probably traceable to an essay on "Pet Heaven," written by Wallace Sife in the 1980s:

> Just this side of heaven is a place called Rainbow Bridge. When a pet dies—one that's been especially close to someone here, that pet goes to Rainbow Bridge. There are meadows and hills for all of our special friends so they can run and play together. There is plenty of food, water and sunshine, and our friends are warm and comfortable, fear and worry free . . .
>
> But the day comes when one suddenly stops and looks into the distance. His bright eyes are intent, his eager body quivers. Suddenly he begins to run from the group, flying over the green grass, his legs carrying him faster and faster.

You have been spotted, and when you and your special friend
finally meet, you cling together in joyous reunion, never to be
parted again . . .

Then you cross Rainbow Bridge together.[10]

Some presentations of the text, which is distributed by many pet cemeteries and organizations offering pet-loss counseling, hint at an American Indian source for the legend; but no specific source has been put forward. A Google search ("rainbow bridge" + pet) makes it clear that the
Rainbow Bridge legend, unlike so many other American attitudes and
practices regarding animals, developed on this side of the Atlantic. Well
under 10 percent of the 53,700 hits deal with Britain.

Dog grooming tells the same story. Dog owners preparing their animals for shows became expert groomers in the nineteenth century, and
specific recommendations were put forward in *Kennel Secrets* by "Ash-
mont," a pen name for Perry Joseph, published in Boston in 1893. But
America's "doggie barbershops," as they were called before World War
II, catered to owners who just wanted to pamper their pets. According
to one listing, there are now over seventy pet grooming schools in the
United States and five more in Canada, as opposed to only two in the
United Kingdom.

The trend in the United States favored a celebration of the bond
between pet owners and pets—the more sensitive postdomestic term is
"companion animals." Hunters still use hunting dogs and seeing-eye dogs
assist the blind, but the stereotype of the American pet owner, as repeatedly seen in movies and television commercials, is the person who baby-
talks, pampers, communes with, dresses up, fusses over, and deeply
mourns his or her pet.

By contrast, in Britain, the animal welfare concerns that gained
prominence early in the nineteenth century maintained a prominence in
public discussion that had no parallel in the United States. The hunting
of foxes, badgers, and other wild mammals persisted as a key issue. The
League for the Prohibition of Cruel Sports was founded in 1924 by
Henry Amos and Ernest Bell, who were frustrated by the RSPCA's failure to address the matter. Eight years later, Bell and animal liberation
pioneer Henry Salt ("Have the lower animals 'rights'? Undoubtedly—if
men have.")[11] organized the National Society for the Abolition of Cruel
Sports (reorganized as Call for the Wild in 1984) to focus on public edu-

cation. With the end of World War II, the League began seriously to lobby Parliament. In the 1970s, League members got elected to the RSPCA council, and a campaign by the League and the RSPCA to outlaw the hunting of badgers passed Parliament in 1973, but with a loophole allowing trappers to escape prosecution by claiming they were after foxes. The campaign against hunting with dogs, that is, fox hunting, has continued to the present day, with Scotland finally enacting a ban in 2002, and England in 2004.

Though the United States, like many European countries, followed Britain's lead in enacting humane legislation and forming societies for the prevention of cruelty to animals in the nineteenth century, nothing resembling the campaign against fox hunting and related activities captured the public interest through the first two-thirds of the twentieth century. Hunting and gun owning were too well established in American life. Postdomestic anxiety about hunting burst out only in the 1970s, in a blizzard of publicity about Canadians, Norwegians, and Russians clubbing baby seals for their white pelts. The resulting save-the-seals campaign, like the simultaneous outcry against whaling, differed from the British assault on fox hunting in that the fox hunters were fellow Englishmen, while the seal clubbers and whalers were mostly not Americans.

Further detailing of the differences in tone and trajectory between British and American postdomesticity would only reinforce the point that particular circumstances and histories influence the ways in which people reshape their thinking about animals in the waning days of the domestic era. The argument has been made, however, that because a more general transition from late modernity to postmodernity subsumes all of the changes I have been associating with postdomesticity, nuances like these are unimportant. The British-trained sociologist Adrian Franklin, a professor at the University of Tasmania in Australia, presents the case for a postmodern alternative approach most astutely in *Animals and Modern Cultures* (1999). Drawing on a panoply of theoretical constructs devoted to constructing and deconstructing modernity, Franklin contrasts the work of historian Harriet Ritvo, whose work I, as a historian, find very appealing, with that of the British historical sociologist Keith Tester, who published *Animals and Society: The Humanity of Animal Rights* in 1991.[12]

Ritvo's technique centers on the significance of variations in human-animal relations, about which these [general sociological] theories have little to say. Her critique suggests that the only way we can understand change is by looking closely at the local and culturally contingent nature of change. Tester's critique is more penetrating. While acknowledging the critical significance of the historical and cultural variations, he builds on the contributions of social anthropology and Foucault to identify the essentially human and social content of human-animal relations in modernity. By suggesting that all cultural groups use animals to think through human conflicts and problems, Tester's analysis requires us to look closely at those who propose and enact change in human-animal relations, and the relationship between their views and social divisions of the day. Tester's approach was never applied rigorously to an analysis of change in the twentieth century, but class and cultural divisions and conflict were identified as the critical social contents of much reform in this area. As we consider more recent change we must add the salience of gender, ethnicity and nation. Tester's framework will be broadened in order to consider the links between changing human-animal relations and theories of postmodernity—in the same way that earlier change was linked to modernizing themes.[13]

After analyzing twentieth-century attitudes toward pets, hunting and fishing, the livestock and meat industries, and "the zoological gaze," or animals as a spectacle, Franklin concludes:

> We can identify two paradigm states of human-animal relations in the twentieth century, which correspond, approximately, to the social conditions of modernity and late or postmodernity. Relations in modernity were characterized by a relatively fixed and restricted series of interactions, with a relatively narrow range of species. Relations were dominated by the anthropocentric priorities of human progress and animals were largely the subject of human consumption and human entertainment. Sentiments were restricted to a narrow range of highly anthropomorphized and neotenized [i.e., bred for characteristics of immaturity] animals while most others were of interest as objects of use or scientific knowledge (the value of which was also tied to human progress). Neo-Romantic and neo-Darwinian doctrines originating in the nineteenth century continued to define a range of possible popular relations with animals in the twentieth century. While the for-

mer placed animals at the pinnacle of a human aesthetic of nature, the latter placed humans alongside animals as creatures of instinct, natural hunters and killers. Both doctrines, however, preached the conservation of animals and their habitats, which resulted in an uneasy alliance with respect to the preservation and use of "wild areas." They were essentially urban ideas and practiced by urbanites with new powers to visit natural areas and to commune with or consume animals—or both.

Postmodern relations with animals are the reverse, more or less. Postmodernity can be described as the fragmentation of the idea of progress and of the priority of humanity. The decentred sensibilities of postmodernity were caught up in acts of reflexive remodeling in relations to a range of "Others" (including people of different race, gender, age and sexual orientation) and, in turn, this reflexivity dissolved the former certainty of anthropocentricism in relations to animals. We found relations with animals to be expressive of new values: empathy, understanding, support, closeness. Sentiments expanded to include all or most forms of animals (how can we choose between them?); understanding and empathy extend to animals other than those with superficially human-like characteristics; our relations were dominated by a wish to know more about them but not merely for our advantage, and by our uncertainty as to the lines which separate humans and other animals.[14]

Aside from the density of the theory-laden prose, I see little to disagree with in Franklin's characterization of a nineteenth- and early twentieth-century society focused on the consumption of animal products, and to a lesser degree on blood sports as entertainment, and indifferent toward most other animal matters. Nor would I take issue with his analysis of an emerging alternative viewpoint in the late twentieth century that evinced greater interest in and empathy with animals of all sorts and questioned the primacy of human interests in the human-animal relationship. This is indeed what I have described as the passage from late domesticity to postdomesticity.

Where I disagree with Franklin is in his association of these two states with modernity on the one hand and late modernity/postmodernity on the other. Given the enormous weight of French and German theorists in the construction of models of both modernity and postmodernity, one would expect to find them abundantly cited. In fact, the only non-Anglo-Saxon 800-pound theory-gorillas whom Franklin draws into his analysis are Claude Lévi-Strauss, Jean-Paul Sartre, Pierre Bourdieu, Michel Foucault, and Norbert Elias—with the briefest of nods to Jean Baudrillard. However, none of these thinkers ever devoted a book to the question of animals or made them central to their theorizing. The fact that Franklin's bibliography contains eighty-seven books published in Britain, thirty-five published in the United States, ten published in Australia, and none published elsewhere reflects more than just a preference for working with English-language materials. Franklin's second paradigm does not, in fact, correspond to postmodernity in the continental European circles that have had the most influence in defining that much-debated cultural condition.

Animal liberationist Tom Regan introduces the book *Animal Others: On Ethics, Ontology, and Animal Life* in a way that makes the gap between Anglophone and continental thought very clear: "It has been my privilege to be one voice in the choir of analytic philosophers pressing for consideration of 'the animal question' . . . Here, for the first time, we have a volume where the tools of philosophy fashioned on the continent are used to explore the contours of our knowledge of, and encounters with, other than human animals."[15] Though Heidegger, Merleau-Ponty, Derrida, and others are cited in the papers that compose the book, the authors of the papers, along with Regan and the editor, H. Peter Steeves, all teach or study in the United States or other Anglophone countries.

This is not to say that animals are never included by continental philosophers in their discussions of problematic "Others." But the proposition that animals should receive a special theoretical consideration because they fall into the same category as women, children, people with disabilities, peoples of color, "Orientals," and gays and lesbians has so far found little resonance beyond the United Kingdom, the United States, Canada, Australia, and New Zealand.

It is possible, of course, that the Anglo-Saxon world simply represents the cutting edge of a new sensibility that will ultimately be adopted and given high priority in all postmodern circles. Would a country-by-country census of pet lovers and vegetarians, of wildlife rescuers and genetic engineering protesters, of humanized fictional animals and animal biographies, or of audiences for pornographies of blood and sex show a steady growth in these indicators in all industrial countries? From available evidence it does not seem so.

I do not believe that the mentality of postdomesticity can be predicted from a historical analysis of modernity alone. By assuming that it can, and by limiting his historical and geographical vision to the rise of modern society in Europe from the sixteenth century onward, Franklin violates his own construction of the late modern/postmodern paradigm of human-animal relations. "Our [paradigm two] relations," he writes, "were dominated by a wish to know more about [animals] but not merely for our advantage, and by our uncertainty as to the lines which separate humans and other animals." Yet by concentrating on Tester's insistence on identifying "the essentially human and social content of human-animal relations in modernity," Franklin loses sight of the animals themselves. Changing patterns of human-animal relations do indeed teach us about human societies, whether they are predomestic, domestic, or postdomestic. But they also reflect changing realities as to the place of the human species among all animal species. What our prehistoric forebears thought about animals thousands of years ago, what our great-grandparents thought about animals a century ago, what we think about animals today, and what our grandchildren will think about animals in decades to come has significance beyond our use of animals in human social rituals or economic processes. The fauna of the Earth have a past and a future of which we are but a part.

11. The Future of Human-Animal Relations

Where are human-animal relations headed? If the postdomestic era I have described is at all like the eras that preceded it, its development over the coming centuries cannot be extrapolated from its initial manifestations. In the short run, however, certain points of conflict between what is emerging and what is passing away are evident. Inspired by deep feelings of moral responsibility, supporters of animal liberation, many of them vegetarians or vegans, cannot be expected to abandon their cause and go back to eating Big Macs. Ever more forceful advocacy for their cause must be expected, and their moral stance is certain to gain increasing respect. Judging from past moral crusades in American history, it seems certain that activists on animal issues will increasingly seek to shape public policy. While many Americans are yet not prepared to see the cause of animal liberation succeeding to the righteous mantle of abolitionism, feminism, and civil rights—one could add temperance if it had not become discredited—it would not be surprising to see a reconsideration of this position in the coming years.

Collaboration between animal rights activism and a concern for ecology and the environment will seem logical to some activists, but not to all. Ecologists, for example, usually focus on the interaction of wild flora and fauna and have less to say about domestic species. Environmentalists, on the other hand, are often as concerned about the noxious effluents of animal-processing facilities as they are about preserving wild spaces. Yet neither ecologists nor environmentalists are likely to concern themselves, as some postdomestic animal activists do, with the extinction of domestic animal breeds. The prospect of losing forever some wild bird or insect that differs only minutely from a similar species arouses strong feelings, while the almost equally rapid disappearance of much more distinctive varieties of chicken or pig has yet to excite broad concern. Nevertheless, of the 4,184 (out of 6,379 listed) domestic animal breeds for which population data are listed in the Global Databank for Farm Animal Genetic Resources maintained by the Food and Agriculture Organization, 740 are already extinct and 1,335 are in danger of extinction—numbers that make up 49 percent of the total.[1]

From the point of view of the FAO, the rapid pace of extinction raises fears that there will be insufficient genetic diversity to deal with future problems of maintaining product yields. According to Irene Hoffmann, the Chief of the Animal Production Service: "The existing animal gene pool may contain valuable but unknown resources that could be very useful for future food security and agricultural development. Maintaining animal genetic diversity allows farmers to select stocks or develop new breeds in response to environmental change, diseases, and changing consumer demands."[2] Her concern, of course, is rooted in the product-oriented history of animal husbandry in the late domestic era.

As postdomestic concerns deepen, however, domestic animal breeds may come to be accorded the moral worth normally ascribed to wild species. And agricultural life as it was experienced before the rise of the factory farm may become as intriguing as trekking into the wilds to look at birds and mammals.[3] A perusal of Web sites describing programs worldwide to preserve local domestic breeds already reveals a mix of motives in which product-oriented biodiversity competes with a less utilitarian concern for preserving rare members of the earth's faunal community.[4] The Okeefe Ranch and Interior Heritage Society in British Columbia, for example, sees preservation as more than just a genetic diversity program:

> It is also important to preserve rare breeds from a heritage perspective. Many of the endangered breeds of livestock played a significant role in the development of Canada as an agricultural producer. The breeds were carefully developed and preserved by our ancestors. The preservation of these breeds for the generations to come is just as important as the preservation of buildings and artifacts of the past.[5]

Yet some facts will not alter in the foreseeable future. Urbanism, with its unavoidable isolation from animals, will remain a fact of postdomestic life. And most postdomestic people will continue to draw upon print and electronic media for animal experiences that extend beyond owning a pet or engaging in birdwatching. What those media will deliver will be but a pale substitute for the direct contact with animals that the human species has known for tens of thousands of years. The idea of a Jane Goodall gaining the trust of a group of chimpanzees or of a Biruté Galdikas communing with the orangutans she devoted her life to protecting will hint at what things were like in predomestic times. But their intrepid exploits have all been done in the name of science, which raises the question of whether the spiritual experience of animals that was part of predomesticity and eventually faded to nothingness in the domestic era is beyond recovery. The start of an answer may possibly be found in a consideration of the current state of human-animal relations in Japan.

The Japanese Way

Specialists on Japan are tired of hearing that Japanese society, psychology, or economic organization differ from that of the rest of the world. For every theory of European exceptionalism that has been used to "explain" why so much of the world's money, industry, and military might resides in European and American hands there is a parallel theory "explaining" why Japan, unlike the rest of the non-European world, has been able to pursue a separate path to modernity and in the process snag for itself a surprisingly large share of the world's money and industry. However, proving that the special qualities described by such theories actually exist and that they actually do explain what they are supposed to explain is very difficult.

Nevertheless, the history of human-animal relations in Japan is unique among complex literate societies. Though the Japanese have owned and used some domestic species for many centuries, their involvement with domestic animals in general was never extensive or intensive enough to give rise to a full-fledged domestic mentality. As the fourteenth-century essayist Kenko put it:

Domestic animals include the horse and the ox. It is a pity we must bind and afflict them, but unavoidable, since they are indispensable to us. You should certainly keep a dog; dogs are better than men at watching and protecting a house. However, every house already has a dog anyway, so you need not search for one especially for this purpose.

All other birds and beasts are useless.[6]

By useless, however, Kenko did not mean that animals were devoid of spiritual worth. The Confucian humaneness rooted in Mencius's story, related in chapter 7, of the king who out of compassion spared an ox on the way to sacrifice, comes out in the following comment:

As a rule, people who take pleasure in killing living creatures or making one creature fight another, are themselves akin to the beasts of prey. If we carefully observe the countless varieties of birds and beasts, even tiny insects, we shall discover that they love their children, long to be near their parents, that husband and wife remain together, that they are jealous, angry, greedy, self-seeking, and fearful for their own lives to an even worse degree than men because they lack intelligence. How can we not feel pity when pain is inflicted on them or people take their lives?

A man who can look on sentient creatures without feeling compassion is no human being.[7]

Just as the American Indian cultures of the Western Hemisphere that encountered European domestic animals only in the sixteenth century still retain many predomestic—that is, spiritual or affect-oriented—attitudes toward animals, Japanese culture today is able to draw on attitudes toward animals that seemingly derive from predomestic traditions, as reinforced by the Confucian principle of humaneness, Buddhist reverence for sentient life, and the Shinto belief in animal spirits. Thus not only are the postdomestic anxieties so evident in Britain and America comparatively insignificant in Japan, but cultural expressions of human-animal relations point to a future that may be quite different from that brewing in the Anglophone world. In support of these conclusions, I shall first outline the historical posture of the Japanese toward land animals, and then offer some illustrations from contemporary culture of their continuing access to spiritual animal traditions.

Despite the ubiquity of domestic pigs in most of eastern and southeastern Asia as well as the Pacific islands, including Japanese-owned Okinawa, the Japanese traditionally raised no pigs. Hunting wild boar, however, is an ancient practice that continues today. Sheep and goats, either domestic or wild, were similarly unknown. The horses that served as military mounts and draft animals were mostly raised in the territory of the Emishi on the island of Honshu's wild northeastern frontier. The Emishi are thought by many scholars to be the ancestors of the indigenous non-Japanese Ainu people who once lived in northern Honshu but now live still farther to the north on the island of Hokkaido. The Ainu are a foraging people who are known to sacrifice bears, wolves, and owls.

Oxen were more common than horses as plow and cart animals, and palanquins carried by human bearers were preferred for elite personal transport. Even in the late nineteenth century the emperor traveled by palanquin. Though they raised both cattle and horses, the Japanese seldom ate either beef or horsemeat. Moreover, they did not consume milk products. Without a dairy industry, young male animals were castrated and used for labor rather than being slaughtered for veal. As a consequence, such beef and horsemeat as was consumed came from worn-out work animals and was of very low quality.

The dogs mentioned by Kendo were like the pariah dogs of India: ubiquitous in villages and residential neighborhoods, but undifferentiated by breed and mostly unowned and unexploited. In contrast to the neighboring Koreans, whose delight in dog soup overrode public-relations pressure to hide the practice from foreigners attending the 2002 World Cup, the Japanese do not normally eat dog meat. The overall disinclination of the Japanese to adopt the dietary regimens and animal husbandry practices of China and Korea is all the more remarkable in light of the phenomenal amount of cultural borrowing from those cultures that took place in other aspects of life.

These traditional practices began to change after Commodore Matthew Perry's 1854 fleet visit forced Japan to open up to foreign influences. Woodcuts of the period show a particular interest in the pet dogs brought in by European visitors. Dietary habits, however, were slow to change. Palace documents record the precise date on which the westernizing Meiji emperor (1868–1912) first tasted beef and drank milk, and neither became common at his dinner table. Indeed, after a century of exposure to the West, industrial growth, and urbanization, culminating in the spread of American cultural practices introduced by the post–World War II military occupation (1945–1951), by 1965 annual per capita meat consumption, excluding seafood, was still only 14 pounds, a level comparable to that of some of the world's poorest countries. Thirty years later, after an astounding economic boom had transformed Japan into a leading economic power, Japanese meat consumption had risen to 67.5 pounds, with pork and chicken more popular than beef, but this figure was still little more than one-third the American level.

In the Buddhist tradition, some of Japan's early emperors tried to curtail the killing of animals. Dr. Hoyt Long reports the following entries from early chronicles:

- 675 C.E.: Emperor Temmu restricts the use of certain hunting devices (for example, pitfalls, spear-traps, and fish-traps) and the eating of cow, horse, dog, and monkey meat.
- 741 C.E.: Emperor Shomu orders prohibitions against hunting and fishing on the fast days of the month.
- 764 C.E.: A proclamation is issued in an attempt to alleviate the emperor's illness and extend his life; it calls for a five-month moratorium on the killing of living things and the use of deer or wild boar as sacrificial tribute items.
- 780 C.E.: A proclamation is issued which calls for an end to the use of dogs and hawks in hunting practices and suggests that the use of any animal or fish meat as ritual offerings should be stopped. Though the political reasons underlying this proclamation are unclear, it can be interpreted as an extension of recent prohibitions on eating meat made against monks and nuns.[8]

Preference for seafood was probably more important than these occasional bans in limiting the amount of meat in the Japanese diet. As vegetarians from the West have been baffled to learn, despite their Buddhist religious tradition, Japanese have a difficult time understanding a vegan's aversion to eating all animals. The Japanese word for vegetarian is directly borrowed from English, and attempts to expound vegetarian lifestyles reportedly find an uncomprehending reception. One foreign visitor laments, "Being vegan in Japan is extremely tough. It is probably the most difficult place I have ever been to try and eat a vegan diet. . . . As far as eating out . . . I understood that just about all noodle dishes were made with fish flakes and meat stock. . . . I quickly gave up eating Japanese and went to Indian restaurants."[9] Another vegetarian laments, "I have a very hard time going to restaurants here. Some might be willing to accommodate me if I tried, but I find I'm too shy to even ask. The fact that none of my other friends is vegetarian makes it more difficult. While there are a growing number of people who eat fish but avoid meat, true vegetarians like me are still thought of as radical."[10] The president of the Japan Vegetarian Society adopted his dietary practice after experiences in the United States and cites Seventh Day Adventist dietary rules as a primary influence.[11]

Westerners sensitized to postdomestic animal issues might also find it odd that in a country that has never depended heavily on land animals, hunting and trapping are licensed activities that are neither commonly indulged in nor actively protested against. Whale hunting, on the other hand, stirs national feelings. Whale meat is a traditional food, and the Japanese government has frequently opposed international restrictions. But this has not prevented Japanese scientists from expressing great interest in the dolphin communication theories of John C. Lilly, with their implicit recognition of dolphins as very advanced mammals.

Pet ownership also follows a peculiarly Japanese trajectory. For animals to have around the home and value for their striking appearance, Japanese have traditionally favored fish. The selective breeding of carp with red, orange, yellow, and black markings began in the seventeenth century among farmers who were raising the fish for meat. The ornamental carp were known as *koi* or *nishikigoi*. In time, seventeen major breeds, each with several subbreeds, came to be recognized.[12] The rarest of these command very high prices. Though Americanization after World War II spurred an increased interest in dogs, fish remain the favorite animals. In 1996, 21.1 percent of Japanese families—almost half of all pet owners—owned goldfish (*kinyo*) or *koi*, as compared to just 12 percent of American households keeping fish of any sort.

Dogs and cats have recently gained popularity as pets in the context of a boom in pet ownership of all kinds that began in the early 1990s. By 1996, 49.1 percent of all Japanese households had some pet. This figure approaches the 59 percent pet-ownership level of the United States. The Japanese electronics industry has also developed virtual pets and robot pets, including imaginary beings like the Tamagochi ("Loveable Egg") animal.[13] In all of these cases, however, the notion of an animating spirit is more pronounced than in Western pet traditions.

Attitudes toward dogs exemplify this difference. Prior to the nineteenth century, dogs showed little variation in breed and served primarily as hunters, watchdogs, and contestants in organized dog fights. Naturalists debated the issue of how dogs differed from wolves. In 1908, dog fights were banned, and in 1931, the Akita became the first Japanese breed to be officially recognized. Nine Akitas were identified as "national treasures." Since then, nine other breeds have been recognized by the Japan kennel club: about half look like Akitas, and aside from one import from China, the other half stem from interbreeding with imported Western dogs.[14]

Pet cemeteries, grooming salons, and dog shows have come into being to service the growing popularity of dogs as pets. Newly developed cemetery practices betray the special quality of the Japanese pet sensibility. Instead of stone monuments set in a grassy park, pet cemeteries allocate small niches to cremated remains and feature photographs of the deceased animal as the primary memorial. In a presentation analyzing the genre of deceased pet photographs, anthropologist Richard Chalfen writes:

> In Buddhism there are different sects and some sects believe that animals are reincarnations of their great ancestors. For this reason, the owners of the pet cannot let others take care of their pet after it dies. They think that an evil spell will be cast upon the family if they don't bury the animals properly. This Buddhist sect allows people to put the ashes of the human being and the pets in the same family altar. Other Buddhist sects will be furious if they saw a picture of a dog in the *butsudan* (family altar). Because they believe that animals have their own heaven, paradise, or kingdom after they die and the same goes for human beings.[15]

The development of these distinctive funeral practices derives in part from an idea of dog spirits that long preceded modern pet keeping. In the waning years of the Tokogawa shogunate, before Admiral Perry and the opening to the West, a popular writer named Kyokutei Bakin (1767–1848) penned *The Eight Dog Chronicles* (in Japanese, *Nanso Satomi Hakkenden*—literally "The Chronicles of the Eight Dog Heroes of the Satomi Clan of Nanso") in 106 volumes from 1814 to 1842. Enjoying phenomenal popularity in its own time, the serial was transformed into a televised puppet drama in 1973 and an anime cartoon epic (420 minutes) in 1993.

The root of the story lies in the Lotus Sutra, a book containing teachings of the Buddha that was translated into Chinese in 405 C.E. and went on to become a key text in Chinese and Japanese Buddhism. Among the stories it contains is that of the dragon king's eight-year-old daughter. (Dragons [*nagas*] were one of the eight kinds of nonhuman beings spoken of in Buddhist folklore.) When a learned monk scoffs at the suggestion that a little, nonhuman female could ever achieve enlightenment, a state that earlier Buddhist teachings describe as the labor of a lifetime and open to men only, the girl replies: "Employ your supernatural powers and watch me attain Buddhahood. It will be even quicker than that!"

> At that time the assembly all saw the dragon girl in the space of an instant change into a man and carry out all the practices of a bodhisattva, immediately proceeding to the Spotless World of the south, taking a seat on a jeweled lotus, and attaining impartial and correct enlightenment. With the thirty-two features and the eighty characteristics, he expounded the wonderful Law for all living beings everywhere in the ten directions.[16]

The translator remarks: "Once again the Lotus Sutra reveals that its revolutionary doctrines operate in a realm transcending all petty distinctions of sex or species, instant or eon."[17]

The Eight Dog Chronicles opens in 1441.[18] Yoshizane, the leader of the Satomi clan, vanquishes his foes and becomes a benevolent ruler. However, he reneges on a promise to spare the previous ruler's wife, and with her execution looming, the woman levels a curse: the members of the Satomi clan will become "dogs of worldly desire." A few years later, Yoshizane adopts a male puppy and names it Yatsufusa ("Eight Spots"). What he does not know is that after the dog's mother was killed, the dog was nursed by a raccoon, and the spirit of the executed woman passed from the raccoon into the dog.

More years pass and Yoshizane makes a rash promise to give his daughter to whoever will rid him of an enemy general. Yatsufusa brings in the general's head, and Yoshizane's daughter, Fusehime, insists that her father remain true to his promise—as he failed to do years before—even though it will mean her marrying a dog. So dog and daughter go off into the mountains as husband and wife to live alone in the wilds. The daughter takes with her nothing but the clothes on her back, a knife with which to kill herself if the dog assaults her sexually, and a text of the Lotus Sutra, along with brush, ink, and paper to make additional copies:

> Feeling lonely and depressed, Fusehime spent her first night at the front of the cave reading the Lotus Sutra by the light of the moon. Around her neck she wore the string of crystal prayer beads she had received as a girl from the mountain god En no Guoja. Shortly after the dog had killed her father's enemy, the eight largest of the beads—each of which had earlier displayed a written character

214 / The Future of Human-Animal Relations

with one of the eight Confucian virtues—had suddenly shown eight characters forming the words "Animals can achieve enlightenment". . . . Early the next morning, Yatsufusa left the cave and went down into the valley. There he picked berries, fern roots, and other edible things and brought them back to Fusehime between his teeth and placed them before her. He did the same thing the next day, and the next. After he had been doing this for more than a hundred days, he gradually began to listen to the words of the Lotus Sutra that Fusehime was chanting. Eventually his [carnal] desire seemed to clear from his mind, and he never again stared at Fusehime in that way.[19]

Meanwhile, a suitor in the court of Fusehime's father discovers where she and the dog are living and undertakes to kill the dog and rescue Fusehime. What no one knows, however, is that Fusehime has, without any sexual contact, become pregnant and is carrying in her womb eight "empty," or formless, souls. When the suitor reaches the cave, he kills Yatsufusa and unintentionally inflicts a mortal wound on Fusehime. Fusehime then contributes to her own demise:

Fusehime reached for her short sword, unsheathed it, and thrust it into her belly. She moved the blade sideways, cutting herself open in a straight line. A strange white mist rushed out of the wound. Undulating, the mist enveloped the string of 108 crystal prayer beads around her neck and lifted them up into the air. Suddenly the string broke and fell to the ground, carrying with it a hundred clattering beads. The eight larger beads remained in the air, giving off light and circling. Their paths crossed as if they were bright comets passing through the sky. . . . As they [her father, the suitor, etc.] watched entranced, a harsh wind roared down from the mountains and carried off the eight soul-lights in different directions until they disappeared from sight. Finally, only the early evening moon remained above the mountains in the east. This was the beginning of the eight dog-heroes who would appear separately in the world and years later gather together in the Satomi clan.[20]

The remainder of the saga tells how the eight dog-heroes—each has a name starting with *inu*, the Japanese word for dog—make their way in the world, identify one another, and reclaim the rights of the Satomi clan.

The Eight Dog Chronicles provides a background for understanding the development in the twentieth century of a "national dog" as the embodiment of Japanese warrior culture. Building upon an incident in which dogs accompanying a military unit were believed to have died heroically in combat alongside their trainers, the Japanese militarists of the 1930s declared the dogs to be Akitas—they were actually German Shepherds—and to be worthy models of national loyalty. Children were all exposed to the story of these "modern" dog-warriors, and there was no room for doubting that dogs could act consciously on behalf of the nation.[21] It was in this connection, unrelated to any definition proposed by dog breeders, that Akitas were recognized as "national treasures" in 1931.

Cats make a similar spiritual transfer from premodern to modern times. The practice of placing a figurine of a Maneki Neko, or "Beckoning Cat," as a protective spirit at the entrance of inns and restaurants dates back for centuries. Legend holds that one stormy night, a cat saved an emperor (or a samurai, or just a traveler, according to variants of the legend) from being struck by lightning when it beckoned to him from the doorway of an inn and caused him to get off his horse. Shinto belief credited the cat with being a divine spirit (*kami*), and the "beckoning cat" became the "patron saint," as it were, of places of public accommodation. In addition, Buddhist monasteries commonly kept cats and some had cat cemeteries.

Though Maneki Neko figurines are still readily available, the modern transformation of the cat as a benevolent spirit manifests itself in the Hello Kitty (pronounced in Japanese *Harro Kitei*) phenomenon. Hello Kitty is a cartoon figure, a mouthless white kitten with a red hair-ribbon. The Sanrio Company introduced the character in 1974 and it is now featured on all sorts of consumer products, from toilet paper to kitchen appliances to fax machines, earning Sanrio one billion dollars a year in royalties.[22] The overwhelming popularity of this animal icon in Japan and among many youthful Americans is all the more startling in view of its having no history or story. Unlike Mickey Mouse or Bugs Bunny, there are no Hello Kitty movies or comic books. Hello Kitty is a spirit icon more than a humanized cartoon animal, and as such it far outdistances its companion figures like Keroppi the frog, Pochaco the dog, and Bad Batz-Maru the penguin, among others, in popularity.

More generally, the feline spirit has a strong affinity for the feminine in Japanese popular culture. Whether in comic books and video games or on Internet sites, representing girls with cat ears and tails is common-place. Unlike the Catwoman character in the United States, however, there is nothing inherently sinister or dangerous about a female in her cat incarnation.

In addition to keeping in touch with the domestic animal spirits of pre-modern times, Japanese popular culture is able to draw unselfconsciously on shamanist traditions that have long disappeared in most other parts of the world. I will cite two examples. Hayao Miyazaki's animated feature film *Princess Mononoke* (1997) won the Japanese "Best Picture of the Year" award and set box office records. It enjoyed a much more modest success in its American release. The film tells the story of a young Emishi (Ainu) prince in the wild north who finds himself caught in a struggle between Lady Eboshi, whose ironworks are denuding the hillsides and polluting the air, but who provides jobs to lepers and redeemed prosti-tutes, and Princess Mononoke, a shamanistic girl who lives with wolves and stands militantly alongside the animals and forest gods in defending the wilderness. The prince rides a reindeer; the princess rides a wolf.

Beneath this environmental parable lies a Buddhist story of great antiquity, one of a number of tales designed to illustrate *ongaeshi*, or the act of repaying a favor. According to Hoyt Long, "the standard plot structure of these tales, in which a human rescues from peril a member of the animal kingdom and is then rewarded in some way by the grateful animal, relies on interaction between humans and animals (e.g., the sharing of language, the sharing of moral principles)."[23] No specific men-tion of this narrative tradition is made in the film, and it was unknown, of course, to American audiences.

In the film, the god of the forest takes the daytime form of a magnif-icent deer with fantastic antlers. Far, far away, the Japanese emperor has heard of this magical deer and has sent a wily and unscrupulous hunter to kill it and bring back its head. Valuing the patronage of the emperor, the Lady Eboshi undertakes to help the hunter kill the deer. A further unspoken resonance with Japanese culture links the deer to the predo-mestic, pre-Buddhist Yayoi era (circa the fourth century B.C.E. to the third century C.E.), when the shoulder blades of deer were used as div-inatory oracle bones. According to Long:

> There is overwhelming evidence that for inhabitants of provinces
> surrounding the capital, deer served an essential symbolic role as
> mediator between the secular and spiritual worlds. For example,

there are many accounts of place name origins that involve the sighting of a deer as the impetus for naming the location, an indication that deer were seen as closely tied to the land gods of a particular region. Other accounts reveal that deer were considered exceptional listeners, so exceptional that their ears were thought to be a means by which human's prayers could be heard by the gods. The overlap of the deer's mating and growth cycle with the harvest cycle of rice [a Yayoi innovation] seems to have contributed to the practice in certain provinces of sacrificing deer in ceremonies for agricultural prosperity. We also know that the deer, as a manifest symbol of the land gods occupying an area, was closely connected to the power of a ruler. This power was reaffirmed through ceremonial hunts in which a ruler symbolically usurped the power of the local gods by killing the deer. Despite the fact that the deer's spiritual potential was often realized by the sacrifice of its own life, it is apparent that whether living or dead, the deer retained an intimate connection to the spiritual world as mediator with and messenger of the gods.[24]

The Buddhist tale of a divine deer originated in India and was rendered into Chinese before it reached Japan. A deer with white horns and nine-colored hair once lived in the forest, unknown to the people of the surrounding kingdom. One day a man was caught in the torrent of a river and the deer rescued him. The man asks what he can do to repay the favor and the deer simply asks him to keep his existence secret. The man complies with this request until the Queen dreams of the deer and demands of the King that he capture it. The man learns of the reward the King is offering and volunteers to lead the hunt. Taken by surprise while asleep, the deer accepts its fate and prepares to die. Then the King observes that it is no ordinary deer and declines to shoot. When the deer finds out who has led the hunt, he chastises the man for forgetting the deer's kindness in rescuing him from the river. Hearing the tale, the King bans the killing of all deer in his realm under penalty of death.

After that, the rain fell at the appropriate times in the kingdom and no wild winds ever blew. Within the kingdom there was no more sickness, the five grains grew in abundance, and there was not a poor person in the land. So it is that those who forget *on* [an act of kindness] are of the human realm and those who help humans are of the animal (*kemono*) realm.[25]

In *Princess Mononoke*, the hand of the King's huntsmen is not stayed. Lady Eboshi kills the divine deer and the forest begins to die. But the wily hunter's attempt to bring the deer's head back to the emperor fails, as the Emishi prince and Princess Mononoke help the angry forest god to retrieve his head. Once again the forest blossoms, but the irontown of Lady Eboshi is swept away by the god's wrath.

Hayao Miyazaki strayed far from the edifying Buddhist legend in conceiving of his animated environmental parable. Yet he was able to draw the substance of the story from the inner resources of Japanese religious culture. He did not have to borrow from somewhere else to find a spiritual linkage between humans, animals, and the environment, as Disney had to do, mining African tales for *The Lion King*.

My second example is Haruki Murakami's prizewinning novel *A Wild Sheep Chase*, published in 1982. It presents a different take on the Japanese capacity to conceive of human-animal relations outside the paradigms of domesticity and western postdomesticity. Critics who have celebrated the international character of Murakami's fiction have noted its seemingly acultural construction, in which Japan often seems to be only an incidental setting. The protagonists, often nameless, swig Heinekens and ponder the lyrics of Beatles songs. But Murakami's imagined sheep is all Japanese.

The story involves a quest for a sheep that appears in an advertising photograph shot somewhere on the island of Hokkaido in the far north, Japan's symbolic wild frontier. A billionaire industrialist with a shady background pays a partner in the small advertising company to find the sheep, but does not tell him why it is important. In searching for the sheep, the rootless and aimless protagonist uncovers the history of sheep-raising in Japan. Sheep had been introduced to Hokkaido before World War II as a military project, to produce wool for army uniforms. The project enjoyed some minor success but faded away after Japan's defeat. However, according to Murakami, among the sheep that had been imported from Manchuria was a singular animal of great malevolence, a seemingly immortal sheep that could take full mental possession of a human being. In thrall to this supernatural sheep, the victim of the moment enjoyed great success up to the time when the sheep chose to abandon him. After this, life was not worth living.

As the protagonist nears his goal in the wintry mountains, he encounters the Sheep-Man, a hermit visionary who dresses as a sheep and communes with them. Following clues from this shamanistic figure, the protagonist finally discovers that the demonic sheep is the incarnation of militaristic evil, which in this telling entered Japan from abroad, having in earlier centuries inspired the likes of Genghis Khan. The unnamed billionaire industrialist, whom the sheep has abandoned and who is now on his deathbed, attained his fortune through the sheep's machinations and became a Class A war criminal, one of many who were identified but not tried after World War II. More recently, he had been a financial supporter of neofascist movements.

Could a Western novelist born into a domestic society, with or without a postdomestic sensibility, ever have imagined a sheep as the metaphor of militaristic genius and evil incarnate? Anglophone writers would have to contend with their own language. Usages like "sheepish," "mutton-headed," "wooly thinking," "like a flock of sheep," and "like sheep to the slaughter" derive from a domestic view of sheep as extraordinarily stupid and totally governed by herd instincts. The average Japanese reader, having no sheep in his or her cultural background, would not be burdened by such stereotypes. To be sure, an absurdist writer, in a moment of irony, might happen upon the notion of a metaphorically omnipotent sheep. But turning the conceit into an allegory in which Japan's turn toward militarism is attributed to foreign influences, those influences symbolized by Japanese importation of an unfamiliar domestic animal, is a tour de force that could only make sense in Japan. Murakami's novels do indeed transcend national identity, but *A Wild Sheep Chase* conveys a distinctly Japanese message that is not at all obvious to non-Japanese readers: beware of foreign borrowings that bring short-term riches but carry with them the virus of (revived) militarism.

In both *Princess Mononoke* and *A Wild Sheep Chase*, the shamanistic character supports rather than motivates the plot. The Sheep-Man appears again as an oracular, advice-giving figure in Murakami's *Dance, Dance, Dance* (1994). What this signifies is the openness in contemporary Japanese culture toward souls crossing or living astride the human-animal boundary. And this in turn may foreshadow a very different future for Japanese human-animal relations than can currently be visualized for the postdomestic West. Postdomesticity as it has so far developed problematizes the human-animal divide in its science, its philosophy, and its politics. But it never truly erases it. A companion animal or a fictional flock can be humanized and animals can be seen as metaphors for human dilemmas. But for all the talk of humankind being a species of animal, the legacy of domesticity has shut the door on specific humans actually being or becoming animals, except in cases like Kafka's *Meta-morphosis*, where irony is the dominating motif. The many millennia of the domestic era effectively erased once-vital memories of animals and human-animal hybrids as mediators with or dwellers in the unseen spirit world.

The Future of the Postdomestic Imagination

In *Princess Mononoke* and *A Wild Sheep Chase*, animals have great spiritual power. Humans, some of them shamanistic and half-animal themselves, can commune with animals, and animal characters can carry the burden of serious allegory without being marinated in the treacle of Disney cuteness. The giant hog of Jane Smiley's novel *Moo* (1995), placidly consuming its swill in an Iowa State University barn, flirts with such weightiness, but the context of ag-school faculty politics and experiments to improve milk yields is thoroughly postdomestic.

Despite the efforts of postdomestic philosophers and scientists to erase the human-animal divide inherited from the domestic era, no work of imagination has yet recovered the predomestic spiritualization of animals that informs the work of Miyazaki and Murakami. Both of the Japanese examples draw on the place of animals in Japanese history and use spiritualized animals to address contemporary concerns, and both were phenomenally well received. No domestic or postdomestic writer or artist in the West has achieved anything comparable. Nor does the path taken by Miyazaki and Murakami look promising for non-Japanese. Western domestic and postdomestic audiences have difficulty appreciating the weight of Miyazaki's and Murakami's animal characters.

Are there other directions to travel that do not depend on the peculiar Japanese innocence of domesticity's final degradation of animals? Donald Kingsbury's Hugo-nominated science fiction novel *Courtship Rite* or *Geta* (1982) visualizes a human society on a faraway planet in a future so distant that recollections of migration from Earth have virtually disappeared. The story focuses on social relations of two sorts: multiple-partner marriages and ritual cannibalism. The latter practice evolved because the native fauna and flora of the planet are for the most part poisonous to humans. Hence, all human sustenance comes from the handful of domestic plant species the first settlers brought with them. If they brought animals as well, they didn't survive. So aside from a few vegetarians, humans satisfy their taste for animal protein and fat through eating one another. As distasteful as the subject might seem, the visualization of meat eating as a form of reverencing and remembering the animal provider of the meat—in this case a human being—effectively conveys a sense of the role that sacrifice and meat eating may have played in late predomestic and early domestic society.

The story also raises the question of how real-life humans of the twenty-first century will solve the problem of food supply in planning and possibly carrying out the colonization of other parts of the solar system. Science fiction generally populates other planets with their own fauna and provides on-board pets, most often cats, for space travelers, who make their meals from stuff that comes out of machines or from the harvest of hydroponic gardens. Meat animals convert vegetable matter into food with too little efficiency to make their off-planet export plausible. Thus a nearly total termination of human-animal relations may be in store for the tiny number of persons who eventually spend a significant portion of their lives away from Earth. We may hope that they will not react to this by deciding to eat one another.

Frank Di Silvestro's *Boy Jesus and His Dog* (1998) appeals to an entirely different segment of the postdomestic audience, American Catholic children. As the story begins, Mary is concerned about Jesus feeding food scraps to wild dogs.

> Day and night in Nazareth and its outskirts wild dogs in noisy packs haunted the streets, alleys, and garbage dumps. When humans approached them too closely, they snarled with the intention of maiming them. Because these dogs were pests and scavengers, Israelites loathed and viewed them with total disgust. They were filthy and likely they would have killed these feral animals, but they served a good purpose. They daily devoured the garbage and waste thrown in the streets. They fought ferociously with the jackals, leopards, wolves, and vipers that occasionally came down from the hills to prey upon the livestock.
>
> Many years went by before the descendants of these wild dogs became tame and man's best friend. From time to time, however, an amenable dog was domesticated. Shepherds made occasional use of dogs to help guard and handle their sheep. But most dogs in those ancient days generally distrusted human beings. They had no familiarity with the human-dog bond we have today. Yet, in

spite of their savagery, they developed a trusting relationship with boy Jesus. Only he could safely approach them.[26]

Then an angel carrying a dog in its arms appears in a dream and tells Jesus that there is one dog who needs his love. Jesus finds the dog and names it Angel. His painstaking efforts to win the animal's confidence come to naught, however, when Angel runs away. But the prodigal eventually returns, battered and starving, and Jesus is thrilled. This time he successfully wins Angel's love.

> Angel sat contentedly beside Boy Jesus with his head resting on the boy's thigh and his tail lazily thumping the ground. In silence, Joseph had been staring thoughtfully at the dog. Finally he said, "A dog's love is sometimes even greater than a human being's love."
>
> Joseph's words touched Mary's heart. Resting her eyes on the dear animal, she added, "And Angel's love is unconditional."
>
> In response to their words, Boy Jesus said, "His love comes from God the Father."
>
> "All love does," Mary sweetly reminded her son.
>
> "Yes, yes," the boy quickly agreed. "All love does."
>
> Joseph was still staring thoughtfully at the dog as he now said, "Jesus, you have the best friend in the world right there at your side . . ."
>
> As Mary gazed at the heavens, a long silence ensued. Then, as if stating a divine prophecy, she announced, "Someday, dogs like Angel will bring love and happiness to people all over the world."
>
> Joseph also gazed at the glorious sky, responding in the same prophetic tone: "And dogs will be cherished as loving companions. They'll be loyal helpers and watchful protectors."
>
> "And dogs will be faithful friends to people everywhere," Boy Jesus also prophesied as he closed his eyes. He saw in the future countless children and adults enjoying the undying love and companionship of dogs everywhere in the world. As he slowly opened his eyes and looked heavenward, his heart was filled with great joy. For he knew his Heavenly Father had been sharing his glorious vision.[27]

The plot twists when a refugee from the revolt against Roman rule of a false Messiah appears and announces that Angel is really his long lost dog Olive. " 'When I left home to follow Judas,' Jacob continued, 'I left everything behind, including my dog. I felt it was God's plan that I sacrifice Olive for the love of my Messiah.' "[28] Boy Jesus is deeply saddened to see Angel (now Olive again) depart with Jacob, but a potter consoles him with the gift of a jug bearing a likeness of Angel and Boy Jesus together—the same picture that is on the book's cover. Boy Jesus says, " 'I feel Angel is with me right now.' 'So do I,' Mary said, 'His spirit is in that jug.' "[29]

The Romans arrest Jacob as a rebel and sentence him and Olive to death. Boy Jesus rushes forward to offer his life for theirs, but the Roman commander declares both Jacob and the dog are innocent. Subsequently, Jacob falls ill. He gazes at his beloved Olive and then says to Jesus that he only wished he had lived long enough to see the true Messiah. Jesus replies, "Jacob, you've seen the Messiah. You're looking at him. . . . I promise you this . . . you and Angel will be with me in paradise."[30]

Unlike the works by Miyazaki and Murakami, *Courtship Rite* and *Boy Jesus and His Dog* have not enjoyed runaway market success and wide acclaim. Their tortured plot contrivances testify to the challenge authors face in respiritualizing meat eating, on the one hand, and raising postdomestic idolization of pets to a divine level, on the other. Few readers are prepared to suspend their disbelief sufficiently to embrace Kingsbury's vision of slaughtering below-average children for meat, and only those who are prepared to finesse two millennia of Christian theology will feel comfortable with pet dogs inheriting the kingdom of Heaven along with their masters. What these works testify to is not an emerging postdomestic understanding of human-animal relations but rather the obstacles the postdomestic imagination confronts in trying to reach beyond the themes of domestic animal exploitation, affection for pets (short of divinization), and the narration of human stories using humanized animal characters.

The future of human-animal relations in real-world terms will be determined by the worldwide expansion of exploitation in a late domestic mode and the reaction to that expansion by increasingly angry postdomestic activists. At the present time, neither camp has reason for optimism. There is no middle ground between meatpackers and vegetarians, hunters and mink liberators, pharmaceutical companies and opponents of experimentation on animals. Philosophers, scientists, writers, and filmmakers have been drawn into the maelstrom. But in the imaginative realm, the heritage of the late domestic era, with its herds of symbolically degraded beasts being transformed into industrial commodities, has left the creative mind with little to build upon. It will take true genius to rediscover the magic of the predomestic era, when animals communed with gods, half-animal beings commanded respect, and killing inspired awe and incurred guilt.

Notes

1. Postdomesticity: Our Lives with Animals

1. Lois Gordon and Alan Gordon, *The Columbia Chronicles of American Life, 1910–1992* (New York: Columbia University Press, 1995), 558.

2. The 1650–1500 B.C.E. laws of the Hittites, who lived in what is today Turkey, show uncommon nuance: "If anyone have intercourse with a pig or a dog, he shall die. If a man have intercourse with a horse or a mule, there is no punishment. But he shall not approach the king, and shall not become a priest. If an ox spring upon a man for intercourse, the ox shall die but the man shall not die. One sheep shall be fetched as a substitute for the man, and they shall kill it. If a pig spring upon a man for intercourse, there is no punishment." In Oliver J. Thatcher, ed., *The Library of Original Sources*, vol. 3, *The Roman World* (Milwaukee: University Research Extension Co., 1901), 9–11. As quoted and edited online by J. S. Arkenberg, "Ancient History Sourcebook," http://www.fordham.edu/halsall/ancient/1650nesilim.html.

3. Havelock Ellis, *Studies in the Psychology of Sex*, vol. 3 (1900–1913; repr., New York: Random House, 1936), 79.

4. Sheila Fitzpatrick, "Sex and Revolution: An Examination of Literary and Statistical Data on the Mores of Soviet Students in the 1920s," *Journal of Modern History* 50, no. 2 (June 1978): 275.

5. Ibid., 267–268.

6. Ellis, *Studies*, 3:72–73.

7. See Lisa Sigel, "The Autobiography of a Flea," http://eserver.org/cultronix/sigel/.

8. Dick King-Smith, *Babe: The Gallant Pig* (New York: Crown, 1985). Originally published in Britain as *The Sheep-Pig* (London: Victor Gollancz, 1983).

9. Michael Pollan, "Power Steer," *New York Times Magazine*, March 31, 2002.

10. Thomas More, *Utopia*, ed. and trans. by David Wootton (Indianapolis: Hackett, 1999) 104.

11. *Telegraph* (Calcutta), October 5, 1998.

12. http://www.gallupindependent.com/9–06–01.html#anchor1.

13. For a thorough and largely materialistic analysis of food taboos, see Frederick Simoons, *Eat Not This Flesh: Food Avoidances from Prehistory to the Present*, 2nd ed. (Madison: University of Wisconsin Press, 1994); and, by the same author, *Plants of Life, Plants of Death* (Madison: University of Wisconsin Press, 1998).

14. Mindy Sink, "Losing Meat, but Keeping a Child's Diet Balanced," *New York Times*, July 25, 2000, F7.

15. Poll carried out by Suzanne Schneider in the context of my course "Domestic Animals and Human History" at Columbia University in the spring semester of 2004.

16. United Nations Development Programme, *Human Development Report 1998* (New York: Oxford University Press, 1998), 50.

17. Prehistorian Colin Tudge cites estimates of 10 percent animal-based calories for the diet of australopithecines, our earliest ancestors, and 20 percent for their *homo erectus* successors. See his *The Time Before History: Five Million Years of Human Impact* (New York: Simon & Schuster, 1996), 194–255. For a convenient reference to the ages of our hominid ancestors, see "Origins of Humankind," http://www.pbs.org/wgbh/evolution/humans/humankind/i.html.

18. This sort of analysis is used by anthropologist Marvin Harris to explain India's sacred cows and other animal phenomena in his *Cows, Pigs, Wars, and Witches: The Riddle of Culture* (New York: Random House, 1974). Harris's utilitarian approach to all animal questions runs counter to many of the basic arguments in this book.

19. Isidore Geoffroy St. Hilaire, *Acclimatation et domestication des animaux utile* (Paris: Librairie Agricole de la Maison Rustique, 1861), 126–138.

20. Upton Sinclair, *The Jungle* (1906; repr., New York: Bantam Classics, 2003).

21. For example, see Eric Schlosser, *Fast Food Nation: The Dark Side of the All-American Meal* (Boston: Houghton Mifflin, 2001).

22. The pioneer historian in this field is Alfred W. Crosby Jr. See his *The Columbian Exchange: Biological and Cultural Consequences of 1492* (Westport, Conn.: Greenwood Press, 1972). Many other historians have added to the story. One work that stresses more recent species introductions into the United States is Kim Todd and Claire Emery, *Tinkering with Eden: A Natural History of Exotics in America* (New York: W. W. Norton, 2001).

23. Tom L. McKnight, *The Camel in Australia* (Melbourne: Melbourne University Press, 1969).

24. For accounts of major field primatologists see Sy Montgomery, *Walking with the Great Apes: Jane Goodall, Dian Fossey, Birute Galdikas* (Boston: Houghton Mifflin, 1991).

25. Edward O. Wilson, *Sociobiology: The New Synthesis* (Cambridge: Harvard University Press, 1975).

26. New York Times News Service release, May 10, 2000, www.naplesnews.com/00/05/features/d458440a.htm.

27. Stanley Godlovitch, Roslind Godlovitch, and John Harris, ed. *Animals, Men, and Morals: An Enquiry into the Maltreatment of Non-Humans* (New York: Taplinger, 1972).

28. Peter Singer, *Animal Liberation: A New Ethics for Our Treatment of Animals* (New York: Avon Books, 1975).

29. Jeremy Bentham, *An Introduction to the Principles of Morals and Legislation*, ed. J. H. Burns and H. L. A. Hart (London: Methuen, 1982), chapter 17, section 1. The full text is available online at "Classical Utilitarianism Web Site," http://www.la.utexas.edu/research/poltheory/bentham/ipml/.

30. Michael P. T. Leahy, *Against Liberation: Putting Animals in Perspective* (London: Routledge, 1991). I discuss Leahy's views in chapter 2.

31. Keith Tester, *Animals and Society: The Humanity of Animal Rights* (London: Routledge, 1991).

32. As summarized by Adrian Franklin in *Animals and Modern Cultures: A Sociology of Human-Animal Relations in Modernity* (London: Sage Publications, 1999), 29.

33. See, for example, Andrew Linzey and Dan Cohn-Sherbok, *After Noah: Animals and the Liberation of Theology* (London: Mowbray, 1997); and Robert N. Wennberg, *God, Humans, and Animals: An Invitation to Enlarge Our Moral Universe* (Grand Rapids, Mich.: William E. Eerdmans, 2003).

34. Charles Patterson, *Eternal Treblinka: Our Treatment of Animals and the Holocaust* (New York: Lantern Books, 2002). http://www.powerfulbook.com/.

35. BBC News, "Animal Rights, Terror Tactics," http://news.bbc.co.uk/1/hi/uk/902751.stm.

36. North American Animal Liberation Front Press Office, "2001 Year-End Direct Action Report," 18, http://www.animalliberation.net/library/2001DirectActions.pdf.

37. Ibid., 10.

2. The Stages of Human-Animal Relations

1. Richard W. Bulliet, *The Camel and the Wheel* (Cambridge: Harvard University Press, 1975), 2.

2. E. Sue Savage-Rumbaugh, *Ape Language, From Conditioned Reflex to Symbol* (New York: Columbia University Press, 1986).

3. For a representative book on this topic, see Jonathan Marks, *What It Means to Be 98 Percent Chimpanzee* (Berkeley: University of California Press, 2002).

4. René Descartes, *Selections*, ed. Ralph M. Eaton (New York: Charles Scribner's Sons, 1927), 358–360.

5. The *Oxford English Dictionary* cites the usage by Darwin himself: *Voy. Nat.* viii. (1879), 150: "Animals that readily enter into domestication."

3. Separation: The Human-Animal Divide

1. *The Epic of Gilgamesh*, trans. N. K. Sandars (Baltimore: Penguin Books, 1960), 60–66.

2. Genesis 3.5.

3. Genesis 3.7.

4. Even Alfred Russel Wallace, who with Darwin cofounded evolutionary theory, fell prey to the idea that "survival of the fittest" could explain the supposed superiority of Europeans and inferiority of savages. See Ross A. Slotten,

The Heretic in Darwin's Court: The Life of Alfred Russel Wallace (New York: Columbia University Press, 2004), 281–287.

5. *The Cambridge Encyclopedia of Hunters and Gatherers*, eds. Richard B. Leland and Richard Daly (Cambridge: Cambridge University Press), 1999.

6. Charles Lamb's newspaper essays were collected in 1823 in Charles Lamb, *Essays of Elia*, with a foreword by Philip Lopate (1823; repr., Iowa City: University of Iowa Press, 2003).

7. Mary Douglas, *Implicit Meanings: Essays in Anthropology* (London: Routledge, 1975). See specifically chapter 1, "Social and Religious Symbolism of the Lele" and chapter 2, "Animals in Lele Religious Symbolism."

8. Paul Shepard, *Coming Home to the Pleistocene* (Washington, D.C.: Island Press/Shearwater Books, 1998), 171–172.

9. Ibid., 145.

10. Ibid., 162.

11. For a forceful assertion of this position, see Carol J. Adams, *The Sexual Politics of Meat: A Feminist-Vegetarian Critical Theory* (New York: Continuum, 1990).

12. Shepard, *Coming Home*, 30–31.

13. John C. Lilly, *Man and Dolphin* (Garden City, N.Y.: Doubleday, 1961), as quoted on the John C. Lilly homepage: http://www.tomigaya.shibuya.tokyo.jp/lilly/mandolph01.html.

14. *Mousterian Bone Flute*, ed. Ivan Turk (Ljubljana: Znanstvenorazisko-valni Center Sazu, 1997). Photographs of this and another Paleolithic bone flute may be found in Randall White, *Dark Caves, Bright Visions: Life in Ice Age Europe* (New York: American Museum of Natural History, 1986), 115.

15. Douglas Gilbert, *American Vaudeville: Its Life and Times* (New York: Whittlesey House, 1940), 58.

16. Personal communication from Dr. Jean-Marc Oppenheim, an expert horse trainer.

4. Predomesticity

1. Current evidence suggests that zebu cattle (*bos indicus*) with their distinctive humps became domestic in Pakistan as early as other subspecies became domestic farther west. See Richard Meadow, "Early Animal Domestication in South Asia," in *South Asian Archaeology*, edited by H. Haertel (Berlin: D. Reimer, 1979), 143–179. Evidence pointing to local cattle domestication in northeastern Africa is summarized in Brenda Fowler, "African Pastoral: Archaeologists Rewrite History of Farming," *New York Times*, July 27, 2004, F2.

2. Dutch art of the Golden Age affords an apparent exception, but the luxuriant paintings of dead game, fruits and vegetables, and banqueters posing with full wineglasses and plates laden with roasted cranes and other birds relate less to dining habits than to the social ambitions of the owners of the paintings.

3. André Leroi-Gourhan, *The Dawn of European Art: An Introduction to Palaeolithic Cave Painting* (Cambridge: Cambridge University Press, 1982), 45.

4. Eberhard Wagner, Kurt Wehrberger, et al., *Der Löwenmensch: Tier und Mensch in der Kunst der Eiszeit* (Sigmaringen: Ulmer Museum-Jan Thorbecke Verlag, 1994).

5. Mathias Guenther, "From Totemism to Shamanism: Hunter-Gatherer Contributions to world Mythology and Spirituality," in *The Cambridge Encyclopedia of Hunters and Gatherers*, edited by Richard B. Leland and Richard Daly (Cambridge: Cambridge University Press, 1999), 426.

6. Ibid., 429.

5. Where the Tame Things Are

1. For a bibliography on the complex topic of reindeer domestication, see the Suggested Reading.

2. Jared Diamond, *Guns, Germs, and Steel: The Fates of Human Societies* (New York: W. W. Norton, 1997), 165.

3. Ibid., 166–168.

4. Kim Todd, *Tinkering with Eden: A Natural History of Exotics in America* (New York: W. W. Norton, 2001), chapter 11.

5. Thomas Bewick, *A General History of Quadrupeds* (repr., Leicester: W. H. Smith, 1980), 170–171.

6. Diamond, *Guns, Germs, and Steel*, 166.

7. Information on this experiment comes from R. J. Berry, "The Genetical Implications of Domestication in Animals," in *The Domestication and Exploitation of Plants and Animals*, edited by Peter Ucko and G. W. Dimbleby (London: Duckworth, 1969), 207–217.

8. Cat bones have been found on the island of Cyprus in association with a human burial datable to 7500 B.C.E. Though the bones are indistinguishable from those of a wild cat, Cyprus has no native wild cat species. Hence the find is taken as evidence of deliberate human cohabitation with cats. See J.-D. Vigne, J. Guilaine, K. Debue, L. Haye, and P. Gerard, "Early Taming of the Cat in Cyprus," *Science* 304 (April 9, 2004): 259.

9. Carl O. Sauer, *Seeds, Spades, Hearths, and Herds: The Domestication of Animals and Foodstuffs*, 2nd ed. (Cambridge: MIT Press, 1969).

10. Lyudmila N. Trut, "Early Canid Domestication: The Farm-Fox Experiment," *American Scientist* 87 (March–April 1999): 160–169.

11. Paul S. Martin and H. E. Wright Jr., eds., *Pleistocene Extinctions: The Search for a Cause* (New Haven: Yale University Press, 1967).

12. For a flavor of the challenges to the theory, see among many examples, David Choquenot and D. M. J. S. Bowman, "Marsupial Megafauna, Aborigines, and the Overkill Hypothesis: Application of Predator-Prey Models to the Question of Pleistocene Extinction in Australia," *Global Ecology & Biogeography* 7, issue 3 (May 1998); D. K. Grayson and D. J. Meltzer, "Clovis Hunting and Large Mammal Extinction: A Critical Review of the Evidence," *Journal of World Prehistory* 16 (2002): 313–359; or at the popular level, William K. Stevens, "New Suspect in Ancient Extinctions of the Pleistocene Megafauna: Disease," *New York Times*, April 29, 1997.

13. Vine Deloria Jr. presents a particularly strong rejection of the theory from the standpoint of later Native American attitudes toward animals in *Red Earth, White Lies* (Golden, Colo.: Fulcrum, 1997).

14. http://www.washington.edu/newsroom/news/2001archive/10–01archive/k102401.html

15. *Encyclopedia Britannica*, 11th ed., 12:648.

6. Domestication and Usefulness

1. Claude Lévi-Strauss, *The Savage Mind* (Chicago: University of Chicago Press, 1966), 14–15.

2. A. Rudolf Galloway, "History of the Canary," in *Canaries, Hybrids, and British Birds*, edited by John Robson and S. H. Lever (London, 1900). As cited at http://members.madasafish.com/~grahamwhite/download/history.html.

3. Martha Chaiklin, "Feathered Friends: Japanese Demand for Exotic Birds in the 18th Century" (paper delivered at conference on animals in Japan, Columbia University, New York, April 22, 2001), 8. To be published in Gregory Pflugfelder and Brett L. Walker, eds., *JAPANimals: History and Culture in Japan's Animal Life* (forthcoming).

4. Much of the following discussion is informed by the work on secondary uses by archaeologist Andrew Sherratt. A summary presentation of his views may be found in Andrew Sherratt, "The Secondary Exploitation of Animals in the Old World," *World Archaeology* 15, no. 1 (1983): 90–102.

5. Ibid., 93–94. Sherratt dates the earliest use of wool in Europe to 3000–2500 B.C.E.

6. H. Epstein offers a marvelous assortment of pictures of sheep breeds in H. Epstein, *The Origin of the Domestic Animals of Africa* (New York: Africana, 1971), 2:21–191.

7. Valerie Fildes, *Breasts, Bottles, and Babies: A History of Infant Feeding* (Edinburgh: Edinburgh University Press, 1985).

8. Sherratt, "The Secondary Exploitation of Animals," 94–95.

9. Frederic L. Pryor, "The Invention of the Plow," *Comparative Studies in Society and History* 27, no. 4 (October 1985): 727–743.

10. Sherratt, "The Secondary Exploitation of Animals," 91–92.

11. The argument for early cattle domestication in North Africa is put by Douglas J. Brewer, Donald B. Redford, and Susan Redford in *Domestic Plants and Animals: The Egyptian Origins* (Warminster: Aris & Phillips, 1994), 77–90. Richard Meadow presents reasons for thinking that the domestication of humped cattle (*bos indicus*, a subspecies of *bos primigenius*) took place in northwestern India independently of cattle cultures farther west. See Richard Meadow, "Early Animal Domestication in South Asia," in *South Asian Archaeology*, edited by H. Haertel (Berlin: D. Reimer, 1979), 143–179.

12. Richard Lobban and Michael Sprague, "Bulls, and the W3S Sceptre in Ancient Egypt and Sudan," *Anthrozöos* 10, no. 1 (1997): 14–22.

13. The two best introductions to this complicated field are Stuart Piggott, *The Earliest Wheeled Transport, From the Atlantic Coast to the Caspian Sea* (Ithaca, N.Y.: Cornell University Press, 1983); and Mary Littauer and Joost H. Crouwel, *Wheeled Vehicles and Ridden Animals in the Ancient Near East* (Leiden: E. J. Brill, 1979).

14. On pack oxen, see X. de Planhol, "Le boeuf porteur dans le Proche-Orient et l'Afrique du Nord," *Journal of the Economic and Social History of the Orient* 12, no. 3 (1969): 298–322. There is a good deal of scholarly debate over whether the light horse-drawn chariots shown in Saharan rock art ever existed in reality, but in any case, they seem to date from after 1200 B.C.E. and thus have nothing to do with early domestication.

15. Richard W. Bulliet, *The Camel and the Wheel* (Cambridge, Mass.: Harvard University Press, 1975), chapters 2–3.

16. See article on "Wagon" in J. P. Mallory and D. Q. Adams, *Encyclopedia of Indo-European Culture* (Chicago: Fitzroy Dearborn, 1997), 625–628.

7. From Mighty Hunter to Yajamana

1. The mother goddess scenario was put forward in 1896 by Eduard Hahn, in *Die Haustiere und ihre Beziehungen zur Wirtschaft des Menschen*. It played an influential role in early debates on domestication. Its weaknesses in view of accumulating archaeological evidence are succinctly summarized in Frederick J. Simoons and Elizabeth Simoons, *A Ceremonial Ox of India: The Mithan in Nature, Culture, and History* (Madison: University of Wisconsin Press, 1968).

2. Jean Jacques Rousseau, *The Social Contract and Discourses* (London: J. M. Dent, n.d.), 207.

3. Robert L. Kelly, *The Foraging Spectrum: Diversity in Hunter-Gatherer Lifeways* (Washington: Smithsonian Institution Press, 1995), 296.

4. Ibid., 296–297.

5. Ibid., 302–303.

6. Ibid., 304.

7. Lawrence H. Keeley, "Hunter-Gatherer Economic Complexity and 'Population Pressure': A Cross-Cultural Analysis," *Journal of Anthropological Archaeology* 7 (1988): 373–411.

8. See chapter 11 for a more extensive discussion.

9. Simoons, *A Ceremonial Ox of India*, 55.

10. Ibid., 152.

11. Ibid., 153–154.

12. Ibid., 232–233.

13. Ibid., 181.

14. Theodore de Bary and Irene Bloom, eds., *Sources of Chinese Tradition,* 2nd ed. (New York: Columbia University Press, 1999), 8–9.

15. Ibid., 73–74.

16. Ibid., 120–121.

17. "The *Aitareya Brahmana* states that the man, horse, ox, goat and ram are sacrificial animals and that the flesh of the *kimpurusa* [sacrificed human victim?], *gauramrga, gavaya,* camel and *sarabha* (young elephant), which were not meant for sacrifice, should not be eaten. D. N. Jha, *The Myth of the Holy Cow,* London: Verso, 2002, 31.

18. Richard Meadow, "Early Animal Domestication in South Asia," in *South Asian Archaeology,* edited by H. Haertel (Berlin: D. Reimer, 1979), 143–179.

19. Anthropologist Mary Douglas describes a wide array of complex affective relations between the Lele of central Africa and the animals of the forest, but also points out that the Lele had little interest in the domestic animals they had acquired. See Mary Douglas, *Implicit Meanings: Essays in Anthropology* (London: Routledge, 1975).

8. Early Domesticity: My Ass and Yours

1. Claudine Fabre-Vassas, *A Singular Beast: Jews, Christians, and the Pig* (New York: Columbia University Press, 1997).

2. Regarding the title of this section of the chapter, many works discuss the ancient "donkey libel" against Jews and Christians and its possible Egyptian origins. For an exhaustive application of Egyptological lore to the question, see the three articles (in Dutch) by B. H. Stricker, "Asinarii," *Oudheidkundige Mededelingen uit het Rijksmuseum van Oudheden te Leyden*, n.s., 46 (1963): 52–75; 48 (1967): 23–43; 49 (1968): 22–53. On Tertullian and the term *onocoetes* (see below), see Jean-G. Préaux, "Deus Christianorum Onocoetes," in *Collection Latomus* 44, *Hommages à Léon Herrmann* (Bruxelles-Berchem: Latomus, Revue d'Études Latines, 1960), 639–654. E. Bickermann explores the Jewish side of the question in "Ritualmord und Eselskult," *Monatschrift für Geschichte und Wisenschaft des Judentums*, n.s., 35 (1927): 255–264.

3. Apuleius, *The Golden Ass*, trans. Jack Lindsay (Bloomington: Indiana University Press, 1962).

4. Ibid., 231.

5. The image may be accessed online at http://www.cowart.info/ Monthly%20Features/Ugly%20pix/Ugly%20%20pix.htm.

6. Geraldine Pinch, *Votive Offerings to Hathor* (Oxford: Griffith Institute, Ashmolean Museum, 1993).

7. *Rigveda Brahmanas: The Aitareya and Kausitaki Brahmanas of the Rigveda*, Arthur Berriedale Keith, trans., Harvard Oriental Series 25 (1920; repr., Cambridge, Mass.: Harvard University Press, 1998), iv:7–9. The "double seed" probably refers to the donkey's ability to impregnate both another donkey and a horse.

8. Adolf Erman, *Die Religion der Ägypter* (Berlin: Walter de Gruyter, 1934): 404–405.

9. Èxodus 11.13.

10. Martin Noth, "Das Alttestamentliche Bundschliessen im Lichte eines Mari-Textes," *Gesammelte Studien zum alten Testament* (Munich: Chr. Kaiser Verlag, 1960), 142–154, along with the added note by Folker Willesen, "Die Eselsöhne von Sichem als Bundesgenossen," *Vetus Testamentum* 4 (1954): 216–217.

11. Studies of cattle-keeping among the peoples living around the southern reaches of the Nile also indicate that wealth in livestock was not solely related to consumption of meat and milk. For example, see Douglas J. Brewer, Donald B. Redford, and Susan Redford, *Domestic Plants and Animals: The Egyptian Origins* (Warminster: Aris & Phillips, 1994), 78.

12. My thanks to Dr. As'ad Busool for this information.

13. Numbers 22:21–31.

14. I am grateful to Sara M. Averick for informing me that the story can be found in the *Midrash Agada* on the Book of Genesis in *Breshit Rabba*.

15. Judges 13:3–5.

16. Judges 15:14–17.

17. *The Interpreter's Bible* (New York: Abingdon Press, 1953), 2:789–790.

18. Suliman Bashear, "Riding Beasts on Divine Missions: An Examination of the Ass and Camel Traditions," *Journal of Semitic Studies* 36, no. 1 (1991): 37–75.

19. I Kings 1:32–48.

20. Zechariah 9:9.

21. George Amoss, Jr., "The Power of Suffering Love: James Nayler and Robert Rich," (Quaker Electronic Archive and Meeting Place, 1996). Online at http://www.qis.net/~daruma/index.html.

22. Luke 19:30–36.

23. John 12:14–16.

24. Bashear, "Riding Beasts on Divine Missions," 48.

25. Genesis 49:10–12.

26. Bashear, "Riding Beasts on Divine Missions," 48.

27. Abu Nu'aim al-Isfahani, *Kitab dhikr akhbar Isbahan*, S. Dedering, ed. (Leiden: E. J. Brill, 1931–1934), 2:54, 2:183.

28. According to a personal communication dated January 1985 from Prof. F. de Jong of the University of Leiden, Turkish Shi'ite (Bektashi/Alevi) verses mentioning Duldul occur in the following publications: Abülbaki Gölpinarli, *Alevi-Bektasi Nefesleri* (Istanbul: Remzi Kitabevi, 1963), 76, 112, 114, 262, 305; Cahit Oztelli, *Bektasi Gülleri. Alevi-Bektasi Siirleri Antolojisi* (Istanbul: Milliyet Yayinlari, 1973), 22, 30, 207, 223, 227, 236, 249, 258, 260, 262, 340; and Kemal Samancigil, *Alevi Sairleri Antolojisi* (Istanbul: Gün Basimevi, 1946), 255. I am most grateful to Prof. de Jong for this information and for his further directing my attention to a publication by F. von Luschan, "Die Tachtadschy und andere Ueberreste der alten Bevölkerung Lykiens," in *Archiv für Anthropologie* (Braunschweig: Friedrich Vieweg, 1891). Among a people in southwestern Turkey (Lycia) whom von Luschan believed preserved very early pre-Islamic religious beliefs—they eat pork, drink wine, and consider rabbits taboo—he nevertheless discovered (34) the notion that Ali could be reincarnated as a donkey.

29. Bashear, "Riding Beasts on Divine Missions," 59.

30. The figurine is in the National Archaeological Museum in Athens. It is reproduced with an erroneous caption in John P. McKay, Bennett D. Hill, and John Buckler, *A History of Western Society*, 3rd ed. (Boston: Houghton Mifflin, 1987), 157.

31. *Le Man, Kronik Hastaliginiz* (Istanbul), issues 82, 107–111, 113, 128, 132, 137, 182.

32. Apuleius, *The Golden Ass*, 59–60.

33. Ibid., 101–102.

34. Ibid., 144–145.

35. Ibid., 180–182.

36. Ibid., 193.

37. Lucian, *True History and Lucius, or The Ass*, trans. Paul Turner (Bloomington: Indiana University Press, 1974).

38. Ibid., 223–225.

39. Ibid., 106–107.

40. *The Apocryphal New Testament* (Philadelphia: Gebbie & Co., [n.d.]), 38–59. Full text available online at "Wesley Center Online," http://wesley.nnu .edu/noncanon/gospels/infarab.htm.

41. Different versions of this text with varying names locate this story differently. It is in 7.1–27 in the print version cited in the previous note. But because it is easier to access, I have quoted the text from the online version, where it is chapters 20–21.

42. Bashear, "Riding Beasts on Divine Missions," 59.

43. *A Midsummer Night's Dream*, Act IV, Scene 1.

44. Jan Kott's essay "Titania and the Ass's Head," in Jan Kott, *Shakespeare Our Contemporary* (New York: W. W. Norton, 1965), 213–236 most notably restates the element of bestial sex in the scene. He has been followed by directors like Peter Brook (1970) and Richard Jones (2002).

45. An anti-Lutheran tract by Johanne Nas has a frontispiece depicting Luther in a tall, conical hat riding backwards on an ass. (Nas, Johanne, *Praeludium In Centurias hominum, sola fide perditorum: Das ist, Newer Zeittung Vorgang, und langerwarter Enderung, von der grossen Gloggen zu Erfurdt, darmit man newlichst das Lutterthumb, ohn sonder groß Miraculum, vom Weinfaß außthaet leiten . . .* (Ingelstad: Wolfgang Eder, 1588).

46. Tamer el-Leithy, "Public Punishment in Mamluk Society" (master's thesis, Cambridge University, 1997), 18–19. My thanks to Dr. el-Leithy for making this available.

47. Igor Rotar, "Afghanistan Special Report: Radical Islam in Northern Alliance Territory," Keston News Service, November 2, 2001.

48. *The Complete Etchings of Goya*, foreword by Aldous Huxley (New York: Crown, 1943).

49. This picture can be found in *Culturefront* (New-York Historical Society, Spring 1998), 6.

50. Margaret Bent and Andrew Wathey, *Fauvel Studies: Allegory, Chronicle, Music, and Image in Paris, Bibliothèque nationale de France, MS français 146* (Oxford; New York: Clarendon Press, 1998).

51. Nigel Longchamp, *Mirror for Fools: Book of Burnel the Ass* (Notre Dame, Ind.: University of Notre Dame Press, 1963).

52. Cited in "New Advent" Web site from *The Catholic Encyclopedia*, vol. 1, 1907. See http://www.newadvent.org/cathen/01798b.htm.

53. Karen Silvia de León-Jones, *Giordano Bruno and the Kabbalah: Prophets, Magicians, and Rabbis* (New Haven: Yale University Press, 1997), 112.

9. Late Domestic Divergences

1. See note 22 of chapter 1. See also Elinor G. K. Melville, *A Plague of Sheep: Environmental Consequences of the Conquest of Mexico* (Cambridge: Cambridge University Press, 1994).

2. Sally McMurry, *Transforming Rural Life: Dairying Families and Agricultural Change, 1820–1885* (Baltimore: Johns Hopkins University Press, 1995).

3. Wayne A. Conaway, "Global Business Basics—Strange Tastes," *Industry Week* (April 6, 2002). Online at http://www.industryweek.com/Columns/ASP/columns.asp?ColumnId=864.

4. Eric Weddle, "Day Job: Slaughterhouse Human-Resources Director," *New Yorker* (April 6 and May 1, 2000): 146.

5. Servio H. Lence, "A Comparative Marketing Analysis of Major Agricultural Products in the U.S. and Argentina" (unpublished manuscript, April 2000). My thanks to Prof. Lence for permitting me to use the material in his article.

6. Harriet Ritvo, *The Animal Estate: English and Other Creatures in the Victorian Age* (Cambridge: Harvard University Press, 1987), 50.

7. Frank G. Menke, *The New Encyclopedia of Sports* (New York: A. S. Barnes, 1947), 247.

8. Joseph Strutt, as cited in Ritvo, *The Animal Estate*, 150.

10. Toward Postdomesticity

1. Alfred Ollivant, *Bob, Son of Battle* (New York: Doubleday & McClure, 1898). Originally published as *Owd Bob, the Grey Dog of Kenmuir* (London: Methuen, 1898). Full text is available as a Project Guttenberg online edition: http://digital.library.upenn.edu/webbin/gutbook/lookup?num=2795. See specifically page 9.

2. *The History of Pompey the Little; Or, The Life and Adventures of a Lap-Dog*, written by Francis Coventry in 1751 is earlier, but the author uses his canine protagonist only as a witness for his descriptions of the manners and foibles of the time.

3. Harriet Ritvo, *The Animal Estate: English and Other Creatures in the Victorian Age* (Cambridge: Harvard University Press, 1987), 93.

4. A show in Tervueren, Belgium, in 1847 is sometimes cited at the first in the world, but it featured only hunting dogs and, more importantly, had no follow-up. The first dog show in the Arab world was held in Beirut in 1972.

5. Frances Power Cobbe, *Vivisection in America* (London: Swan, Sonnenschein and Co., 1890), 5–6, as reproduced online at "Victorian Women Writers Project: An Electronic Collection," Perry Willett, general editor, http://www.indiana.edu/~letrs/vwwp/cobbe/viviamer.html.

6. Ibid.

7. Ronald L. Numbers, *Darwin Comes to America* (Cambridge: Harvard University Press, 1998). Online at http://www.meta-library.net/history/darwinus-body.html.

8. One Internet directory (http://www.northhillswoodworking.com/cemetary.html) lists forty-one.

9. One Internet list of pet cemeteries (http://dog.top-info.ch/dog/blackboard/tod/list.htm) lists four for Switzerland, thirteen for France, and thirty (plus fourteen crematoria) for Germany.

10. My deep thanks to Linda Stein for telling me about Rainbow Bridge and sharing information with me. The text of "Pet Heaven," which is similarly worded but does not use the phrase Rainbow Bridge, may be found online at http://www.aplb.org/frameset4.htm.

11. Quoted in Paul A. B. Clarke and Andrew Linzey, eds., *Political Theory and Animal Rights* (London: Pluto Press, 1990), 141.

12. Keith Tester, *Animals and Society: The Humanity of Animal Rights* (London: Routledge, 1991).

13. Adrian Franklin, *Animals and Modern Cultures: A Sociology of Human-Animal Relations in Modernity* (London: Sage Publications, 1999), 6.

14. Ibid., 188–199.

15. H. Peter Steeves, ed., *Animal Others: On Ethics, Ontology, and Animal Life* (Albany: State University of New York Press, 1999), xii–xiii.

11. The Future of Human-Animal Relations

1. "One Third of Farm Animal Breeds Face Extinction" (December 5, 2000), http://www.fao.org/News/2000/001201-e.htm. I am grateful to Margot Pollans for bringing this and other sources dealing with the preservation of domestic breeds to my attention.

2. "Loss of Domestic Animal Breeds Alarming" (March 31, 2004), http://www.fao.org/newsroom/en/news/2004/39892/.

3. For an indication of how this might transpire, see Brian Donahue, *Reclaiming the Commons: Community Farms and Forests in a New England Town* (New Haven: Yale University Press, 1999).

4. See, for example, Jordan Danchev, "The Preservation of Autochthonous Breeds of Domestic Animals in Bulgaria," http://www.worldwildlife.org/bsp/publications/europe/bulgaria/bulgaria22.html; or the French organization Pronatura-France (http://pronaturafrance.free.fr/anglais.html); or the rare breeds collection at Mount Vernon, the home of George Washington (http://www.mountvernon.org/learn/explore_mv/index.cfm/ss/33/cfid/420171/cfto-ken/35717869).

5. http://www.okeeferanch.bc.ca/rare_breeds.html.

6. Kenko, *Essays in Idleness*, trans. Donald Keene (New York: Columbia University Press, 1967), 101.

7. Ibid., 108.

8. Information contained on supplementary materials accompanying a lecture by Dr. Hoyt Long. See note 23 below for fuller information.

9. http://www.vegsource.com/travel/asia/messages/262.html.

10. http://www.metropolis.co.jp/tokyofeaturestoriesarchive299/293/tokyo featurestoriesinc.htm.

11. International Vegetarian Union Web site: http://www.ivu.org/members/council/mitsuru-kakimoto.html.

12. For additional information and pictures of each variety go to: "Koi Encyclopedia/Talking Dictionary," http://www.koi.com/reference/encyclope dia/.

13. For more see the "Virtual Pet Homepage," http://virtualpet.com/vp/index.htm.

14. Details are available on the Japan Kennel Club Web site: http://www.jkc.or.jp/japanese_dog/index_e.html.

15. Richard Chalfen, "The Case of 'doubutsu no haka no shashin': The Use of Snapshots in Japanese Pet Cemeteries" (paper presented to the annual meeting of the International Visual Sociology Association, University of Bologna, Bologna, Italy, July 8th-12th, 1996). The text of the paper is available online at http://astro.temple.edu/~rchalfen/BOLOGNA.html.

16. *The Lotus Sutra*, trans. Burton Watson (New York: Columbia University Press, 1993), 188.

17. Ibid., xix.

18. Discussion of this text is based on Haruo Shirane, ed., *Early Modern Japanese Literature: An Anthology, 1600–1900* (New York: Columbia University Press, 2002), 886–909.

19. Ibid., 892–893.

20. Ibid., 899.

21. Aaron Skabelund, "Fascism's Furry Friends?: Dogs, National Identity, and Racial Purity in 1930s Japan" (paper presented at conference on animals in Japan, Columbia University, April 22, 2001), 5. To be published in Gregory Pflugfelder and Brett L. Walker, eds., *JAPANimals: History and Culture in Japan's Animal Life* (forthcoming). Further discussion of the dog in modern Japan may be found in Aaron Skabelund, "Loyalty and Civilization: A Canine History of Japan, 1850–2000" (doctoral dissertation, Columbia University, 2004).

22. K. Belson and B. Bremner, *Hello Kitty: The Remarkable Story of Sanrio and the Billion Dollar Feline Phenomenon* (Singapore: John Wiley & Sons [Asia], 2004).

23. Hoyt Long, "Grateful Animals, Inferior Beasts: Buddhist *Ongaeshi* Tales and Changing Conceptions of the 'Animal' in Early Japan" (paper presented at conference on animals in Japan, Columbia University, April 22, 2001), 5. To be published in Gregory Pflugfelder and Brett L. Walker, eds., *JAPANimals: History and Culture in Japan's Animal Life* (forthcoming).

24. Ibid., 7–8.

25. Ibid., 11. Long's translation from *Konjaku monogatari*.

26. Frank Di Silvestro, *Boy Jesus and His Dog: An Inspired Work of the Imagination* (n.p.: Stories and Songs Children Love, 1998), 2.

27. Ibid., 72.

28. Ibid., 78.

29. Ibid., 97.

30. Ibid., 127.

Suggested Reading

Since the subject matter of this book stretches from the emergence of humankind to the day after tomorrow, the number of relevant bibliographical titles is almost limitless. The readings listed here, most of which are also cited in the notes, are designed to provide a more general look at what is available on the issues of postdomesticity and domestication in particular.

General

Of the myriad books that address animals in general, three afford an illuminating comparison between how animal issues have struck popularizing writers at different times. During the heyday of domesticity, Thomas Bewick wrote *A General History of Quadrupeds*, (1790, repr., Leicester: Windward, 1980). R. A. Marchant's *Man and Beast* (New York: Macmillan, 1968) came out at the very end of the domestic era in America. Roger Caras, *A Perfect Harmony: The Intertwining Lives of Animals and Humans Throughout History* (New York: Fireside, 1996) reflects a more postdomestic sensibility. The most insightful sociological overview of contemporary attitudes toward animals is Adrian Franklin, *Animals and Modern Cultures: A Sociology of Human-Animal Relations in Modernity* (London: Sage Publications, 1999). The discussion of animals in Japan draws heavily on the papers in Gregory Pflugfelder and Brett L. Walker, eds., *JAPANimals: History and Culture in Japan's Animal Life* (forthcoming). I am grateful to the editors for making these papers available to me.

Postdomestic Attitudes

The following represents only a sampling of the vast output of writing about human-animal relations that has appeared since the 1960s:

Food Issues

Pollan, Michael. "Power Steer." *New York Times*, March 31, 2002, section 6.
Schlosser, Eric. *Fast Food Nation: The Dark Side of the All-American Meal.* New York: Perennial, 2001.
Spencer, Colin. *The Heretic's Feast: A History of Vegetarianism.* Hanover, N.H.: University Press of New England, 1996.
Walters, Kerry S., and Lisa Portmess. *Religious Vegetarianism: From Hesiod to the Dalai Lama.* Albany: State University of New York Press, 2001.

Philosophical and Theological Issues

Adams, Carol J. *The Sexual Politics of Meat: A Feminist-Vegetarian Critical Theory.* New York: Continuum, 1990.
Benton, Ted. *Natural Relations: Ecology, Animal Rights, and Social Justice.* London: Verso, 1993.
Clarke, Paul A. B., and Andrew Linzey, eds. *Political Theory and Animal Rights.* London: Pluto Press, 1990.
Franklin, Julian H. *Animal Rights and Moral Philosophy.* New York: Columbia University Press, 2004.
Leahy, Michael P. T. *Against Liberation: Putting Animals in Perspective.* London: Routledge, 1991.
Linzey, Andrew, and Dan Cohn-Sherbok. *After Noah: Animals and the Liberation of Theology.* London: Mowbray, 1997.
Mason, Jim. *An Unnatural Order: Uncovering the Roots of Our Domination of Nature and Each Other.* New York: Simon & Schuster, 1993.
Noske, Barbara. *Humans and Other Animals: Beyond the Boundaries of Anthropology.* London: Pluto Press, 1989.
Regan, Tom. *All That Dwell Therein: Essays on Animal Rights and Environmental Ethics.* Berkeley: University of California Press, 1982.
Singer, Peter, and Tom Regan, eds. *Animal Rights and Human Obligations.* Englewood Cliffs, N.J.: Prentice-Hall, 1976.
Singer, Peter. *Animal Liberation.* New York: New York Review, 1975.
Singer, Peter, ed. *In Defence of Animals.* Oxford: Blackwell, 1985.
Steeves, H. Peter, ed. *Animal Others: On Ethics, Ontology, and Animal Life.* Albany: State University of New York Press, 1999.
Wennberg, Robert N. *God, Humans, and Animals: An Invitation to Enlarge Our Moral Universe.* Grand Rapids, Mich.: William E. Eerdmans, 2003.

Scientific Practices

Sperling, Susan. *Animal Liberators: Research and Morality.* Berkeley: University of California Press, 1988.
Savage-Rumbaugh, E. Sue. *Ape Language: From Conditioned Response to Symbol.* New York: Columbia University Press, 1986.

Ecological and Environmental Issues

Donahue, Brian. *Reclaiming the Commons: Community Farms and Forests in a New England Town.* New Haven: Yale University Press, 1999.
Jackson, Dana, and Laura Jackson. *The Farm as Natural Habitat: Reconnecting Food Systems with Ecosystems.* Washington D.C.: Island Press, 2002.

Domestication and Domestic Species

Modern literature on the topic of domestication as a process draws heavily on archaeological and anthropological evidence and generally takes for granted the materialistic approach developed by domestic society. The standard work covering all domestic species is Frederick E. Zeuner, *A History of Domesticated Animals* (New York: Harper & Row, 1963). For a briefer and more up-to-date work that deals only with mammals, see Juliet Clutton-Brock, *A Natural History of Domesticated Mammals*, 2nd ed. (Cambridge: Cambridge University Press, 1999). Douglas J. Brewer, Donald B. Redford, and Susan Redford, *Domestic Plants and Animals: The Egyptian Origins* (Warminster: Aris & Phillips Ltd., n.d.) offers insights, based on recent research, that question the centrality of the Fertile Crescent that largely underlies the arguments made by Zeuner and Clutton-Bruck. For the most up-to-date surveys of the Fertile Crescent itself, see the articles contained in Billie Jean Collins, ed., *A History of the Animal World in the Ancient Near East* (Leiden: E. J. Brill, 2002). Three other regional works by H. Epstein, *Domestic Animals of China* (New York: Holmes & Meier, 1971); *The Origin of the Domestic Animals of Africa* (New York: Holmes & Meier, 1971); and *Domestic Animals of Nepal* (New York: Holmes & Meier, 1977), contain a good deal of data and a great number of valuable illustrations.

Alternative ideas relating to the domestication process may be found in Carl O. Sauer, *Seeds, Spades, Hearths, and Herds: The Domestication of Animals and Foodstuffs*, 2nd ed. (Cambridge: MIT Press, 1969); and the various articles contained in Peter J. Ucko and G.W. Dimbleby, eds., *The Domestication and Exploitation of Plants and Animals* (London: Gerald Duckworth, 1969).

Brief but interesting descriptions of particular domestic species may be found on the Internet at "Breeds of Livestock," maintained by the Department of Animal Science at Oklahoma State University (http://www.ansi.okstate.edu/BREEDS/). Information on where domestic species fit into their several families, along with extensive bibliographies, can be found at "The Ultimate Ungulate Page: Your Guide to the World's Hoofed Mammals" (http://www.ultimateungulate.com).

Many books and articles devoted to single species or groups of animals, with an emphasis on domestication and human-animal interaction, have been cited in the notes. The following is a classified listing of many of them:

Bovids: Cattle, Water Buffalo, Mithans, Yaks, etc.

Lincoln, Bruce. *Priests, Warriors, and Cattle: A Study in the Ecology of Religions*. Berkeley: University of California Press, 1981.
Simoons, Frederick J. *A Ceremonial Ox of India: The Mithan in Nature, Culture, and History*. Madison: University of Wisconsin Press, 1968.

Camelids: Camels, Llamas, etc.

Bulliet, Richard W. *The Camel and the Wheel*. Cambridge, Mass.: Harvard University Press, 1975.
Flannery, Kent V., Joyce Marcus, and Robert G. Reynolds. *The Flocks of the Wamani: A Study of Llama Herders on the Punas of Ayacucho, Peru*. San Diego: Academic Press, 1989.

Gareis, Iris. "Llama und Alpaca in der Religion der rezenten Bewohner des zentralen und südlichen Andengebietes," *Münchner Beiträge zur Amerikanistic*, vol. 6. Munich: Klaus Renner Verlag Hohenschaftlarn, 1982.

Kent, Jonathan D. *The Domestication and Exploitation of the South American Camelids: Methods of Analysis and Their Application to Circum-Lacustrine Archaeological Sites in Bolivia and Peru*. Dissertation, Washington University. University Microfilms International, 1982.

Miller, George C., and Richard L. Burger. "Our Father the Cayman, Our Dinner the Llama: Animal Utilization at Chavin de Huantar, Peru." *American Antiquity* 60, no. 3 (1995).

Schmidt-Nielsen, Knut. *Desert Animals: Physiological Problems of Heat and Water*. New York: Dover, 1979.

Canids: Dogs, Dingos, etc.

Clutton-Brock, Juliet. *Dog*. London: Dorling Kindersley, 2000.

Ibn al-Marzuban. *The Book of the Superiority of Dogs Over Many of Those Who Wear Clothes*. Translated and edited by G. R. Smith and M. A. S. Abdel Haleem. Warminster: Aris & Phillips, 1978.

Meggitt, M. J. "The Association between Australian Aborigines and Dingoes." In Anthony Leeds and Andrew Peter Vayda, eds., *Man, Culture, and Animals: The Role of Animals in Human Ecological Adjustments*, 7–26. Washington, D.C.: American Association for the Advancement of Science, 1965.

Trut, Lyudmila N. "Early Canid Domestication: The Farm-Fox Experiment." *American Scientist* 87 (March–April 1999): 160–169.

Caprids and Ovids: Goats and Sheep

Levy, Thomas Evan. "The Emergence of Specialized Pastoralism in the Southern Levant." *World Archaeology* 15, no. 1 (1983): 15–36.

Cervids: Deer, Caribou, Reindeer, etc.

Anderson, Robert T. "Dating Reindeer Pastoralism in Lapland." *Ethnohistory* 5, no. 4 (Autumn, 1958): 361–391.

Hatt, Gudmund. "Notes on Reindeer Nomadism." *Memoirs of the American Anthropological Association* 6, no. 2 (April–June, 1919): 75–133.

Ingold, Tim. "Reindeer Economies: And the Origins of Pastoralism." *Anthropology Today* 2, no. 4 (August 1986): 5–10.

Laufer, Berthold. "The Reindeer and its Domestication." *Memoirs of the American Anthropological Association* 4, no. 2 (April–June, 1919): 91–147.

Mirov, N. T. "Notes on the Domestication of Reindeer." *American Anthropologist* n.s. 47, no. 3 (July–September, 1945): 393–408.

Equids: Horses, Donkeys, Mules, etc.

Clutton-Brock, Juliet. *Horse*. London: Dorling Kindersley, 2000.

Barclay, Harold B. *The Role of the Horse in Man's Culture*. London: J. A. Allen, 1980.

Gladitz, Charles. *Horse Breeding in the Medieval World*. Portland, Ore.: Four Courts Press, 1997.

Langdon, John. *Horses, Oxen, and Technological Innovation: The Use of Draught Animals in English Farming from 1066 to 1500*. Cambridge: Cambridge University Press, 1986.

Hänsel, Bernhard, and Stefan Zimmer, eds. *Die Indogermanen und das Pferd: Festschrift für Bernfried Schlerath*. Budapest: Archaeolingua, 1994.

Dent, Anthony. *Donkey: The Story of the Ass from East to West*. London: George G. Harrap, 1972.

Felines

Clutton-Brock, Juliet. *Cat*. London: Dorling Kindersley, 2000.

Clutton-Brock, Juliet. *Cats: Ancient and Modern*. Cambridge: Harvard University Press, 1993.

Swine

Fabre-Vassas, Claudine. *A Singular Beast: Jews, Christians, and the Pig*. New York: Columbia University Press, 1997.

Birds

Galloway, A. Rudolf. "History of the Canary" in *Canaries, Hybrids, and British Birds*, edited by John Robson and S. H. Lever. London, 1900.

Levi, Wendell M. *Encyclopedia of Pigeon Breeds*. [n.p.]: Wendell Levi Publishing Co., 1965.

Levi, Wendell M. *The Pigeon*. [n.p.]: Wendell Levi Publishing Co., 1981.

Other Animals

Delort, Robert. *The Life and Lore of the Elephant*. New York: Harry N. Abrams, 1992.

Digby, Simon. *Warhorse and Elephant in the Delhi Sultanate*. Reprint. Oxford: Oxford University Press, 2005.

Morales, Edmundo. "The Guinea Pig in Andean Economy: From Household Animal to Market Commodity," *Latin American Research Review* 3: 129–143.

Morales, Edmundo. *The Guinea Pig: Healing, Food, and Ritual in the Andes*. Tucson: University of Arizona Press, 1995.

Index